Mrs. J. Herbert Tritton

A History

of the

World's Young Women's
Christian Association

by

ANNA V. RICE

———

The Woman's Press
New York

Copyright 1947, by

THE WORLD'S YOUNG WOMEN'S

CHRISTIAN ASSOCIATION

Printed in the United States of America
by Parish Press, Inc., New York 13, N. Y.
10

To the women WHOSE VISION, COURAGE, AND CONVICTION FOUNDED AND DEVELOPED THE WORLD'S YOUNG WOMEN'S CHRISTIAN ASSOCIATION, AND TO THEIR SUCCESSORS WHO, IN A NEW AND REVOLUTIONARY AGE, CARRY FORWARD ITS WORK IN THE SAME SPIRIT OF FAITH AND ADVENTURE.

PREFACE

This book is a history, not of the Young Women's Christian Association the world around, but of the world organization that unites and seeks to develop and extend the Movement in all lands. Some account of Association work as it grew during forty years preceding the forming of a world organization has been necessary as background. Further than this, events in the life of the Associations of different countries have been recounted only in their relation to, or their effect upon, the work of the World Movement.

Assistance in gathering material, especially regarding the early history of the Associations, has been given by women of many countries. Present-day leaders of many National Associations who have read the manuscript either in its entirety, or that part of it which deals with the work in their own countries, have given helpful suggestions and made possible the correction of many inaccuracies. Special thanks are due to Miss Ruth Rouse, President from 1938 to 1946 of the World's Council, and to Miss Ruth F. Woodsmall, its General Secretary, both of whom gave invaluable criticism and help throughout the process of writing; to Miss M. Marianne Mills of the World's Y.W.C.A. staff, without whose indefatigable labor in securing the necessary documents and reports in spite of the difficulties of wartime communications the task could not have been accomplished; to Miss Gladys E. Bretherton of the national staff of the Y.W.C.A. of Great Britain and a former member of the World's staff, who did the indexing; and to Miss Lucy T. Bartlett, formerly on the national staff in the United States and a member of the World's staff during the war, who prepared the manuscript for the press. Such value as the book may have would have been impossible of achievement without the aid of these many experienced leaders of the Association.

Certain important phases of the work of the world organization, as, for example, its financial support and the development of its financial policy, have for various reasons been little stressed. They should find a larger place in a later history.

The faces of many women who have made outstanding contributions to the World Movement will not be found among the limited number of photographs which it has been possible to include, and this is a matter of deep regret.

ANNA V. RICE

Fulton, New York
March 1, 1947

Foreword

Biographies are rarely written during the life of the individual, but this history of the World's Young Women's Christian Association is in reality a biography of a living movement which has just passed the turn of a half-century. More than a mere chronicle of events, this is a vivid account of the vision and creative ability of many individual women joined in a world-wide enterprise. Beginning in 1855, through the faith and insight of two Englishwomen who were filled with the desire to serve girls and women in a wartime period of special need, the same idea found expression in other countries; other leaders also felt the impulse to service, and Associations were formed.

The pioneers of four countries—Great Britain, Norway, Sweden, and the United States of America—united to form the World's Young Women's Christian Association in 1894. In a day when international organizations were very rare, they saw, beyond national and even international boundaries of effort, the far horizon of a new world movement. Since this pioneer beginning, the outreach of the Y.W.C.A. has steadily widened, so that today there is some form of Association work in sixty-five countries.

With London as headquarters until 1930, and then Geneva, the World's Y.W.C.A., at the center of this expanding movement, unites the National Associations in a fellowship of women and girls of many nations and races. These fifty years have brought far-reaching social and political changes that have vitally affected the life of women. Constantly the World's Y.W.C.A. has been forced to face the implications of its unchanging Christian purpose for new circumstances. Ever under the compulsion of new demands and ever deeply rooted in the Christian faith, the leaders of the World's Young Women's Christian Association have met the tensions of their day. Faith and adventure move together through Miss Rice's narrative. With skill and clarity she traces the ever-widening interests of the movement, which brought new imperatives for action and courageous decisions at successive World's meetings. It is an inspiring account of the vitality of the Christian faith to adjust to the needs of successive generations.

The Young Women's Christian Association has moved today far from the sheltered security of the mid-Victorian drawing-rooms of the founders. But the present developments were implicit in their wide vision of a movement which should touch the life of women and girls in all its aspects—physical, mental, and spiritual—and bind them together in a fellowship world wide. That vision has been in great measure realized in these fifty years. Their spirit of adventure has been the touchstone of the achievement of the World's Y.W.C.A. Their synthesis of prayer and service is still the source of its strength.

The leaders of the World's Y.W.C.A. today, who build on the foundations laid by its founders, are grateful to Miss Rice for her vivid portrayal of the rich heritage they have received, and for the inspiration that it brings for the yet unwritten pages of the future. The World's Y.W.C.A. was singularly fortunate to have had Miss Rice, formerly the General Secretary of the National Board of the Young Women's Christian Associations of the United States, and a member of the World's Council, undertake this important work, for which she had such unique gifts. Her long experience with the Association, her intimate understanding of its problems and possibilities, her close personal contact with leaders in many countries, have enabled her to draw the essentials from the wealth of historical material available, and to interpret with simplicity and power the unfolding life of the World's Association. In this history Miss Rice has made a lasting contribution to the whole movement.

RUTH F. WOODSMALL
General Secretary, World's Y.W.C.A.

Geneva
Switzerland, 1947

Contents

LIST OF ILLUSTRATIONS

because stakes were larger and weapons more powerful than any known before. Along with a great increase in knowledge of the world and a growing sense of world interrelationship went a new intensity of desire for national dominance and control of world resources. In a century that on the whole was one of unusual peace and prosperity, the fear of war and the preparation for war grew apace.

On the other hand, the shift from a civilization based on handicraft to the machine age in industry brought with it the possibility, and in large areas the actual achievement, of an abundance of wealth, comfort, leisure, educational and cultural opportunity such as the world had never before experienced. It also brought poverty, misery and degradation, creating new social and economic problems for the solving of which past experience offered little appropriate guidance.

In the intellectual and religious outlook the changes were no less revolutionary. The Christian faith, in both its Roman Catholic and its Protestant forms, found itself challenged by other great philosophies and faced with a skepticism born of new knowledge that could not be satisfactorily combined with theories long held to be fundamental to religious belief. The new scientific discoveries seemed to reveal a universe of very different nature from that set forth by theologians. The Christian conception of human life as fundamentally dependent on a mysterious, largely unknowable Divine Source which created it and by which alone it was sustained, was, by the marvelous achievements of the human mind, which surprised and staggered man himself, subtly supplanted by confidence in man's own powers. A trend toward secularism removed religion from its controlling place at the center of corporate life to the area of individual choice and commitment. It was a century in which, in many ways and in many areas, the Christian faith lost ground in Europe.

But here again the contradictory effects of the age were manifest, for the very things that stimulated reaction against Christianity were also creative of new life within it. New scientific and historical knowledge led to new and rewarding study of the Bible; new views of the world stimulated fresh thought in the fields of theology and Christian philosophy. Even more characteristic of the century than new abstract thought forms was the urge to missionary enterprise, born of Christian conviction and made possible by the new means of world contact and the new wealth produced by industry and world trade. Gradually, too, particularly in the latter half of the century, there came a consuming concern for the adaptation of the message of Christianity to the new order of life in the western world and for the remolding of that order in terms of the Christian ethic.

These changes were true of all western Europe in varying degrees and with varying emphases. They transformed Germany into a country of

2

highly developed, industrialized, urban civilization and produced in her universities and theological schools those great leaders in scientific and historical research who made her the Mecca for students from all lands in the later decades of the nineteenth and the early years of the twentieth centuries. They broke the hold of the Roman Church upon the political life of France. They made of small countries like Sweden, Denmark and Switzerland model states of freedom, social progress and well-being.

Nowhere on the eastern shores of the Atlantic did these new forces combine with one another in an amalgam making at the same time for steady, if often belated, progress in the spread of prosperity at home and widening influence abroad as they did in Great Britain. Nowhere did the Christian religion retain to so large an extent its hold on life as a whole, together with much reinterpretation and adaptation, or issue in so vigorous a missionary zeal as in Great Britain.

Across the Atlantic, too, a new continent was coming into power. As yet the peoples of the nations lately established there were more absorbed in their own internal development, its problems and its almost unbelievable opportunities when coupled with the new mechanical means for exploitation, than in world affairs. The original incentive of their settlement— the desire to escape the trammels of Europe and build a new way of life in new soil—was still dominant. Yet the ties with Europe were many and inescapable. Of these ties, those with England were far the strongest: in Canada by conscious, cherished tradition and by political unity; in the United States by race, language and cultural heritage. Although, as the century advanced, more and more emigrants came to North America from other European countries, nevertheless the influence of the United States and Canada, as these countries were irresistibly drawn into world life, tended to strengthen and extend the power of those ideas that were characteristically Anglo-Saxon.

This Anglo-Saxon dominance was expressed not only in political and economic fields but also in the religious and humanitarian movements that arose in the latter half of the century. Particularly was this true in the field of Christian missions. Whereas in the eighteenth century Germany had led the world in missionary activity, in the nineteenth century the stream of evangelists, teachers, doctors and Christian social workers who poured into the lands of the Orient from the West were overwhelmingly Anglo-Saxon, first British and later American. This extraordinary expansion of Christianity which makes it possible to designate the nineteenth century as "the Great Century" in the history of Christian missions, while it received notable contributions from the Roman Catholic Church and from continental countries, was, in the main, an expansion from within Protestant Christianity, a spread of Protestant ideas, forms, methods, as these had developed in predominantly Anglo-Saxon lands.

3

The great social welfare movements of the century also, whether under religious or non-religious auspices, were largely of the same origin. The anti-slavery movement, the settlement movement, the struggle for the protection of children and workers in industry and for control of the white slave traffic, while they all owed much to the advanced social experimentation undertaken here and there on the Continent, especially in Germany, were on the whole the product of Anglo-Saxon initiative.

In both England and America there appeared during the latter half of the century a series of remarkable revivals of religion. These revivals expressed themselves in a warm, evangelical type of Christian experience, a chief characteristic of which was personal dedication to the doing of God's will in daily life. From these revivals came much of the impetus to missionary undertakings, including the formation of such organizations as the Student Volunteer Movement for the recruiting of missionaries among the young men and women of the universities. From them came the movement of evangelism which Christians from Great Britain, often laymen, carried on in the Roman Catholic countries of Europe. From them also sprang, directly or indirectly, many of the movements for social amelioration or reform.

Among the revolutionary effects of the new age in Europe, and particularly in England, one of the most revolutionary was the new status progressively attained by women. First recognized in the economic field, through the necessities of an industrial age, and expressing itself also in the opening to women of new educational opportunities, it was, by the latter part of the century, reaching out into a variety of fields of social and religious significance. Within Protestant Christianity in the years from 1850-1900 there was a remarkable increase in the activities of women in evangelism, missionary enterprise and practical service. This steady, unpremeditated stepping forth into public life by women, under the pressure of changing circumstances, was not the least significant of the changes wrought in human life by this extraordinary century.

It was, then, in line with general historical trends that in 1894 a world organization of women, thinking in terms of evangelism and of social service, should have had its inception in Great Britain, where the Y.W.C.A., which had been in existence since 1855, was already world-conscious and world-connected, and that it should have been seconded and supported by a sister movement in the New World which was just beginning to look beyond itself.

It was equally to be expected that the new organization should be Protestant in origin, in temper, and in method. The nineteenth century was as truly the century of Protestantism as it was the century of Europe or of England, and nowhere did Protestantism enjoy so dominant a position as in

Great Britain, the United States, and the countries of northern Europe, two of which, Norway and Sweden, joined with Great Britain and the United States to make up the original four in the World's Y.W.C.A.

The World's Young Women's Christian Association, then, is a product of European Christian culture, but its beginnings were within that type of European culture that developed most fully in Great Britain. It embodied the vitality, the vigor, the freedom, the evangelical conviction, the practical ethical temper, and the adventurous pioneering spirit that were the marked characteristics of nineteenth century Anglo-Saxon Protestantism. Moreover, while the World's Y.W.C.A. was rooted in European, and particularly in English social and religious culture, it was, from the first, because of the part taken in its leadership and its financial support, largely influenced by the New World across the Atlantic. This New World was, in the nineteenth century, largely ignorant of the Old World's past; it abounded in ideas, movements and methods born of a new country cut off from close connections with its origin. On the venture on which those who organized the World's Y.W.C.A. embarked in 1894, this new-world element was bound to have a profound effect, sometimes disturbing because unfamiliar, but at the same time stimulating because of its freshness, the earnestness of its conviction, and the vastness of its resources.

The course of development of great movements, the form they take, and the specific tasks they assume are determined by two major influences. One is the impress of their origin. The creative moment in which a movement is born stamps irrevocably upon it a character which it henceforth bears. If it repudiates that character it is no longer that movement, but has become a different one. The second is the pressure of changing circumstances, the altered environment, the new historical situation within which a continuing movement lives and grows. These things force change upon it. The two influences are often in conflict, hence the life of great movements is always one of inner tension and struggle. At the same time, these opposing influences are the means of clarification, enrichment, and deeper penetration into fundamental issues, so that the movement that sustains the conflict over the years may reap whatever of truth the original insight held, corrected, reinterpreted and enlarged by the wider experience of succeeding years.

The history of the World's Y.W.C.A. is the as-yet-unfinished story of one such movement within the world-wide Christian community. It was created out of a specific soil—the Christian experience as it expressed itself at a given moment and in a given place—but it grew and is still growing under conditions extraordinarily and increasingly different from those within which it arose.

Women are obviously going to have their day in this old country, where they have had to keep so much in the background in the days that are passing, if not already passed. But if they are to come more and more to the front in the social, the commercial, the literary and even in the political life of the country, how doubly important that they should themselves be won for Christ, and use whatever additional influence he may in his providence assign to them for the advancement of his Kingdom as well as for the general improvement of the social conditions of the world.
W. HAY M. H. AITKEN, Canon of Norwich: Foreword to
Girls of Yesterday and Today, by Lucy M. Moor.

CHAPTER 1
THE Y.W.C.A. BEFORE 1894:
GREAT BRITAIN AND
THE BRITISH EMPIRE

WHEN the World's Young Women's Christian Association was organized in 1894 there was already a considerable history of Y.W.C.A. work in many countries. In Great Britain, in North America and in Norway the work had already attained the status of a national (or international in North America, where Canada and the United States had united) organization. The same was practically though not technically true in Sweden. In Germany several lines of work that had recently united in a national Y.W.C.A. were already strong and well organized. France, which claims the distinction of having started the first Association group anywhere in the world, in the year 1849, had in 1894 a large number of such groups and a certain amount of district organization. There was a quite well developed work in Denmark and many little groups were active in Switzerland, while at least a few "branches for scattered members" were to be found in Hungary, Italy, Belgium and Spain, and one was in Malta. Outside Great Britain, North America, and the continent of Europe, the Association had already been planted or had sprung up spontaneously in Egypt and in Palestine; in Australia, New Zealand and South Africa; in India, Burma, Ceylon and Malaya; in British Guiana, Grenada and Argentina.

Two separate movements, both arising in the year 1855 and coming together into one body some twenty-two years later, formed the Y.W.C.A. of Great Britain. The first of these was a quiet, unpublicized, wholly

7

spiritual movement that originated in the mind and heart of Emma Robarts, youngest of five daughters of a retired merchant living on an estate in the little village of Barnet. Miss Robarts, who with her sisters had already conducted a school for girls on their father's estate, became at the age of thirty-seven deeply concerned for individual young women whom she knew, and through them, for all young women. Neither by opportunity nor by temperament was she fitted to step out into such activities as were even then beginning to open up for women, but she did bring together a little group of her friends, who pledged themselves to pray each Saturday night for relatives and friends and for young women as a whole.

The idea proved to be a creative one, and quickly spread, until within the next few years Prayer Unions had sprung up in many communities. There was no formal organization. The members met in small groups, and these groups, as well as the individuals who composed them, were bound together chiefly by correspondence, of which Miss Robarts and some of her closest colleagues carried a voluminous amount. The members of the Prayer Unions were Christian young women, largely girls of leisure and education, and the aim was to win such girls to a more complete dedication to Christ and to a life of Christian service. It was a work almost private in character. Miss Robarts feared publicity and set herself against it. Indeed, so intimate and personal a work as she sought to encourage would have been destroyed by being noised abroad. Yet the very success of the Prayer Unions suggested the need of extending the circle of the fellowship in order to give more outlet for the service to which they called young women.

In 1876 one of the Prayer Unions, in which Miss Lucy Moor was a leader, laid before Miss Robarts a plan for an outer circle, made up, not of fully consecrated young women, as were the Prayer Unions, but of any young women, "even though only nominally Christian," who cared to associate themselves with others. To Miss Robarts this seemed a sweeping and dangerous departure from the spiritual purpose of the Prayer Unions. She feared the publicity involved and the lessened depth of spiritual fervor which the broadened base might bring. Still, she gave her consent to the new venture, and some of the Prayer Unions began to reach out beyond themselves.[1]

In this same year 1885 there was living in London another young woman, a woman of prayer and of deep Christian devotion but of quite different temperament from Miss Robarts. The Honorable Mrs. Arthur Kinnaird, already the mother of several children and the wife of a man of great public spirit and wide philanthropic interests, was by every in-

Lady Kinnaird

Miss Emma Robarts

stinct a woman of affairs, vigorous, able, practical-minded, whose loving spirit reached out in every direction. She was concerned for the weak little Protestant churches which she saw when she traveled on the continent of Europe; for Africa, because of what she heard of the sufferings of African slaves;[2] for India, "which, though she never saw it, she loved intensely."

With Mrs. Kinnaird, to know of a need was immediately to do something about it. She helped to place matrons on ships for the protection of young women emigrating to British colonies. She was the moving spirit in the establishment of a home in London to serve temporarily the young women who, to the consternation of their parents, were following Florence Nightingale across Europe to nurse the British soldiers wounded in the Crimean war. It was but a step from meeting this emergency need to the founding of a permanent home in London for young women coming up from the provinces to find employment in the city. From this as a beginning Mrs. Kinnaird was instrumental in opening other homes in many parts of London.

In connection with these homes a variety of activities—Bible classes and religious meetings, educational classes in many subjects, social activities, employment agencies and clubs—were soon initiated. The need was great, the response of the young women was immediate, and the situation that led to these first London ventures existed in every city where industry and trade were transforming life. By the time Miss Robarts' Prayer Unions were feeling themselves pushed to enlarge their fellowship and undertake new forms of service, the work begun by Mrs. (now Lady) Kinnaird had spread to large proportions. Boarding homes, restaurants, employment agencies, traveler's aid, libraries, clubs, had sprung up in many cities. There was no formal connection between these activities in different places. The London work was a whole by itself but its general lines were reproduced by women conscious of similar needs elsewhere.

In the year 1876 or 1877, Lady Kinnaird, desiring to deepen the spiritual life of the expanding work in London, planned to relate it to a group of Christian women who would, in a very special way, carry it on their hearts in prayer. It was called to her attention that in the Prayer Unions, some of whose members were already connected with the London work, such a group already existed. The result was a conference of Lady Kinnaird with Miss Robarts and the uniting of the two movements in London. "Evidently no greater formality was needed to bring about this union than the mutual agreement of the two leaders over a cup of tea."[3]

Both the Prayer Unions and the Homes and Institutes of the London work had previously used the name "Young Women's Christian Association", copied from the already well-known Young Men's Christian Association, and though the name at first chosen for the new organization was the rather cumbersome one of "The London Young Women's Institute Union and Christian Association", the united work soon became known simply as the Young Women's Christian Association.

The first step toward a National Association was taken in 1884, when the London work and that which had grown up in other cities and towns of the United Kingdom were brought into relationship with one another by the formation of a United Central Council, on which were representatives from the Councils of London, South of England and Wales, North of England, Scotland and Ireland. One of the earliest actions of this United Central Council, taken in January 1885, was the organization of two committees for the extension of the work beyond the British Isles. One of the committees, called the Foreign and Continental Division, was charged with work for girls from other countries who were in Great Britain and with work on the Continent. The other, known as the Extra-European and Colonial Division, was entrusted with the extension of the Association to the British colonial territories and to other lands outside Europe.[4]

In the decade from 1884 to 1894 the program at home and its outreach into other countries grew rapidly. What were the outstanding characteristics of the British Association in this, its creative period?

In the first place, it was fundamentally not only a Christian but an evangelistic movement. Practically all the early leaders came from those within the Church of England or in the Free Churches who were known as "Evangelicals". Their Christian experience had been deeply influenced by the religious revivals of the middle of the century and especially by the preaching of Dwight L. Moody, who had come to England from America in the early 1870s, and by the Keswick Movement. They burned with a great faith in the power of the gospel to redeem and save individual lives and to provide also the cure for the social ills of mankind, and they took with great seriousness their responsibility for winning men and women to this faith. The following statement adopted at the formation of the United Central Council embodies phrases taken from earlier statements of both the Prayer Unions and the London work:

Basis

A living union with Christ our God and Saviour, the only principle of action being the love of God shed abroad in the heart by the Holy Ghost, uniting in prayer and work those who desire to extend his kingdom by all means that are in accordance with the word of God.

Objects

I. Union for prayer for young women.
II. Work amongst young women of all classes by all means that are in accordance with the word of God, namely:

10

1. To unite together for prayer, mutual help, sympathy, and instruction in spiritual things young women of all classes who truly love and desire to serve the Lord Jesus Christ.

2. To seek to win to a knowledge of Christ our sisters all around us who are strangers to the joy of his salvation.

3. To draw together for mutual help, sympathy and instruction young women of all classes.

4. To promote the moral, social and intellectual well-being of all through the various agencies.

5. To provide Christian friends for all young women, especially those who come from the country into the town.

6. To afford protection to those who need it, and thus to help them to avoid the dangers and temptations which they meet.[5]

The earnestness with which this evangelistic purpose was carried forward is shown by the number of Bible classes and religious meetings, and by the references to "lady missioners" who were invited to hold evangelistic services in London during the annual Week of Prayer which the Y.W.C.A. observed with the Y.M.C.A. Miss Moor, writing of the Association in the early 1880s, says that sometimes "an effort was made to move a whole town by a series of meetings in different centers." As an illustration of this she records the story of the General Mission held in Birmingham in 1882. "The town," she says, "was divided into 26 centers, and 430 meetings were held during a fortnight." There were ladies' drawing-room meetings and special gatherings for different classes of workers— mothers, nurses, factory girls, school girls, servants and others. "The town was thus besieged at all points; there was hearty cooperation, and all ecclesiastical differences were, for the time, merged in the hearty desire to win young hearts and bring them into obedience to Christ."[6]

Besides its emphasis on Bible study and special evangelistic effort, the Y.W.C.A. very early developed short training courses in "personal work". These, and also camps and conferences for workers in which the purpose was first of all the deepening of the inner life and consultation regarding methods of evangelism, were an important part of the program.

A second notable feature of the British Association, characteristic of both the Prayer Unions and the Institutes from their earliest days, was its entire disregard of denominational lines. This is strikingly illustrated in the account of the Mission in Birmingham just quoted.

A third characteristic was the place taken by voluntary unsalaried leadership. Its work was almost wholly carried on by "Honorary Secretaries", women of social standing who carried correspondence, kept accounts, taught Bible classes, held evangelistic meetings, traveled over the British Isles and sometimes far beyond, in the interests of the work. In

11

these later years of professional service one marvels that so much could be undertaken and carried through by women who were at the same time deeply involved in family and social responsibilities.

Still a fourth mark of the Y.W.C.A. in Great Britain was its missionary interest. That this interest should be strong is not surprising; it was the natural outgrowth of the Association's strongly evangelical character and its evangelistic emphasis. Moreover, these were years of expanding missionary activity in the churches. An organization that had as one object the calling of young women into Christian service, would inevitably lead many to the mission field and be itself a center of education and support for missionary work. Moreover, Lady Kinnaird's interest in missions led her to cultivate an interest in missionary projects in her Y.W.C.A. work. At the first World's Y.W.C.A. Conference in London, in 1898, the report of the missionary activity of the Associations in Great Britain could claim that from among their members 496 missionaries were working abroad under various church boards, and that the Association's branches were at that time themselves supporting between fifty and sixty missionaries. The writer of the report remarks that there had even been "some fear that our various [missionary] Societies would find in our branches a happy hunting ground and descend upon us without leave or license," but this fear, she concludes, had proved "foolish and groundless."

From the standpoint of the future development of the Y.W.C.A. as a world movement, that which is most significant about this missionary interest of the British Association is that it included from the first a sense of obligation to promote Association work itself outside its own country. Miss Annie M. Reynolds, the first General Secretary of the World's Y.W.C.A., writing of those early days, says: "Great Britain alone of any country, so far as we have been able to ascertain, had from the beginning, committees upon which devolved the heavy responsibility of extending the work in other lands."[7]

These committees were, of course, the already mentioned Foreign and Continental Division and the Extra-European and Colonial Division.[8] Much of the work which they fostered had begun long before in the same spontaneous response to evident need which had inspired the first work at home. As early as 1857, a Foreign Prayer Union, known as the "Friday Evening Union", had been formed in Geneva, Switzerland, by several young women from different countries, and in 1878 an English branch of this Union united with the Y.W.C.A. Prayer Unions, thus establishing an international connection. Moreover, the British movement itself was faced even in its earliest days with the numbers of girls from continental countries, French and German especially but also Swedish, Norwegian, Spanish, Italian, who were employed in various capacities in England and whose need of friendly counsel and comradeship was often very great. There was a German branch of the Y.W.C.A. in London in 1885, and a French branch was started only a little later. The minutes of the Foreign and Continental Division between the years 1885 and 1890 record such things as a discussion about printing invitations to join the Association in Spanish, and the announcement that a lending library of two hundred volumes had been opened in London, with books in French, German, Italian, Swedish and Norwegian.

There were also many young English women abroad. In the continental countries almost every sizable city had a few English girls, frequently as governesses. British people were great continental travelers, and as Y.W.C.A. leaders from time to time resided or traveled abroad they began to seek out these lonely young compatriots and form them into little Y.W.C.A. groups, which then by correspondence and through use of the Bible readings and Almanacs prepared by the British Association were stimulated and encouraged from the home base.

Also, either through their own initiative or through contact with those in the various continental countries who shared their interest and concern for young women, these British leaders were often instrumental in starting work similar to that in England among the young women of the country as well as for English residents. The minutes of the Continental Division from 1885 to 1894 reveal the fact that through its "correspondents" on the home committee and its "referees" in many countries, usually English women residing more or less permanently there, an extraordinarily large advisory and inspirational correspondence was carried on with Association groups in a great number of European cities. In November 1888 the Committee discussed the possibility of beginning work in Constantinople; in April 1889 the minutes record that "Miss van Epen, who is shortly going to Russia and Finland, was present as a visitor and promised to do what she could to extend the work of the Association in these countries." The Paris exhibition of 1890 led the Committee to sponsor a home in Paris for English girls employed in the exhibition, and later to attempt the establishment of a permanent home there for English and American young women.[9] At the meeting in October 1890, reports were read of work among Italian girls in Florence under the leadership of Miss Cox, and of work in the same town, largely for Scottish girls, carried on by Mrs. Coldstream. In July 1891 Dr. Hermina Welch of Bucharest is present, and "thinks it would not be difficult to find a lady to start a scattered members' branch in Bucharest, as there are a number of English governesses there." The minutes for January 1892 report new branches opened in Spain, progress in the branches in the Riviera, and the fact that a report from the Chaplain at Corfu seemed to show that a branch was not needed there. Later that

13

year there are references to a branch in Hamburg, to openings for the work in Frankfort and Heidelberg, the prospect of a branch in Brussels, and letters from the Associations of Bordeaux and Malta. In Norway and Sweden, too, the Y.W.C.A. leaders were in frequent communication with the Continental Committee of the British Association and appear to have looked to them for help and advice.

The outreach beyond Europe came about in the first instance in the same natural, largely informal and spontaneous way as it had on the Continent. British women going to Australia, New Zealand, South Africa or India as permanent residents or as missionaries, teachers, wives of officials, or just as travelers, carried with them the idea of the Y.W.C.A. as they had known it at home. Finding the need for such work equally pressing in other lands, they set it going, usually along very simple lines—small groups gathered for Bible study, prayer and fellowship, followed shortly by the opening of the most immediately needed services, which, as at home, were always boarding homes, employment agencies, and rooms for social and educational activities.

The minutes of the Colonial Division are entertaining reading and one needs an atlas close at hand. In July 1891 the Committee receives a letter "relative to the proposed branch in Algiers"; word of the opening of branches in Buenos Aires and Montevideo; reports of work from Canada, Australia, Bombay and Calcutta, and is shown a picture of a "working group" in the Singapore Association. The November meeting of the same year appoints a correspondent for the Bahamas, discusses suggestions for furthering the work in India, and receives reports from Cape Town, South Africa; Demerara, British Guiana; Dunedin, New Zealand; Buenos Aires, Argentina; Montivideo, Uruguay; Sydney and Rockhampton, Australia; Barbados and Japan. In February 1893 the Committee considers a request to allow a branch to be formed in Aintab, Asia Minor, and not only grants this but votes to equip it with "20 monthly letters, 100 motto cards and 100 almanacs."

Later meetings that year receive a report from Jerusalem, and word of a new Association in Nazareth. They also deal with the problem of finding a new referee for Syria, and report "the urgent need of a worker in Sierra Leone." In June 1894, just before the World's Committee began its work, Miss Butt, the correspondent for China, reports "the great opening for a lady worker and for a home in Shanghai". The Committee's method of recruiting leadership for such new projects as Sierra Leone and Shanghai was the simple one of inserting a notice of the need in *Go Forward,* the national magazine of the British Association, and waiting for someone to volunteer in response to this.

All these outreaches of the British movement were to separate cities, and

14

for a long time they did not seem to envisage any relationship between the different centers established in a given country, but only a corresponding relationship between such centers and the home base in England. In India, however, things had proceeded rather further than this even before 1894.

The first Association in India is believed to have been started in Bombay by Miss Butt, previously a member in England and a friend of Miss Robarts.[10] It is significant that of the four charter members, Miss Butt was English, Miss McRitchie, Scottish, Miss Vitters, Anglo-Indian (Eurasian), and Miss Sorabji, Indian. Growth was slow, for even within the city of Bombay itself transportation problems made it difficult for the members to meet together. The meetings for prayer and Bible study and the simple services undertaken—sewing for the poor and taking flowers to hospitals —were carried on by separate groups who came together only in quarterly meetings and were otherwise bound to one another by correspondence. In 1881, when the number of members, now 150, made correspondence "a formidable, indeed almost impossible task",[11] the first published report was issued.

The beginning of extension came when Miss Vitters, returning to her home in Poona, opened a branch there. This branch rented a room in which to hold its Bible class and so became the first Association in India to have "quarters" of its own. Gradually Associations came into being elsewhere, especially in the larger cities—Calcutta, Madras, Colombo, Lahore. The early reports all mention the up-hill character of the work under the difficulties that existed in India—the vastness of the need, the great distances, the small number of Christian women capable of and available for leadership. As late as 1898, a report given at the first World's Conference says: "The work has existed in India for nearly twenty-three years, but it has been a very feeble existence, few branches, scarcely any workers."[12]

Such work as there was before the organization of the World's Y.W.C.A. was largely among Anglo-Indian young women, though from the beginning the theory of the Association in India was that of an inter-racial fellowship, and the field of Indian womanhood had impressed itself upon Association leaders. The difficulties of language, of finding Indian leadership, and of adapting to Indian conditions a movement born and developed in countries of so different a civilization, proved, however, handicaps hard to overcome.

In spite of the difficulties, things were stirring there in the early 1890s. In 1890-1891, the Honorable Emily Kinnaird made a sixteen months tour of India in connection with a mission led by an American evangelist, the Reverend George F. Pentecost. She visited many Association centers in India, Burma and Ceylon, and everywhere, with great vigor and conviction, she interpreted the "Association idea", always leaving behind her a larger vision of the possibilities of the work and an awakened sense of responsibility and urgency.

Partly as an outgrowth of Miss Kinnaird's visit and partly because of the example of the Y.M.C.A. and the effect of Dr. Pentecost's mission, a group of Christians in Madras, officials of the Y.W.C.A., missionaries, Y.M.C.A. leaders and others, sent, in 1891, an appeal to both the British and the American Y.W.C.A. to send out to India "some ladies of experience and devotion" who would develop " a more definite and systematic work among the young women of India."[13] The result of this appeal was twofold: first, in November 1893 the British Y.W.C.A. sent to Calcutta Miss Maude Orlebar, the first worker to give her entire time to the Y.W.C.A. in India; second, a meeting was held in London to discuss the needs of the Madras Y.W.C.A. This meeting was attended by Mr. McConaughy, Secretary of the Madras Y.M.C.A., by Mr. and Mrs. Wishard of the United States, just returning from a world tour for the Y.M.C.A., and by Mr. Bierce, President of the International Committee of the Y.M.C.A. of North America. When it was suggested that a woman was needed in Madras "to do among young women a work similar to that which Mr. McConaughy is carrying on among young men," Mr. Bierce is reported to have said: "I think my niece, Agnes Hill, now in Toledo [Ohio] is just the one. She is a member of the Anglican Church, a university graduate, and is experienced in Association work."[14] When in 1894 the World's Y.W.C.A. began to function, Miss Hill was already committed to India, and with her arrival there a new era of Association work began.

These early records of the spread of the Association from England to the Continent and to the far corners of the earth are significant not alone as the story of the beginnings of a world-wide work for young women, but also as a revelation of some of the complications and problems arising, even in those early stages, from aggressive work in the international field. For instance, there arose quite early the question of the relationship between the work started by English women in so many countries of Europe, and the work for young women that was developing quite separately during those same years in those same countries under the leadership of men or women of the country. Some continental groups, while recognizing the stimulus they received from the English leaders, found also a problem in the relationship.

In 1886 the Continental Committee was faced with the desire of the German branch in London, which was largely supported and directed by German women resident in England, to form a separate organization with its own president, instead of remaining a branch of the British movement. A similar question arose in Paris over the relationship between the work carried by French women for French girls and the work started in Paris primarily for English and American young women by members of the British Y.W.C.A. At a meeting of the Continental Committee in the autumn of 1890, it was reported that there was a general opinion in France "that the work among English girls must be disconnected from that among French or foreign ones, and each must have separate presidents."

Both these instances perhaps are indicative of a certain resistance on the part of other nationalities to the easy assumption that the British pattern and the British leadership should become the norm for other countries. Although the British work developed a national organization earlier and was more aggressive than that of the continental countries, and though it contributed a good deal to them, there was an altogether wholesome reaction against any uniform pattern for the Y.W.C.A.

Another set of problems that presented themselves very early had to do with the administration of the basis of membership of the Y.W.C.A. in the varying situations in different countries. Wherever the influence of the British work made itself felt, the basis adopted was that of the British movement—Protestant and evangelical, but also interdenominational.

In 1887 the United Central Council found itself faced with "the consideration of the advisability of admitting members of the Greek Church into the Association." After a long discussion the following resolution was passed: "That the Y.W.C.A., being distinctly a Protestant Association, this Council cannot encourage the admission of members of the Greek Church unless their membership be merely legal, and they be prepared to subscribe to the Basis of the Association."[15] What was meant by a "merely legal" membership is not clear, but the qualifying clause would seem to indicate that though the United Central Council felt that the Protestant character of the Association was something to be guarded, there was also recognition of a common Christian heritage wider than Protestantism, and an unwillingness entirely to close the door of the Association to those non-Protestants whose sympathy with its purpose and basis drew them to it.

This interpretation of the thought in the British Association is strengthened by the decision later made in the Continental Division with regard to Roman Catholic members. When branches were formed in Roman Catholic countries, as in Italy and Spain and certain sections of France, this question came to the fore. In the early months of the year 1890, the Continental Division was forced to consider it. The minutes say: "It being ascertained that there was no definite rule of the Association against it, it was agreed that Roman Catholics should be admitted as members of the general Association, but not of the Prayer Union, the chief reason being that in some countries, such as Spain and many parts of France, the work is entirely among Roman Catholic girls and it would prevent many opportunities for good work, if they were cut off from all benefits of the Association."[16]

On the other hand, as the Association developed in strongly Protestant countries in which virtually the entire population was affiliated with one church, it was the interdenominational feature that presented a difficulty. In July 1892 the Continental Division had to consider a letter from a leader of the Y.W.C.A. in Norway regarding the difficulty she was finding in her attempts to work on any save Lutheran lines. Evidently recognizing the necessity for adaptation to existing conditions, the Committee wrote suggesting that "so long as the basis of the Association is recognized as undenominational, the branches may be worked on denominational lines." At the same meeting, however, a further resolution was adopted: that private effort from England should be used to push the work in other denominations than Lutheran and that the existing Associations in Norway should be duly informed of this decision.

The aggressive work of the British Association outside its own borders, especially its interest in the continent of Europe, is responsible for the establishment in very early days of another practice which was of significance for the development of a world movement—the practice of cooperation with other movements. The particular illustration of this in the period preceding the formation of the World's Y.W.C.A. is the relation of the British Y.W.C.A. to *l'Union internationale des Amies de la Jeune Fille.* This organization, probably the earliest of all international women's organizations, came into being in 1887 as the direct outcome of a Congress held that year in Geneva by the British and Continental Union for the Upholding of Morality. One of the subjects discussed at this Congress was "the fate of young girls who leave their homes to seek a living in foreign countries." The result of the discussion was that a *Union* of some twenty ladies of different nationalities was formed to aid these young travelers. The first President, and the soul of the movement, was Madame Humbert of Neuchâtel, Switzerland. She was followed in this office by Mademoiselle Anna de Perrot, also of Neuchâtel, who had been working among young women since 1855.[17] The headquarters of the organization were in Neuchâtel but the movement spread rapidly into many countries.

The methods by which it carried on its work were simple but extraordinarily efficient: "Every girl on leaving home is given a little book in which are lists of homes and registries in different countries where she may find help and shelter. Besides this, the member interested in her [her *Amie*] writes on a blank page the name and address of anyone in the town to which she is going who is also an Amie, and who will give her advice and be a real friend to her while away from home. . . Every Amie engages herself to help girls, meet them and see them off if asked to do so by an Amie in another place.[18] By 1894 there were branches in thirty countries and a membership of six thousand Amies."

In Great Britain, as the Y.W.C.A. grew, the work of the Amies became incorporated into its program, though in many other countries it remained as an entirely separate organization. The United Central Council worked consistently with the Amies, and when the World's Committee was organized, one of its first concerns was to establish understanding and cooperation between the two international organizations.

REFERENCES

[1] Moor, Lucy, M. *Girls of Yesterday and Today,* 1910, pp. 27-29.

[2] In her book *Reminiscences* (p. 64) Mrs. Kinnaird's daughter, the Honorable Emily Kinnaird, writes: "I well remember those early times when I was six years old and the black ex-slave, Bishop Crowther, came to stay with us and preached in our field, as the Parish Church would not admit him."

[3] Sims, M. S. *The Natural History of a Social Institution, the Y.W.C.A.,* 1935, p. 3.

[4] Later the titles of these two divisions were changed respectively to "The Continental" and "The Colonial" Divisions (*Minutes of United Central Council,* November 16, 1888).

[5] Moor, Lucy M., *Girls of Yesterday and Today,* pp. 71, 72.

[6] *Ibid.,* pp. 80, 81.

[7] Reynolds, A. M. *Ten Years' Record,* 1904.

[8] See p. 10.

[9] Continental Council, Minutes, May 23, 1889; January 23, 1890; February 6, 1890; March 6, 1890.

[10] Wilson, Elizabeth. *The Story of Fifty Years of the Y.W.C.A. of India, Burma and Ceylon,* 1925, p. 1.

[11] *Ibid.,* p. 2.

[12] First World's Y.W.C.A. Conference, Report, p. 116.

[13] For full text of this appeal see Elizabeth Wilson: *The Story of Fifty Years of the Y.W.C.A. in India, Burma and Ceylon,* pp. 15, 16.

[14] *Ibid,* p. 22.

[15] Minutes of United Central Council, November 18, 1887.

[16] Continental Committee, April 1890, Minutes.

[17] Moor, Lucy M. *Girls of Yesterday and Today,* p. 150.

[18] *Ibid.,* p. 157.

*Wir müssen unsere Aufgabe ansehen als ein Ewig-
keitswerk. Viele arbeiten mit all ihrer Liebe und
Hingabe nur deshalb vergeblich und verlieren daher
ihre Freudigkeit, weil sie nicht den Glaubensmut
haben, den Mädchen das Höchste zu bieten und zum
Höchsten zu verhelfen.*

PASTOR BURCKHARDT, erster Präsident des Nationalen
Christlichen Verbandes Weiblicher Jugend.

*Ayons au coeur l'ambition de faire de toute jeune fille
que nous pouvons atteindre une femme forte, pieuse,
pratique; ne négligeons rien de ce qui peut lui être
utile . . . Ah! certes, un tel programme nous entraîn-
era loin. Nous ne pourrons rester "spectatrices oisives"
de la grande mélée entre le bien et le mal qui se
livre sous nos yeux. Il nous faudra prendre résolument
place à coté des nobles âmes qui se donnent pour
faire régner sur la terre un peu plus de justice et
d'amour—et, par conséquent, supporter des opposi-
tions, surmonter des difficultés, nous mettre en avant,
nous des femmes et des jeunes filles. Eh! bien, pour-
quoi pas? Si Jésus Christ nous a affranchies, si, peu
à peu, nous conquérons nos droits à la liberté et
à l'action, n'est-ce-pas pour pouvoir accomplir nos
devoirs?*

JEANNE SEQUESTRA, Rédactrice du *Journal de la Jeune
Fille.* Address, World's Y.W.C.A. Conference, 1906.

CHAPTER 2   THE Y.W.C.A. BEFORE 1894:
THE CONTINENT OF EUROPE

THE FIVE countries on the European conti-
nent which before 1894 had Y.W.C.A. work that had developed into
something approaching a national movement—France, Germany, Norway,
Sweden and Denmark—all had certain similarities to the movement in
Great Britain. On the Continent, as in England, the work, under whatever
name, that eventually became the Y.W.C.A. had its beginnings in each
country within the Protestant Christian body. It was, as in England, closely
related to the changing conditions of life that especially affected women, and
to the evangelical revival within the Protestant churches, which stirred
Christian people anew to evangelistic and social effort. But the conditions
on the Continent, quite different in different countries and all in some

ways strikingly different from the situation in Great Britain, produced in each continental country a Christian movement for young women that was distinctive and expressive of the environment within which it was born and grew to national proportions. It is this wide variety along with certain basic similarities that is of significance for the later development of the World's Y.W.C.A.

The Y.W.C.A. of France is an outstanding example of the differences inherent in a World's Y.W.C.A. movement made up of national units. In contrast to Protestant, Anglo-Saxon Britain, France was a predominantly Roman Catholic and Latin country. In an article in the *World's Y.W.C.A. Quarterly* in later years, Mademoiselle Marie Appia of the French National Association says: "Protestants are in such a feeble minority (there are about 600,000 Protestants out of a population of 38,000,000) and young women are so much less free in the Latin than in the Anglo-Saxon countries, that our work meets with special difficulties."[1]

It is not therefore surprising to find that in France the Y.W.C.A. had smaller beginnings, was slower to develop, and is, even now, smaller in proportion to the size of the population than in Protestant countries. Other factors, too, had an influence on the character of the French Y.W.C.A. It lived and grew not only within a struggling minority group but surrounded by an atmosphere of religious skepticism. This skepticism, a characteristic feature of the nineteenth century, was a far larger factor in the spiritual life of the Continent than in that of Great Britain. For some continental countries, and particularly for France, it was the prevailing temper of the time, and as such strongly influenced the form taken by the spiritual awakening within the Protestant churches. In France this awakening was largely a protest against the secular trend of the period, whereas in Britain the religious trend of the age found expression in the evangelical revival.

Within this environment the impulse toward work for and by young women expressed itself in the years between 1850 and 1890 in the formation of many little parish groups of girls in different parts of France. Though usually led by the pastor's wife, these groups had no formal relationship to the church. Their growth was spontaneous, not promoted from any central headquarters or by church officials. They also arose quite independently of one another, the product of a common impulse to meet a common need. They closely resembled one another in their simple form of organization and their program of weekly meetings for prayer and Bible study. There is a certain similarity in them to the early Prayer Unions in England and there may well have been a conscious modeling of the work after that which had been so fruitful across the channel, for in the decade of the 1870s, links had already been established between the British Unions and similar groups in Le Hâvre, Boulogne, Calais and Paris.[2] There was, however, a fundamental difference between the Prayer Unions as developed by Miss Robarts and her colleagues and the little Christian Associations growing up in France. The former were in the main composed of young women of leisure and of privilege; the latter were made up primarily of simple people, many of them working girls from villages and country districts.

For a long time these parish groups remained quite separate, and local in character and outlook. The first move toward drawing them together in a larger fellowship came in 1891, from a French pastor in southeastern France. Pastor Maillet called a conference at Le Pougin, Ardèche, of representatives from some ten or twelve of these Parish Unions. About sixty delegates attended, and these representatives chose a "District Council", the purpose of which was to relate the groups in the district to one another and to extend the work. They also elected Pastor Maillet President for southeastern France.

It is significant of the recognition given to the leadership of Great Britain in Y.W.C.A. work at this time that Mrs. Gardner James, the President of the Continental Committee of the United Central Council of Great Britain, was present by invitation at this meeting, and that following the conference, she traveled about the districts of Drôme and Ardèche, visiting eight of the Unions.[3] Similar conferences were held in 1892 and 1893, and at the fourth conference, at Nîmes in 1894, a national organization was formed, with forty-nine local Associations affiliated. This conference adopted as the basis of its national organization a translation of the statement that was in use in Great Britain.[4]

The earliest statement of the purpose of the French national movement, probably coming from this 1894 conference at Nîmes, says: "The Association desires to gather together in one group all young women who wish to affirm their faith and combat skepticism, immorality, evil companionships, bad literature, and the moral carelessness to which many young girls are prone, and to build up a social circle where a girl may find sisters who share her needs, where she may find a family if she is alone, and a friend if she is weak and in danger of falling. The Association is founded on the gospel and believes that only in such a faith can there be any life of power or richness."[5]

As the movement grew, the program of the local Unions, except in the larger cities and towns, continued to consist for the most part of Bible study, evangelistic services, and meetings for prayer. To these were added missionary activities, chiefly help for the work of the church in Madagascar. In Paris and Marseilles, and then in other cities, foyers, restaurants and other activities were soon established, temperance work was carried on, thrift societies were organized. The Unions were bound together and kept in touch with one another through a national magazine, *Le Journal de la Jeune Fille.*

Throughout its history the growing French movement has been conscious of the handicap it suffers in comparison with Associations in Protestant countries. Mademoiselle Rourin, then President of the French Association, in a report made at the World's Conference in 1902, said: ". . . we cannot forget that we are working in a Roman Catholic country, often meeting with great difficulties." A hint of another kind of difficulty in early days is given in a still later report, where it was said that the majority of leaders belonged to the class of manual or intellectual workers and the services of young women of leisure were greatly needed.[6] The prestige and the financial backing which came on the whole so generously to the Y.W.C.A. of Great Britain and made possible its expansion along so many lines was largely lacking in the French movement.

It is perhaps to this characteristic of its early leadership that the French Y.W.C.A. owes its strong tradition of democracy. The first District Council was chosen by the girl members of the local groups themselves, and from the first, the local Associations shared in the administration of the whole. The place in district and even in national affairs given to the girls who made up the local groups appears to have been, from very early days, the expression of a recognized fundamental principle. This principle was expressed also in their conviction that "youth should be evangelized by youth."

Like the British, the French movement was always interdenominational. "It is a daughter of the Protestant church. . . . Every denomination and every variety of French Protestantism is represented in the membership. The National Association has no official link with any particular church, but it belongs to the Federation [of Protestant churches]. Membership is open to every girl who accepts the principles and the rules, but there is no confessional work."[7]

The first Y.W.C.A. groups in Germany appeared, as in England and France, in the 1850s, and like them they originated in the concern of Christian women for the increasing number of wage-earning girls away from home. In the beginning the programs were meetings, mostly religious in character, held in homes. When, as their numbers grew and the groups became too large for a home, an effort was made to obtain the use of a parish house for these meetings, the church was not at first hospitable to the idea. Church leaders had not yet come to recognize the need of special work for girls as well as for boys.

It was a young pastor in Berlin, Pastor Johannes Burckhardt, who, intensely interested in work for young people, girls as well as boys, in

1890 first brought the scattered Associations in Berlin together into a district organization. He was also the moving spirit in forming the National Association in 1893, and became its first President, holding this office until his death in 1914. Pastor Burckhardt was deeply concerned that the church should minister more vitally to the needs of youth and that youth should grow up within the church, and committed to its service. Thus under his leadership the ties with the church were greatly strengthened. The Association, however, was never wholly absorbed by the church, but remained a separate organization, supported by voluntary contributions.

Several circumstances tended to bring about the close relationship between the Y.W.C.A. and the established churches which distinguished the German work from that of Great Britain and of France. In the first place, in the later decades of the nineteenth century, Protestant denominational churches, other than those recognized by the government,[8] were very small in membership (or entirely non-existent) in Germany. This fact was bound to make the identification of the Association with the church much more marked than in countries where a variety of sects were found within the Y.W.C.A. fellowship. Second, the large place taken by church deaconesses in the direction of the program of the Association was doubtless a factor in making it what in fact it eventually became, practically the work of the church for young women. Pastor Burckhardt, reporting on the work of the German Y.W.C.A. at the World's Conference in 1906, explains it thus: "The intimate relation between our Associations and the church is primarily due to the fact that the majority of these Associations were founded by ministers of the church and are under the deaconesses. In a sense, therefore, they form part of the work of the church."[9]

Two movements within the church in Germany, the deaconess movement and the *Innere Mission* influenced the development of the German Y.W.C.A. and contributed largely to its special character and quality. The Innere Mission, formed in 1849, carried on a great variety of social and religious activities, seeking especially to serve those groups that had special needs, such as the unemployed, prisoners, and underprivileged children. Through its system of sisterhoods and lay-brotherhoods the Innere Mission carried on an extensive program, which included schools organized to meet the needs of special groups, rescue homes, lodging houses, clubs for working men, and many other activities. Most important of all, it was a great force for the education of the church regarding social and industrial conditions, and a training ground for a large number of workers in the field of social service.

The deaconess movement in the church was even earlier in origin than the Innere Mission, having been started in 1836 by Theodore Fliedner, a pastor of Kaiserwerth, a small village on the Rhine. Its purpose, as described by Pastor Burckhardt in an address given at the Paris World's Conference, was to train young women "to carry out the work of Christian ministrations . . . to the sick, the poor, children, prisoners, etc., to whatever class they belong in our churches and communities."[10] During the more than twenty-five years that Pastor Fliedner spent there, Kaiserwerth became in a remarkable way "a training center and an example for European philanthropy." From it came deaconess homes and many lines of Christian service, not only in Germany but in Protestant communities in many countries on the Continent. Its influence was also strongly felt in England. It was from Kaiserwerth that Florence Nightingale gained the impulse for her vocation and at Kaiserwerth that she received her nurse's training.[11]

In Germany itself there developed a large and well established order of deaconesses, holding a general conference every three years. In 1894 this order numbered some 8000 workers in hospitals, poorhouses, orphanages, and as parish workers. Pastor Burckhardt says that their sphere of action embraced "the entire field of Christian ministrations in so far as they can be performed by women." Thus in the Innere Mission and in the deaconess organization, especially among those deaconesses engaged in parish work, the church in Germany had ready at hand a network of organized social services and a body of trained and experienced social and religious workers. The resources of the Innere Mission and the leadership of the parish deaconesses gave to the Y.W.C.A. a trained professional leadership such as neither the British nor any other continental Associations possessed.

These were not, however, the only determining influences in the development of the German Y.W.C.A. Another was the personality, conviction, enthusiasm and genius of Pastor Burckhardt himself. He was not only intensely interested in youth, he was also concerned to develop in the service of youth the unused capabilities of young women of leisure. For this group he opened a training school, with a six months' course, to prepare them to become leaders of clubs for girls and to administer the other activities of the Y.W.C.A. He had a rare gift for recognizing possibilities of leadership and he had great confidence in what young women could do. Through the Association activities which he entrusted to them, he in effect developed a new profession for women in Christian service. Until this time the work of deaconess had been almost the only opening for them.

Nor was Pastor Burckhardt's vision for the Association confined to one group of girls or to activities of a wholly individual character. He opened work for girls in factories and was instrumental in getting factory owners to install welfare work. He investigated conditions adverse to the best interests of young women and worked for adequate protective legislation. Under his leadership the German National Association set definite standards and endeavored to bring the more backward local units to that level, especially encouraging them to include girls "of any social position and of all callings" among their members.

In the larger cities the work took the form of clubs where, in their own clubrooms, open every evening, girls could have opportunity for education and social intercourse. In smaller places the Association made use of rooms put at its disposal by the parish. A national traveling secretary, and later a large staff of secretaries, visited and advised local Associations. A magazine to give help to inexperienced leadership and another "to create a bond between the members" were among the first projects undertaken by the National Association.

When the World's Y.W.C.A. was formed in 1894, the newly organized national movement in Germany felt that it was not sufficiently well established to take on the responsibilities of membership in a world movement, though it was in hearty sympathy with its organization. In 1898, however, after the first World's Conference, it affiliated with the World's Y.W.C.A. as an active member.

Young Women's Christian Association work in the northern continental countries began twenty to thirty years later than in England, France and Germany. Once started, however, the Association developed more rapidly, so that in Norway, Sweden and Denmark there was, at the time of the organization of the World's Y.W.C.A., work comparable to that of France and Germany. The same causes that gave rise to the Association elsewhere repeated themselves here. The needs of young women in a changing social order were a challenge to new forms of organization, new institutions, new programs designed to meet these needs. The example of the Y.M.C.A. suggested a similar type of work for girls. Through increased travel and the multiplication of contacts between these countries and the rest of the Continent and the British Isles, leaders became aware of how needs like those of their own young women were being met elsewhere.

The beginning in each of the northern countries was simple. In Norway it was in Sunday afternoon meetings in Oslo. In Denmark it was through the efforts of a young nurse, Miss Karen Petersen, who in 1883 brought together in Vejle some young women for such meetings as she knew the Y.M.C.A. held for young men. In Sweden Miss Beatrice Dickson, in the early 1880s, pioneered in holding meetings for working girls in Gothenburg, along lines similar to work she had seen during her visits to England. In Iceland a young clergyman read about Y.M.C.A. and Y.W.C.A. work in a German paper, and thereupon organized his boys and girls together in a Christian Association in 1880.

The Danish Y.W.C.A. was from early days predominantly a rural work, and in very close touch locally—and nationally when a national organization developed—both with the church and with the Y.M.C.A. In the same year in which the first Y.W.C.A. group was formed in Vejle in 1883, a "Committee for Christian Work with Adolescents" appointed by the Innere Mission of the State Church, named a clergyman, the Reverend Carl Moe, as secretary for both Y.M.C.A. and Y.W.C.A. work. When the World's Y.W.C.A. was organized in 1894, Denmark had as yet no national Association. However, the Copenhagen Association, which had been organized in 1889 through the initiative of a young member from Vejle who was taking nurse's training in Copenhagen, was in 1896 accepted as a corresponding member of the World's Association and was represented on the World's Committee by its President, Mr. Kjaer.[12]

In contrast to the Danish work, the work for young women in Norway started almost simultaneously under several different auspices, with the result that in the later years of the nineteenth century this country, with a population of less than two and a half millions, had three Christian organizations national in scope, each having programs of work for young women. The largest of these movements as well as the oldest was founded by a clergyman in 1879, for both boys and girls. It was at first largely rural, but as time went on it opened centers also in the towns. In these centers, special Y.M.C.A. and Y.W.C.A. groups were often organized.

A second organization carrying from its beginning the name Young Women's Christian Association, was started in Oslo in 1887 by Miss Sophie Pharo, with the encouragement and help of the Y.M.C.A. This organization, which was entirely within the Lutheran State Church, developed into a full-fledged city Association in Oslo, and by 1894 had thirty-five branches in cities, towns and a few rural districts.

The third movement, begun in 1890, also in Oslo, was at first called the Young Women's Christian Society. Its founders were two women interested in evangelistic work, the Countess Wedel-Jarlsberg and Miss Birgitte Esmark. Both these women were acquainted with the work of the Y.W.C.A. in England and consciously modeled their work on the British pattern, especially its basis of membership, which was interdenominational. In 1894 this Young Women's Christian Society had ten branches and had formed a national organization. It was this national Norwegian organization that affiliated with the World's Y.W.C.A., in that year.

It was entirely natural that as time went on, these separate movements, all working in the same field, should seek to unite. In fact the oldest youth movement united with the Y.M.C.A. as early as 1886, and became the "Christian Youth Association". Thus there were many young women in a national Christian Association movement of both boys and girls, as well as in a national but strictly Lutheran Y.W.C.A., who were in no way connected with the World's Y.W.C.A. Eventually, however, these different national movements came together, and the young women in all of them became a part of the World's Y.W.C.A. But this is a story of later years.

The first real Young Women's Christian Association in Sweden was organized in Stockholm in 1885 by Mrs. Natalie Meijerhelm, who also had seen and been interested in Y.W.C.A. work in England.

An early report by the General Secretary, Miss Anna Roos, says that the work was carried on "according to the same principles as the English Mother Association from which rules as well as methods are largely taken." It followed the lines, characteristic elsewhere, of an evangelistic and Bible-class program. From the first, however, there were other activities, social and educational, and it was not long before the Stockholm Y.W.C.A. became the center from which similar work spread to other parts of Sweden. Though one in aim with the church, the work in Sweden did not develop on parish lines nor did pastors take the lead in it. Every branch had its own rules and its own Council, while the Council of the Stockholm Association formed the bond that united the branches with one another and also with the Association in England.

One of its most striking features was its missionary program. In 1894 the Stockholm Association organized a special branch called the "Female Missionary Workers", the object of which was the publication of missionary literature. This agency translated and published some English books on missions. It sent out and supported missionaries and provided maintenance for native evangelists and for children in mission lands. It was, in effect, a foreign missionary society organized, administered, and financed by the Y.W.C.A. Through it the Swedish Y.W.C.A., at the turn of the century, was supporting workers or making contributions toward missionary work in India, China, Lapland, the Congo, Mongolia, Thibet, North Africa, Armenia, a Swedish village in the south of Russia, and the McAll Mission in France. Not all the missionary interest of the Y.W.C.A. was channeled through this body. Some of the Asociations gave directly to the great missionary societies of Sweden, but the Female Missionary Workers was the organization through which the Stockholm Association, and others as well, made their contribution. There is no evidence, however, that any of this missionary impulse went, as it did in the Associations in Great Britain, into reproducing the Y.W.C.A. as such in other lands.

In these small strongly Protestant countries, not yet acutely pressed by the social miseries of industrialism but religiously quickened by revivals and sharing largely in the missionary enthusiasm which swept over European Protestantism in this period, it was natural that the Association's

28

evangelistic and missionary program should bulk larger than in other countries. The extensive program of social services, hostels, restaurants, holiday homes, camps, employment agencies, travelers' aid services, clubs, educational classes and recreational features was something to which the Associations were driven or led by force of circumstances, as their deeper acquaintance with young women, begun in the Bible class or the evangelistic meeting, revealed the imperative need.

This summary of the development of Y.W.C.A. work in France, Germany, Denmark, Norway and Sweden, though it covers the field of national or near national work in existence before 1894, does not wholly reveal the extent to which work for young women along Y.W.C.A. lines had already taken root in continental countries.

In French Switzerland such work dates from 1851, though its spread did not become general until after 1875. For a long time the Swiss work was not only almost wholly religious, it was almost wholly local in character, the separate Associations having little or no connection with any outside their own canton. Gradually, however, the Associations throughout the French-speaking cantons developed cooperative activities, and later the German speaking cantons did the same. Reports given at the first World's Conference furnish a vivid picture of the atmosphere within which the early work developed, and the reasons for its special characteristics.

> Our position in such matters (i.e. as joining in a universal Association) is peculiar. Each canton being in some measure a distinct state, having its own autonomy not only in political matters but in all questions of administration, religious bodies have also proceeded in the same way. The Y.M.C.A.s and the Y.W.C.A.s have grouped themselves according to the limits of the cantons.[13]

The same report says that the French-speaking Associations at that time numbered 311, the German-speaking 293. The character and program of these little groups of girls who met together in the towns and villages of Switzerland can be inferred from a report given sixteen years later, but probably describing what was in general true of the Swiss Associations throughout their early history.

> Our people are extremely individual and our Associations are the same. In each little Cantonal Republic the work is carried on in a different way. . . . The social side is not developed in the Swiss Associations. A large number of our Associations adhere faithfully to the old tradition of applying the name "Christian Associations" to strictly religious gatherings, Bible lectures, etc.

Yet even in Switzerland it was not always possible to confine the sense of Christian concern for young women within these limits, for the report continues:

> In our industrial towns the necessity is keenly felt of working for the whole development of the young girl, for her health, her education, even her pleasure, without losing sight of the real object of the Association, religious and spiritual development.[14]

Hungary had work for young women which can be thought of as the forerunner of the Y.W.C.A., dating back to 1884. There was at that time an organization that went by the name of "Sunday's Association" whose members were chiefly women. A second source is found in the "Lorantffy Zsuzanna", organized in 1894 to undertake various types of welfare work for women. Under its auspices a student hostel, a deaconess home, and a hospital were established. The moving spirit in this work was Madame de Szilassy, wife of the statesman Count de Szilassy, "a delightful cosmopolitan, and deeply Christian woman, versed in worldly matters." Madame de Szilassy was the first President of "Lorantffy Zsuzanna", and it is to her conviction, energy and ability that much of its development was due. It was she who on learning about the organization of the World's Y.W.C.A. realized the value for the work in Hungary of a connection with this world movement, a recognition which led in due time to the forming of a National Y.W.C.A. in Hungary and its affiliation with the World's Association.

In the Netherlands, in the early 1880s, following a period of religious revival, work was started in many parts of the country for small groups of girls. These groups were everywhere led by women, often the wives of pastors. Their purpose was religious, yet they also carried on a good deal of social service. The work was largely among village girls—a group could be found in almost every village—but there were some groups in cities as well.

In the meantime, out of the work of the Union Internationale des Amies de la Jeune Fille there developed an organization of girls known as *de Nederlandsche Meijes Bond,* whose members were for the most part country girls engaged in domestic service in the cities, but whose leadership came from a fine group of young women of leisure. In 1894, when the World's Y.W.C.A. was organized, the Meijes Bond, the program of which was closest to that of the Y.W.C.A. in other countries, had only recently organized its National Committee and felt that it was not sufficiently well established to take on the responsibilities of an international affiliation.

30

The founding of an Italian Y.W.C.A. is still another interesting revelation of the threads, issuing from Great Britain for the most part, that were woven together in the latter days of the nineteenth century to form a movement existing under the varied conditions of many countries but possessing a common basis of purpose, program, and mutual understanding. The work for both English and Italian girls undertaken by English women in Florence has already been mentioned, and there was similar work in Rome,[15] but the real beginnings of the Italian Association have a different source.

In the late 1880s or early 1890s, Mr. Schalck, a German who had acquired British citizenship and was engaged in the lace industry in Nottingham, moved his factory to Turin, Italy, in order that his wife, whose health was delicate, might live in a milder climate. Madame Schalck, a French woman by birth, had also lived since childhood in Nottingham. There she had become acquainted with a family of young people, one of whom, Lucy, later the wife of Mr. J. Herbert Tritton, the Chairman of Barclay's Bank and a man of wide interests, became her life-long intimate friend. Mrs. Tritton was for many years the President of the Continental Committee of the United Central Council of the Y.W.C.A. in Great Britain and became in 1894 the first President of the World's Y.W.C.A.

Madame Schalck, in part perhaps through her association with "the world-wide Trittons", became not only deeply interested in the Y.W.C.A. but possessed of a broad international outlook upon it. Italy in 1890 was far behind the northern European countries in the characteristic developments of the late nineteenth century, yet she had recently undergone revolutionary changes that were fast bringing the northern provinces, particularly, into the maelstrom of those same currents of life that had influenced the development of woman's movements in other lands.

The attainment of political unity by Italy in 1870 was a signal for progress in many ways: the extension of manhood suffrage, a new religious freedom, the passage of compulsory education laws, the opening of educational opportunities to women, and the industrialization of many towns in the north. With the larger religious freedom there came a considerable growth in the Waldensian Church, which since the Middle Ages had managed to keep alive in the northern valleys that had been its refuge in days of persecution. Missionaries from Great Britain and the United States also took advantage of the more liberal attitude of the government towards religion. English Methodists and Baptists, American Methodists, Baptists and Seventh Day Adventists all planted small preaching stations in Italy and often opened schools for girls. Protestantism in these years enjoyed a "modest growth" in Italy, but it was often Protestantism of a narrow, sectarian and proselytizing spirit.

Conditions for women too were changing. It is true that higher education, though theoretically open to them, was still a door they rarely entered. Industrialization, however, was rapidly drawing young women in northern Italy into factories, and the new atmosphere of freedom, change and progress was stirring those of more favored background into new activities and interests.

In 1894, in the face of the changing conditions in Italy and just as the World's Y.W.C.A. was coming into existence, Madame Schalck, in collaboration with Signorina Elisa Meynier, a young Italian woman of rare spiritual gifts belonging to a Waldensian family, organized in Turin the first Italian Y.W.C.A. It was largely a gathering together of girls of leisure, meeting for Bible study and for devotional services. Soon, however, educational classes and social service were added to its program. Its membership, at least at the beginning, was made up entirely of "evangelicals". It seems to have been the Waldensian groups among whom the Association spread most quickly, for within two years a conference was held of delegates from twelve Associations in the towns in the Waldensian Valleys, though from the start, Madame Schalck and Signorina Meynier labored to build an interdenominational movement.

In the nineteenth century Spain was, with the exception of Portugal, the country of western Europe least touched by the new spirit of liberalism that was expressing itself in the trend toward constitutional, democratic forms of government, economic industrialization, the rapid spread of education and religious toleration. There was, to be sure, a small minority of educated, liberal-minded citizens, but compared to other European countries, Spain was far behind in spite of its expansion culturally in Latin America. Education was still entirely controlled by the Roman Catholic Church, and for women even primary education was the exception rather than the rule. During the first half of the century, Protestantism was almost non-existent; after the granting of religious freedom in Spain in 1868, missionaries from America and from some of the English free churches established small Protestant communities. The results of this missionary effort were, however, small.

Yet Spain as a field of Y.W.C.A. missionary endeavor seems to have been a particular interest of the Continental Council of the British Association in quite early days. To the strongly evangelical British Association there was the appeal of missionary activity—the desire to bring the study of the Bible and a warm, vital, evangelical experience of religion to Spanish girls. As early as 1888 the Council reports four "regular branches" in Spain,[16] and from then on there are frequent references to work in that country—always small, extremely simple in type, and evidently carried on under great difficulties. As has been noted, the earliest discussions about the relation of Roman Catholic girls to the Y.W.C.A. were in connection with the work in Spain.[17]

The actual leadership for the little Association groups came largely from a school for girls founded in 1881 at San Sebastian by Mrs. Alice Gordon Gulick, the wife of a Congregational missionary from the United States. Mrs. Gulick's aim was to provide the Protestant churches in Spain with women of education and training who could be teachers and church and social workers. Actually her work was of much wider significance, for in 1890 her school adopted the state system of education established for men and boys, which allowed them to study where they pleased and then to present themselves at state centers for examination. In 1892 Mrs. Gulick's girls carried off some of the prizes at these state examinations "to the great disgust of the men", and in 1894 four of her students took A.B. degrees, two of them matriculating the following year at the University and taking the M.A. degree.

The minutes of the Continental Council speak definitely of one Association center in Spain as being carried on by a graduate of Mrs. Gulick's school who was married to a Protestant pastor, and it is probable that both the British Association and Mrs. Gulick looked forward to an increasing leadership in the Association field from her girls. This is the point that Association work had reached in Spain when the World's Y.W.C.A. was organized.

One other country in Europe should be listed among those in which Y.W.C.A. work had been established prior to 1894. That is Russia. Here, however, the work was not for or among Russian girls but for German girls living in Russia, and it drew its leadership from German-speaking Protestants in Russia. Information about this early work comes from a report sent by Baroness Marie Nicolay of St. Petersburg to the third World's Y.W.C.A. Conference, at Paris in 1906. She writes:

> In 1884 five ladies, Sunday-school teachers, felt the necessity of continuing to unite with their former pupils after their confirmation, and of forming a center of Christian influence to shield them from the dangers of the metropolis. Meetings for Bible study were started on Sunday afternoons with the object of bringing the young women to a personal, living faith in Jesus Christ. Soon the feeble beginnings began to grow. Numbers of Protestant young women, flocking to St. Petersburg every year from the Baltic provinces in search of situations, naturally felt forlorn and helpless, surrounded by people speaking another tongue and professing another creed. These willingly availed themselves of our newly organized Evangelical Association. Gradually the ladies in charge started an agency for procuring

situations, a library, a Home with a dressmaking and household work department, and undertook the depositing of the girls' savings in the bank.[18]

The constitution of this work was confirmed by the government in 1891. It provided that the general direction of the work should be in the hands of a committee consisting of one evangelical pastor and five ladies with voting power. Meetings were conducted in German. Bible study "with 'opportunity for discussion', and lectures on various topics, including missions, seem to have made up the usual program."

The first attempt at some union of this German work in Russia with similar organizations in other countries was made, Baroness Nicolay writes, in 1885, when Miss Emilia de Scalon and Countess Maria Pahlen became members of the Union Internationale des Amies de la Jeune Fille. In 1890 Baroness Nicolay herself established contact through correspondence with the Y.W.C.A. in London, and in 1891 connection was made also with Pastor Burckhardt, head of the German movement.

The difficulties under which any such work as that of the Y.W.C.A. was carried on in Czarist Russia were of course very great. It is significant that in spite of handicaps there was in existence a small but vital movement which was desirous of contact with similar movements elsewhere. That such did exist was owing to the conviction and the initiative of that small group of evangelical Christians who were also persons of position and worldy experience and alive to the changing conditions under which youth was living.

REFERENCES

[1] *World's Y.W.C.A. Quarterly.* October 1900, p. 57.

[2] Moor, Lucy M. *Girls of Yesterday and Today,* p. 158.

[3] Continental Council, November 5, 1891, Minutes.

[4] See Chapter I, p. 14.

[5] *Association Chronicles,* 1940 edition, p. 124.

[6] Third World's Y.W.C.A. Conference, 1906, Report, p. 75.

[7] *Association Chronicles,* 1940 edition, p. 125.

[8] The United, the Lutheran, and the Reformed Church.

[9] Third World's Y.W.C.A. Conference, 1906, Report, p. 77.

[10] Third World's Y.W.C.A. Conference, 1906, Report, pp. 139-140.

[11] Latourette, Kenneth S. *The Expansion of Christianity,* Vol. 5, p. 153.

[12] In 1900 the Countess Knuth became the first woman President of the Y.W.C.A. of Denmark. Often spoken of as "the Mother of the Y.W.C.A.", it is to her devotion and initiative that the development of the Danish movement is largely due.

[13] First World's Y.W.C.A. Conference, 1898, Report, "Notes on the Swiss Y.W.C.A.s", p. 153.

[14] Fifth World's Y.W.C.A. Conference, 1914, Report, pp. 303-304.

[15] See chapter 1, pp. 13.

[16] Continental Council, January 4, 1888, Minutes.

[17] See chapter 1, p. 17.

[18] Third World's Y.W.C.A. Conference, Report, p. 86.

Every great revival of religion has certain features which distinguish it from similar manifestations upon other occasions. The historic American revival of 1857-1858 showed three outstanding characteristics: the number and value of prayer circles; the unity of Christians of different denominations; and the large place filled by women as leaders of organized Christian forces.

ELIZABETH WILSON, *Fifty Years of Association Work Among Young Women.*

CHAPTER 3   THE Y.W.C.A. BEFORE 1894: NORTH AMERICA

WHILE the Young Women's Christian Association of Great Britain was developing into a national movement of size and power and reaching out to plant the seed of the Association throughout the length and breadth of the Empire, and while the same impulse was fashioning the Association movement on the Continent in forms that reflected the particular circumstances of each country, there were also developing in the countries on the western shores of the Atlantic, Associations similar in purpose and aim but in some of their features very different from those of the Continent or the British Isles. These were the Young Women's Christian Associations of the United States and Canada.

The first appearance of work that later became the Young Women's Christian Association in the United States was in New York City in the year 1858. It was the direct outcome of the religious revival of 1857. In the winter of 1857-1858 a Union Prayer Circle was formed by Mrs. Marshall O. Roberts, "a young woman of splendid intellect, personal charm and fervent religious life."[1] By the end of the year 1858 this Prayer Circle had become the "Ladies' Christian Association", with thirty-five members; had definitely stated its purpose to be "to labor for the temporal, moral and spiritual welfare of self-supporting young women"; and had begun to hold religious meetings especially for this group.

In 1860 this Association opened a boarding home for young women, and ten years later organized a "Young Ladies' Branch". This branch of younger women took the name of "Young Ladies' Christian Association of the City of New York", rented rooms in a large warehouse, and began the development of a varied program of activities. In 1875 the name was changed to the "Young Women's Christian Association of the City of New York".

The emphasis placed by the Ladies' Christian Association on work for self-supporting young women was due to the rapid expansion of industry in the northern sections of the United States, which was causing a great influx of young women from small towns to the city. At about the same time that New York City was opening its first boarding home, Miss Lucretia Boyd, a deaconess of the Methodist Church, became greatly concerned over the number of girls from the towns and villages and even from the country districts who were coming into Boston to work in the ever-increasing number of factories, and for whom there was no provision for safe and wholesome living. It was to meet this need that in 1866 thirty ladies organized the Boston Young Women's Christian Association. They defined its object in terms closely resembling those used by the Ladies' Christian Association in New York, as "the temporal, moral and religious welfare of young women dependent on their own exertions for support." Rooms were opened, religious meetings, Bible study, educational classes and social recreation were begun. Within a surprisingly few years the Boston Association, like the one in New York, was carrying a program of activities that included a boarding home, traveler's aid, and employment bureau, as well as many religious and educational classes. Included in the last were courses designed to furnish training for work in offices and shops and in domestic service.

In both New York and Boston the central concern of the founders of the Association was for the spiritual welfare of girls, though problems presented by girls thrown without preparation into an entirely new way of life forced provision for their immediate physical, educational and recreational needs more into the foreground than was the case in countries where this change was coming more gradually. The basis of active, that is, voting and office-holding, membership in both cities was membership in a Protestant evangelical church. Both Associations were interdenominational in character, and while control and administration were definitely Protestant and evangelical, their associate membership as well as the wider constituency of non-members whom they served was not bounded by religious lines. Their concern was in the fullest sense for all young women "dependent on their own exertions for support."

The needs that had been so acutely felt in New York and Boston were equally real in other cities, and similar work appeared in many places within the next few years. In the year 1871 eight such Associations sent delegates to a conference for the discussion of common problems, and thirteen others were represented by letter. In 1875 twenty-eight Associations, including some from Canadian cities, met in a conference which reported that thirteen of these twenty-eight already had boarding homes and that their combined membership totaled more than eight thousand.

Not all these organizations went by the name of Y.W.C.A. Indeed, they were more frequently called simply "Women's Christian Associations". This name was not inappropriate, because while in every case it was probably the needs of young women which first inspired the undertaking, some of the Associations assumed tasks for other groups as well—for old ladies, or for children, even, occasionally, for men. In those days, when welfare organizations were few and social work in the modern sense scarcely begun, the Women's Christian Associations pioneered in almost any needy field that presented itself to their energy and conscience. Many lines of philanthropic or charitable work which later were carried by special organizations originated in a Women's Christian Association.

In 1877, at a meeting held in Montreal, Canada, it was agreed that the informal biennial meeting that had become a custom should be established as the regular means of consultation and conference among local Associations. No central administrative body like the United Central Council of the Y.W.C.A. of Great Britain was set up, no plans were made for promoting new organization, or standardizing the work already begun, nor was there any attempt to develop a uniform basis of membership. Many Associations, like Boston and New York, had an evangelical basis. Others, while Christian in motivation and spirit, did not define their basis in evangelical or even in Protestant terms, and had as officers or on their Boards of Managers members of non-evangelical churches such as the Unitarian, and Roman Catholics as well as Protestants. According to the constitution of some of these early Associations, "any woman, upon the payment of the membership fee" might become an active member.[2] The International Conference, as the biennial meeting was now called, since there were in it Associations from both the United States and Canada, endeavored to provide a medium for consultation and exchange of experience rather than to form a close-knit organization.

In 1891 a somewhat more formal plan of organization was adopted, providing for an International Board of Women's and Young Women's Christian Associations, with a permanent Executive Committee and an employed staff. At the same time, the tendency toward a more definite specialization in work for young women was indicated by a resolution directing all organizations formed in the future, and uniting with the International Board, to take the name "Young Women's Christian Association" instead of "Women's Christian Association". Yet no uniform basis was adopted and the vitality of the movement continued to reside in the initiative of the independent local units.

When the World's Y.W.C.A. was organized in 1894, this International Board had member Associations in many cities in the United States and Canada. It was one of the two streams of work for young women which, in the United States, joined together in 1906 to form a new national Y.W.C.A. movement. It was from the beginning and throughout its history primarily an Association supplying institutional services for self-supporting girls under Christian auspices. As such, it was extraordinarily fruitful, a pioneer in many fields, the first and for long the most significant expression among women's organizations, of Christian concern over conditions that were affecting profoundly the lives of multitudes of young women. The strong consciousness of itself as a woman's movement as well as a movement for and of youth which is characteristic of the American Y.W.C.A. today, is to a large extent an inheritance from these early Women's Christian Associations.

While the work of this organization of Women's and Young Women's Christian Associations was growing to large proportions, the developments in higher education for women were preparing the ground in the United States for a second movement among young women which was to have great significance. Partly through the founding of women's colleges but even more through the increasing attendance of women students at the universities, especially in the Middle West, the number of women who had the advantage of higher education was rapidly increased. No other country had so large a proportion of college or university trained women. Also the conditions of university life for women in America were very different from those in Europe. Though some universities were at first grudging in their welcome, all state universities were coeducational in policy. Provision for women students was similar to that for men, and women were included in many of the student activities.

Among these activities the Young Men's Christian Association had an important place, since in both the United States and Canada it had not only a large city work but strong student organizations. As women students began to take their place in the universities, those who were interested in Christian activities became sharers along with the men in the student Y.M.C.A.s. It was not long, however, before some of the women students felt that they would benefit more from an organization of their own than from membership in one that was primarily for men and almost wholly led by them. The result was, quite naturally, the formation of student Y.W.C.A.s.

The first of these student Associations was organized in a Normal School in the State of Illinois in 1872. Four others are known to have started independently in the 1870s. Many of the Y.M.C.A. leaders were in hearty sympathy with this trend. Indeed, there was a conviction among some of them that women did not belong in a Y.M.C.A., and Y.M.C.A. traveling secretaries when visiting the colleges in the early 1880s often urged the women to start their own Association, and helped them in their plans for organization. The moment was ripe for such a movement. The number of women students was large and increasing. The revivals that had influenced church life throughout the country had also stirred the colleges, and Christian women students as well as men were eager for a fellowship that would deepen their spiritual life, and many of them were ready to devote their lives to Christian service. The Y.M.C.A. furnished a pattern for the work and helped to promote the idea.

The organization of student Y.W.C.A.s in the colleges and universities was soon followed, again after the pattern set by the men, by the formation of state-wide committees composed of representatives from the different local college groups. These State Committees carried on advisory correspondence with the local Associations and arranged state-wide conventions for the discussion of common interests, the formation of policy, and the carrying out of joint projects. In 1885 there were such committees in seven of the middle-western states.

The student Y.W.C.A. movement was, like the student Y.M.C.A., entirely spiritual in purpose. Through evangelistic meetings and Bible study it endeavored to win young women to a vital Christian commitment which should express itself in dedication to a life of Christian service at home or on the mission field. Its basis of membership, like that of the Y.M.C.A., was Protestant and evangelical. In a little more than a decade after the first student Y.W.C.A. was formed, the women students were asking for a national organization, such as the Y.M.C.A. already had, with a paid staff, to give unity and direction to their work.

That there already existed another organization working among young women in both the United States and Canada, one which in many places was called by the same name, was recognized. True, it had only a slight touch with students, its work being largely in cities, but the ideas of the students were not bounded by college horizons, and already a number of towns and cities had turned to the State Committees to ask that work similar to that among students be started in their communities. In addition, the impulse to a life of service which the student Association generated, more and more tended to express itself not only in the choice of foreign missionary work as a life profession, a field of service that many were not free to enter, but also in an ardent desire to serve other young women in the communities to which students returned after college days were over. If this growing movement among women students should extend itself to cities, it would definitely enter a field already occupied by an organization similar in name and in general spirit and purpose, though radically different in certain features that the student movement regarded as fundamental.

In 1885 the International Board of Women's and Young Women's Christian Associations, meeting that year in Cincinnati, was approached by student delegates representing the seven student State Committees with a proposal for a union of the two movements into one organization that should promote the work of the Y.W.C.A. in both cities and colleges. It proved difficult at that time, however, to bring together two movements, of which one had an already long-established policy and program, much property and much institutional work, while the other was still very much in the making, with a program and type of organization developed especially for and by a student group. The particular stumbling blocks in the way of union are set forth in a little book called *Young Women*.[3] Looking back upon the two organizations as they existed in 1885, the author says, regarding the work of the Women's Christian Association:

> There was no lack of consecrated Christian service and valuable work on Christian lines of philanthropy . . . no question in regard to the value of the International Conference itself . . . But thus far these conferences had not developed a uniform national membership, nor a concentration of effort on behalf of young women exclusively, such as the college Associations desired to engage in and such as they felt to be peculiarly and appropriately belonging to the Young Women's Christian Association. . . . Also . . . though some of the strongest individual Women's Christian Associations either in their government or their active membership were on an evangelical basis, yet there was no universally adopted test of membership which affiliated all the Associations with the evangelical churches— a test which had proved itself of invaluable service to the Young Men's Christian Association in the remarkable development of their work and efficiency, and which the young women felt to be essential to their own organization.

The difference between the evangelical basis required by the students and the liberty regarding basis allowed by the Women's Christian Association to local units was a fundamental difficulty.

There were, however, other reasons for the failure of the two movements to unite at this time. There was a certain lack of understanding between the age groups represented; between a movement predominantly eastern and one that reflected the temper of the Middle West; between an independently developed woman's movement and one that had strong ties with the Y.M.C.A. Beneath all these factors was a lack of fundamental acquaintance of one organization with the other, and an absence of the joint preliminary study and preparation necessary to an intelligent consideration of the complicated question of union.

The following year, 1886, the student Associations, through delegates elected by their state organizations, formed a National Committee with the purpose of promoting Y.W.C.A. work in both college and city communities. They adopted a constitution embodying the same evangelical basis of membership used by the Y.M.C.A., chose Chicago as the location for their headquarters, and pledged contributions toward a budget that should provide for the setting up of an office and the engaging of a national general secretary.

All the Associations that united to form this new national organization were in colleges or universities, but the first annual report, for the year 1887, written by the General Secretary, Miss Nettie Dunn, states that of the 129 affiliated Associations, fifty-five had been organized that first year, and that of this number, nineteen were in cities. In 1893, the year in which the proposal to form a World's Y.W.C.A. was submitted to the biennial covention of the organization, the number of affiliated Associa tions had increased to 307, of which fifty-two were in cities and 255 in schools, colleges and universities. The number of salaried professional sec- retaries had increased from one to fifty-eight, of whom six were national, seven state, and forty-five local secretaries. The student Associations still greatly outnumbered those in cities, but the city Associations were rapidly taking the lead in the number of employed personnel, in size of their budgets, and in the extent and variety of their program. Moreover, the greater number of local Associations were still in the Middle West.

A movement truly national, even international in scope, was in the making, however. There had been a marked growth in the East; a Pacific Coast Committee had been organized; a few Associations had been formed in the South, and the National Committee had come to be the "International Committee"[4] by the affiliation with it of nine Canadian Associations.

What were the characteristics of this Christian movement literally *of,* *by* and *for* young women? In the first place it was, as was the Christian Association movement in every country, a movement with a central spiritual motive, purpose and emphasis. It was born of the desire to call young women into fellowship with Jesus Christ and into a life dedicated to Christian service. In the first annual report of the organization, that for the year 1887, Miss Dunn, after telling of the growing interest in Bible study and in missions, says: "But the greatest result of this first year of the national work is seen in the fact that the hearts of hundreds, and we may begin to say thousands, of young women from Maine to California and from Canada to Mississippi have been welded together in sympathy and interest in a common work, with a common and well-defined purpose, the evangelization of the young women of the world."

The emphasis of the Associations in universities and colleges continued to be largely on religious activities and spiritual fellowship. In the city Associations, because of the immediacy of the need, it was inevitable that a service program should bulk far more largely than among the students. All the activities for young women which the Women's Christian Association had developed so well and so extensively were reproduced in the city Associations of the new movement. Along with these, however, there was a steady emphasis on the evangelistic purpose that motivated and pervaded the work. The report for city Associations for the year 1893 lists an impressive number of weekly gospel meetings, daily and weekly prayer services, Bible study classes, missionary meetings and workers' training classes. The national magazines for these years, first *The Y.W.C.A. Quarterly* and later *The Evangel,* place a central emphasis on the religious purpose of the Association, with many articles on the spiritual life, on plans for religious meetings, Bible study outlines, and missionary information. As the number and size of the Associations in cities increased, the space given to other phases of program and to the administration of funds and of buildings, to the procuring and training of personnel, to the organization of committee work, in fact to all the processes and problems involved in a large undertaking with many facets, necessarily increased, but the spiritual emphasis continued to hold its central place and to supply the dynamic for the whole.

A second characteristic of this American movement and one in which it differed from the Y.W.C.A. as developed in other countries, was the position and importance of its salaried leadership. Having its origin among students, many of whom were looking forward to professional careers, the Y.W.C.A. itself presented a field for professional Christian service. Especially as it spread in the complicated social environment of the cities, the conviction deepened that it could not well be undertaken without trained leadership. The attitude of the International Committee was expressed by its President, Mrs. John Farwell:

> It is an absolute necessity, in starting an Association in any town, that a young woman familiar with Association work and with training which qualifies her to be a leader and guide of young women, be secured as secretary. And yet there are not many of these to be had, the demand is still far ahead of the supply. But the idea of the Secretaryship as a profession is growing among our workers.[5]

The early development of courses of training for Y.W.C.A. workers was natural, and the first secretaries' training conference was held in 1891. At the 1893 convention, Mrs. William Boyd, who as Corabel Tarr had been the second National General Secretary, gave an address on the Y.W.C.A. secretaryship under the title, "A New Profession for Women and How to Enter It".

A third characteristic, directly related to the emphasis placed on professional leadership, was the persistent effort toward standardization of work. *The Evangel,* the annual reports, and the records of conventions are full of articles, recommendations and addresses on such subjects as "How to Organize an Association", "How to Maintain the Association", "The Work of the General Secretary", and suggestions of program, methods, committee work, conducting board meetings, raising funds—the general business of administering the increasingly large affairs of city Associations.

A pungent and spicy address dealing with these practical matters affecting the reputation and the effectiveness of a women's Christian organization was entitled "Diligent in Business", and given at the 1891 convention by Miss Annie M. Reynolds, at that time State Secretary for Iowa and soon to become the first General Secretary of the World's Y.W.C.A. After touching on many areas of Association activity and stressing the double responsibility for making its methods respected placed upon them by "being women and working in a religious cause," the address concludes: "Let every department of the Association work be carried on according to the best standards of the best workers in similar lines anywhere, secular or spiritual, and this we believe can be done if the fervency of spirit of genuine Christian womanhood be combined in no impossible degree with the energy, punctuality and exactness of a business woman of the world."[6]

Still another significant feature of the American work in these early years was the effort made by the International Committee to gain a comprehensive view of the possibilities before the Association and to instill in the whole Association membership a sense of responsibility for an aggressive policy in relation to them. An address by Miss Tarr, General Secretary of the International Committee, at the 1891 convention on the subject "International Needs and Sources of Supply", reveals how large were their ideas and how far-reaching their aims. She challenges the convention to look at the unorganized fields of work properly within the scope of the Association, and lists them thus:

1. New England, our great manufacturing district where "a few cities are doing good work" but where the field as a whole is almost untouched.

2. Canada, "full of rich promise", which has had but one brief visit in five years.

3. The vast West, whose needs are apparent but barely touched.

4. The South, which knows almost nothing of such work.

5. The colored young women, who are asking for the work.

6. 400 cities large enough for the work, thirty to fifty of them needing it at once and fifteen demanding immediate attention.

7. The young women of foreign lands, "whose claims upon the favored young women of this continent" she said she had not time to mention.

No wonder that she adds: "Who is to plan all this? Who to execute? Who to raise the funds to carry it forward?" and concludes that the International Committee must have more secretaries at once, and that it should double its budget, in order to "enter the doors that are wide open to our work."[7]

Until 1893, although missionary education held an important place in its program and missionary interest and giving were widespread, there were no such large missionary undertakings in the American Y.W.C.A. as had characterized the early days of the Y.W.C.A. in Great Britain and in Sweden. The reason for this is not far to seek. The home field was so vast, so ripe for harvesting, so limitless in its opportunities and its appeals that it consumed all the energy and demanded all the leadership available. Also, America itself had not the kind of world contacts that carried British citizens, both men and women, to the ends of the earth. Though the tide of missionaries from North America was rising, the great adventure of American life in these years was the opening up of the Far West, the rebuilding of the war-torn South following the Civil War of 1861-1865, and grappling with the newly recognized social frontiers in the fields of industry. Yet the recognition of missionary responsibility was ever present. The Student Volunteer Movement, launched in 1886, was a powerful factor in college life and many young women who were members of student Associations became volunteers for the foreign mission field.

Student leaders like Luther W. Wishard of the Y.M.C.A. and his wife, who was a charter member of the International Committee of the Y.W.C.A., were profoundly interested in missions. When in 1889-1893 Mrs. Wishard accompanied her husband on a world tour of the foreign work of the Y.M.C.A., she was officially asked to act as a representative of the Y.W.C.A. Her letters sent to the American Association and published in *The Quarterly* and *The Evangel* reported on the work for young women which she found in the Orient, and stimulated missionary responsibility at home. She wrote at length about the advance in the education of women in Japan, where she found two Y.W.C.A.s already established, and concludes: "The field for special work for young women is open in Japan. The same kind of work that succeeds at home would succeed here."[8] Of China she wrote: "Nowhere could richer opportunities be found for the work of the Y.W.C.A. than in these missionary schools. . . . In view of this it is gratifying to see the organization of the first Y.W.C.A.

in China in the Girls' School of the Southern Presbyterian Church in Hangchow."[9]

The visit of Mr. and Mrs. Wishard to India coincided with the appeal sent to the British and the American Y.W.C.A.s from Madras in 1891, and their conference with British leaders in London on their way home led directly to the appointment of the first foreign secretary from the American Association.[10]

Contacts between the American Associations and those of other countries were slight before 1892 but not altogether lacking. In 1887 Lord Kinnaird, at that time treasurer of the British Y.W.C.A., and his two sisters, the Honorable Emily and the Honorable Gertrude Kinnaird, visited the United States and attended a conference of the International Board of the Women's and Young Women's Christian Associations. Miss Emily Kinnaird says that her mother, Lady Kinnaird, founder of the first Y.W.C.A. in London, planned this trip in the hope that some cooperation between the Y.W.C.A. of America and that of Great Britain might be brought about. This result was not immediately forthcoming, but when Lord Kinnaird and his sisters came again to the United States in 1893 to attend the Chicago World's Fair, they took pains to become acquainted with the leaders of the International Committee, both members and staff.

Both the International Board of the Women's and the Young Women's Christian Associations and the International Committee of the Young Women's Christian Association had been from time to time in correspondence with the British Association, usually with regard to services to be rendered to some young woman passing from one country to the other. For the most part, however, the Y.W.C.A. in the new world knew little of the movement as it had developed in Great Britain, and still less of its growth and its character on the continent of Europe.

It was therefore a momentous step in the history of the Y.W.C.A. in North America when the International Committee decided to accept the invitation of the United Central Council of Great Britain to be represented at an International Conference which they were convening in London in April 1892. The American delegates chosen were Miss Rebecca F. Morse, the experienced, gifted and able chairman of the New York State Committee, and Miss Corabel Tarr, the General Secretary of the International Committee. Their visit to English and Scottish Associations, their conferences with British leaders, and their interpretation of the British Y.W.C.A. to American readers of *The Evangel* were, for the American movement, the beginning of knowledge and, in some small way, of understanding of a great sister movement, so like their own in spirit, motivation and ultimate purpose, so different in some of its methods of work and forms of organization. By that visit of Miss Morse and Miss

Tarr to London in 1892 and by the commitments that resulted from it, the sense of world responsibility inherent in the American Y.W.C.A. from the start but largely latent because of other pressures, was called into life.

REFERENCES

[1] Wilson, Elizabeth. *Fifty Years of Association Work Among Young Women,* 1916, p. 22.

[2] Wilson, Elizabeth. *Fifty Years of Association Work Among Young Women,* 1916, p. 56.

[3] Morse, Rebecca F. *Young Women,* 1901, pp. 17-18.

[4] Later called the American Committee.

[5] International Committee, Y.W.C.A.s of the United States and Canada, Annual Report, 1891, pp. 8, 9.

[6] Third International Convention, Y.W.C.A.s of the United States and Canada, 1891, Report, p. 89.

[7] Third International Convention, Y.W.C.A.s of the United States and Canada, 1891, Report, pp. 76-77.

[8] *The Evangel,* April 1890, p. 2.

[9] *The Evangel,* December 1890, p. 8.

[10] See chapter 1, p. 16.

*Not by might, nor by power, but by my Spirit, saith
the Lord of Hosts.* (Zechariah iv:6)
Motto of the World's Y.W.C.A.

*When the women who knew the Y.W.C.A. in its
early days proposed extension or change they wrote
to each other—we find it in their letters—of "this
great crisis" and "these far-reaching plans". That was
not the lack of a sense of humor. They could judge
proportions very well. They knew their own limitations but they knew the Spirit they were trying to
follow has none.*

Our Eighty Years, Historical Sketches of the Y.W.C.A. of
Great Britain.

CHAPTER 4   ORGANIZATION OF THE WORLD'S Y.W.C.A.

THE FIRST official step toward the formation
of a World's Young Women's Christian Association was taken when
the United Central Council of the Y.W.C.A.s of Great Britain invited the
Associations of other countries to attend an International Conference in
London in April 1892. There had been stirrings in the direction of some
form of international cooperation for a number of years. These were chiefly
within the movement in Great Britain, but they were also in the thoughts
of certain American leaders, and they found a sympathetic response in
some of the continental Associations, notably those in closest contact with
the British movement, Norway and Sweden.

In 1888, the year before her world tour, Mrs. Luther W. Wishard
had accompanied her husband to England on a mission for the Student
Christian Movement and had conferred in London with the Honorable
Emily Kinnaird and other British ladies, and, on her return, with the
International Committee of the Y.W.C.A. in North America "as to the
advisability of establishing correspondence between the National Associations of the two countries by means of which they could be mutually helpful to young women passing from one country to the other."[1]

"It is interesting to note," says Miss Morse in her early account of
the history of the American Y.W.C.A., "in Mrs. Wishard's and Miss
Kinnaird's letters of that time their glance into the exigencies of the
future. Mrs. Wishard, referring to the importance of some official con-

nection between the British and the American Y.W.C.A., says, 'While a World's Committee may, at some distant date, be the medium of union, we agreed that we are not yet ready for so unwieldly a body.' "[2]

It is evident that one of the chief concerns which prompted these leaders to urge some working relationship between the two national organizations was the foreign missionary interest, already strongly developed in the British work and now beginning to come into prominence in the American movement. Mrs. Wishard writes to Miss Kinnaird, "America and Great Britain will stand side by side in the foreign field and their work should not be impeded by lack of harmony in methods and wisdom in the occupation of fields." And Miss Kinnaird, writing to the American worker appointed to be the correspondent with Great Britain, says, "I am sure it will be for the glory of God and the benefit of young women if we can, as far as possible, extend unitedly in foreign lands."[3]

Following Mrs. Wishard's visit to London, the idea of an international organization was approached in Great Britain from another angle also. In November 1889 Mrs. J. Herbert Tritton, Chairman of the Continental Division of the United Central Council of the British Y.W.C.A., recommended to the Council:

> That the Continental Division be empowered to prepare and submit to the next meeting of the United Central Council a report of the best means for organizing the work of the Division so as to make it more international in character.

For the next two years, questions raised by this recommendation came periodically before the United Central Council and the Continental and the Colonial Divisions. The Continental Division seems to have had considerable difficulty in dealing with them. In December 1889 it discussed the advisability of trying to form an International Union "on the same plan as the Y.M.C.A.", but the subject was postponed. In March of the following year Mrs. Tritton reported to them "that the Committee of the Y.M.C.A. do not consider that any definite practical work results from their annual international conferences, but that their indirect value is great as a means of stirring up interest in different countries and as a means of exchange of opinion." The only comment in the minutes is that "further consideration of this question was postponed."[4]

In May 1890 Mrs. Tritton brought the matter before them again, saying that the United Central Council "think an international conference likely to be very beneficial in consolidating the work of the Association on the Continent and they are anxious that the Continental Committee should take any steps they think advisable for arranging for one." This time the Continental Committee acted; it instructed the secretary to write to the Colonial Committee to ask its opinion. This Committee replied that it did not think it could send any delegates to such a meeting, "owing to the great distances they would have to travel." There the matter seems to have rested for another year. It appeared again on the agenda of the Committee for June 1891 in the form of a discussion of "the possiblity of holding meetings for the Y.W.C.A. in connection with the Y.M.C.A. International Conference to be held at Amsterdam," but though it was agreed that the secretary should make further inquiries and report at the next meeting, there is no further reference to it in the minutes. It was uphill work for a committee to take forward steps toward so adventurous an undertaking.

When, however, in 1891 the British and American Associations were faced with the request from missionaries in India for trained Association workers, it became evident that some federation or organization was urgently needed. In the words of Miss Kinnaird:

> Enthusiastic young Y.W.C.A. members working in a non-Christian land felt the need of an Association and we were confronted with the fact that two or three different Y.W.C.A.'s were being started in new lands on the lines of the countries from which the workers came, instead of on lines especially adapted to the country for which they were being started.[5]

In November 1891 the United Central Council took the first decisive step by voting:

> That the Committee appointed to inquire into arrangements for the extension of the work on the Continent be asked to enlarge its inquiries so as to include the work carried on by the Extra-European and Colonial Division, with a view to a closer linking together of the Y.W.C.A. work all over the world, and that it be empowered to take action in the matter.[6]

This time action came promptly. The minutes of the Continental Committee for December 1891 record the decision of the United Central Council to hold an international conference in place of its annual spring meeting the following April, and add that a sub-committee had been elected to make arrangements.

No official record of this significant conference, held in London, April 6 and 7, 1892, is available, but the report of the Executive Committee of the World's Y.W.C.A. to the first World's Conference says:

> At the Conference there were met for the first time, representatives of the Y.W.C.A.s of Australia, France, Great Britain, India, Norway, Sweden, Spain, Switzerland and the United States, some sent as authorized delegates by national committees, others whose deep concern in the work of Christian training of

young women had caused their names to be known beyond their own countries. The gathering was irregular in representation and aim; only a few had a more definite thought in mind than mutual conference and comparison of methods and plans of work, and yet so strongly did the possibility of an international development come before them, and so keenly did all shrink from the thought of going back to the previous self-centered national interest, that the Conference appointed Mme Charles Vernes and Pastor Maillet of France, Miss Esmark of Norway, Miss Rebecca F. Morse and Miss Corabel Tarr (now Mrs. William Boyd) of the United States, and Mrs. F. Barker, the Honorable Emily Kinnaird, Miss Morley and Mrs. J. H. Tritton, all of London, to consider more closely the question of a definite organization. Meetings were held on April 8th and 11th, but no detailed minutes of their sittings (precious as they would be to us) have been preserved. At the close of these meetings it was decided to authorize the English and American members to draw up a constitution which should leave each nation entirely free as to its own national methods, growth, and all national action, and should insist only, as the one essential, that the basis of membership for all officers and voting members be such as would embody the fundamental principles of the Young Women's Christian Association.

It was unanimously felt that here all must be like-minded, but membership of national organizations in the World's Association did not involve any right of interference in national affairs. Two years elapsed before the constitution was finished. The few revisions which it has been found necessary to suggest to you for your action after its use during four years of careful study, is the best tribute to the manner in which the work was done. The National Committees of Great Britain and the United States each formally accepted the constitution in the spring and winter of 1894, and later the National Committees of Norway and Sweden followed.[7]

The powers and work of the small committee of English and American women to whom was delegated the task of drawing up a constitution are further clarified in the first annual report of the General Secretary, Miss Annie M. Reynolds:

The International Conference held in London in 1892 having resolved, after much deliberation, that some closer international bond was desirable, appointed a joint English and American Committee whom they authorized to draw up a constitution and to take such legal steps as were necessary to full organization. After two years of faithful work, the Committee reported in the spring of 1894 that their task was so far complete that they were ready to act upon the provisions of the constitution. The first step was deemed to be the choice of a general secretary as executive officer of the Committee. As, by the terms of the constitution, she must be of some country other than that where the headquarters are located, the choice naturally fell upon an American, your present officer. I reached London, September 1, 1894.[8]

Immediately after her arrival, Miss Reynolds set out for Neuchâtel, Switzerland, to interpret to the conference of the Union Internationale des Amies de la Jeune Fille being held there, the purpose and plans of the World's Y.W.C.A. On her return she gave herself for the remainder of the year 1894 to the numerous details of setting up committees, finding and equipping offices, and planning for the months of travel to be undertaken in the coming year in order to interpret the new organization to the Associations on the European continent.

The first meeting of the Executive Committee was held on November 26, at the home of Mrs. Tritton. Five members were present—Mrs. Tritton, the Honorable Emily Kinnaird, Mrs. E. W. Moore, Mrs. Farmer Hall, and Miss Reynolds. Mrs. Tritton was elected President, Lady Fairfax, Vice President, and Miss Mary Morley, Treasurer. Standing Committees were arranged for the European Continent, for Other Continents, for Publications, for Finance and for Traveler's Aid. Miss Reynolds comments on this meeting: "The certain, even regularity with which the mover of one nomination becomes the seconder of the next and vice versa betrays no faint-heartedness nor faltering in taking up the untried and unknown World's Association work." "The meeting closed," say the minutes, "with much informal discussion."

The profound sense of responsibility that was felt by those who thus began "to act upon the provisions of the constitution" finds expression in the report of the Executive Committee to the first World's Conference, held in London in 1898. There also we have a glimpse of the appearance of that most constant concern of all organizations, whether large or small, their financial support. "Initial responsibility," says the report, "is everywhere the hardest to assume. There is no precedent to guide, no encouraging past to give cheer to the future. It was with a deep sense of our dependence upon Divine Guidance that the committee who drew up the constitution decided to locate the headquarters in London and elect an American as their General Secretary. As the question of expense was necessarily a heavy one, Great Britain and America mutually agreed to be responsible for the expense of the Association until the time of the first international conference. The British and American National Committees appointed their national representatives in the number already stipulated by the constitution. Norway and Sweden, each by its basis entitled to active membership, did the same."[9]

Other National Associations soon followed, and the report of the first World's Y.W.C.A. conference lists seven active members of the World's Association—Great Britain, the United States, Norway, Sweden, Canada,[10] Italy, and India. In addition, the World's Committee had corresponding members in Germany and Denmark and in eight colonial Associations in Australasia and South Africa. There were National Committees also in Germany and in France. In both these countries, however, although the attitude toward the World's Committee was cordial and the expectation of eventual membership was real, there was a conviction of the need for further crystalization of their own work before taking on the wider responsibilities of membership in a world body. The Y.W.C.A. of Germany was affiliated in 1898, shortly after the conference. The Y.W.C.A. of France took a similar step in 1900.[11] The total attendance of 326 voting and visiting delegates at the London conference included representatives from China, Egypt, Finland, France, Hungary, Spain, Switzerland and Turkey, as well as from the seven member Associations.

The most important business of the conference was of course the adoption of the constitution, the first three provisions of which, covering Name, Object and Basis, read as follows:

Art. I. *Name*: This organization shall be called the World's Young Women's Christian Association.

Art. II. *Object*: The object of the Association shall be the federation, development and extension of Young Women's Christian Associations in all lands.

Art. III. *Basis*: The World's Young Women's Christian Association seeks to unite those young women who, regarding the Lord Jesus Christ as their God and Saviour, according to the Holy Scriptures, are vitally united to him through the love of God shed abroad in their hearts by the Holy Spirit, and desire to associate their efforts for the extension of his Kingdom among all young women by such means as are in accordance with the Word of God.[12]

There is reported to have been considerable discussion of the question whether the organization should be called the *International* or the *World's* Y.W.C.A. The latter title, it is said, was chosen because of a feeling that the word "international" emphasized cooperation between wholly separate entities, whereas the word "world" emphasized unity.

In its statement of basis the World's Y.W.C.A. followed closely the statement known as the Paris Basis, which had been adopted by the Y.M.C.A. at its first World's meeting in Paris in 1855.[13] It embodied substantially the statement of basis which had been framed by the British national movement at its organization in 1884,[14] which was also the one in use in France. The American movement had at this time no comparable statement of basis but it was in harmony with the World's Y.W.C.A. basis, since it was composed exclusively of evangelical local Associations, i.e., Associations whose voting and office holding members were "limited to young women who are members in good standing of an evangelical church."

Other articles in the constitution provided (1) for active and corresponding membership in the World's Association, the former being restricted to Associations of those countries that had achieved a national organization; (2) for a representative World's Committee; (3) for an Executive Committee, at least seven members of which should reside at headquarters; and (4) for a General Secretary who should be a woman, other officers and members to be either men or women. It was further stipulated that the General Secretary should be of a nationality other than that of the country in which the headquarters of the World's Committee were located, unless otherwise decided by four-fifths of the Committee, and it provided for the holding of a world's conference "at the call of the World's Committee."[15]

The first three Articles—Name, Object and Basis—having been adopted separately with delegates from England, India, Italy and Sweden speaking to the basis, the conference voted unanimously that "all further consideration of the constitution and by-laws be referred to the Executive Committee."

The constitution thus trustingly received at London in 1898 from the hands of the Executive Committee remained in force, with some changes in its by-laws, for twenty years. It was revised at the fifth World's Y.W.C.A. Conference at Stockholm in 1914, on the eve of the first World War, because of a changed situation within the movement itself, created by its own growth and expansion.

The fact that an Executive Committee largely resident in London and therefore almost wholly British, and an American General Secretary, would give to the Associations of Great Britain and the United States preponderant influence in the forming of the policies and program of the World's Y.W.C.A. did not seem to trouble the conference. Perhaps it did not occur to them, or perhaps they recognized it as natural in view of the less developed state of the Y.W.C.A. in other countries. In any case, there was set by the provisions of this early constitution a pattern of a world movement largely Anglo-Saxon in character. Only by slow degrees and often by painful processes has the World's Y.W.C.A. taken to itself and made its own those approaches to life and religion, those methods of work and forms of expression more characteristic of the various nations of the continent of Europe, of the Orient, and of Latin America which were, or were to become, its members. That the British and the American elements should predominate and should determine the development was in line with the character of the period. To them must go the credit for the vision, the energy and the daring to promote a world movement. But it was bound to be for a long time a world movement with a strongly Anglo-Saxon coloring.

The financial responsibility for the new organization, as the report of the Executive Committee to the London conference pointed out, was assumed by Great Britain and the United States jointly for the period from its beginnings in 1894 until the first conference. For this, each of these National Associations agreed to provide £300 annually. Miss Morley, the Treasurer, says that in Great Britain this sum was raised "chiefly by means of large subscriptions from a few generous supporters." In America also somewhat more than half the first year's £300 was received from "personal subscriptions and donations from individual friends of the work, in answer to written or spoken appeals." But, in addition, the American members of the World's Committee, Miss Morse and Mrs. William Boyd, cannily made the necessity of raising funds an opportunity for an experiment in mass education. They laid the responsibility on the shoulders of the International Committee, the State Committees, and the summer schools. They canvassed individual secretaries and committee members. They even placed responsibility on the general membership of local Associations, sending out $5.00 dime banks to be filled by many small gifts, and recommending the setting aside of a special day of prayer for the World's Y.W.C.A. work, and the holding of special meetings with missionary addresses and social entertainments such as Oriental teas, with the dime banks an integral part of all these programs. The first annual report of the American members records that $600 (£127) was raised by these various methods and that eighty-one local Associations contributed to this amount.

It was not an easy task. The American members of the World's Committee admit that "at times it has been difficult to secure the money because of the financial depression," and Miss Morley also feels it necessary to warn the London conference that "the large gifts from individuals in Britain cannot be looked for in equal amounts continuously," and that "the time has come when the future must be faced and the World's Y.W.C.A. placed upon a secure financial basis."

No very definite plans for the realization of this much-to-be-desired end seem to have been placed before the conference, which cheerfully voted to increase the annual budget from £600 to £800. A conference delegate wrote: "We did not feel that sufficient time was given to finance, but perhaps that time is to be more practically given to this question when we return to our own Associations. We were reminded that it was a most enjoyable thing to sit in our chairs and vote maganimously that £800 a year should be raised!" But she concludes: "We have a steadfast purpose, too, that by the grace of God we shall take our share in the monetary cost of this blessed work . . . let us at least see that we bear our share, each one, however small it may be, in making it possible for those whom we have placed in office for another three years rightly and efficiently to carry out this great trust."[16]

Thus, not suddenly but by a long and patient process the World's Y.W.C.A. was formed: by the work of leaders over the years from 1884; by vote of an informal international meeting 1892; by beginning to function on the basis of a provisional constitution in 1894; and by the formal completion of the work of organization through the adoption of a constitution and a budget in a conference of duly elected representatives of seven National Associations in 1898.

REFERENCES

[1] Morse, Rebecca F. *Young Women*, p. 33.

[2] Morse, Rebecca F. *Young Women*. pp. 33, 34.

[3] *Ibid.*, p. 34.

[4] Continental Committee, Minutes, December 1889, and March 1890.

[5] First World's Y.W.C.A. Conference, London, 1898, Report, p. 71.

[6] United Central Council, Y.W.C.A. of Great Britain, November 1891, Minutes.

[7] First World's Y.W.C.A. Conference, 1898, Report, pp. 47, 48.
[8] First Annual Report, for 1895, p. 8.

[9] First World's Y.W.C.A. Conference, 1898, Report, p. 48.
Note: Actually the National Committee of Sweden did not act until 1896, when the Swedish National Association was officially organized. It seems probable that the Stockholm Committee, acting in lieu of a Swedish National Committee, took the step in 1895 (see chapter 2, p. 28).

[10] The Y.W.C.A.s of Canada withdrew from their connection with the Y.W.C.A.s of the United States and formed the National Y.W.C.A. of Canada in 1895.

[11] See chapter 2, pp. 23, 26, 27.

[12] Constitution, see Appendix I, p. 272.

[13] The Paris Basis of the Y.M.C.A.: "The Y.M.C.A. seeks to unite those young men who regarding Jesus Christ as their God and Saviour, according to the Holy Scriptures, desire to be his disciples in their doctrine and in their life, and to associate their efforts for the extension of his Kingdom among young men."

[14] See chapter 1, p. 10.

[15] See Constitution, Appendix I, p. 272 ff.

[16] First World's Y.W.C.A. Conference, 1898, Report, p. 19.

If any readers want to catch the inspiration of these pages they are asked to call a halt and think back lest the history should seem commonplace and the facts make but little impression. . . . The women of whom it gives the history were women ahead of their time; they were born early in the last century, before the penny post, the penny paper and a penny-a-mile were thought of; they were pioneers to whom the present had no time limit, but was a possession whose value lay in its influence on the future.
The Honorable Emily Kinnaird: Prefatory Note to *Girls of Yesterday and Today*, by Lucy M. Moor.

CHAPTER 5   THE FOUNDERS

THE ORGANIZATION of the World's Young Women's Christian Association was formally completed in the first World's Conference of June 1898. Yet it is true to fact to place its birthday in the year 1894, for in September of that year, when Miss Reynolds arrived in London from the United States, it began to function, albeit its constitution was provisional and its Executive Committee was self-appointed.

The four-year period between that date and the holding of the first World's Conference was one of laying foundations for future work. There was little precedent to go by. In spite of the long contact of the Y.W.C.A. of Great Britain with Associations in many parts of the world, in spite of the 1892 conference, and the official commitment of the national movements of Great Britain and the United States to the undertaking, and in spite of the assurances of cooperation already given by Association leaders in Norway and Sweden and the expressions of sympathetic interest from leaders in France, Germany and elsewhere, the vision of a world fellowship of Christian women as an active, vital force was still the possession of only a few.

The immediate responsibility for bringing that vision to earth in the form of a tangible organization rested almost entirely upon the shoulders of a small number of leaders in Great Britain and America. Behind them was the financial commitment of each of the two National Associations to support the work until the first conference, but this was an act of faith, and its justification lay largely with the little group who made those first momentous decisions. For this reason it is fitting at this point to give some picture of these pioneers of faith: Mrs. J. Herbert Tritton and the Honorable Emily Kinnaird of London, Miss Rebecca F. Morse and Miss Corabel Tarr (Mrs. William Boyd) of the United States; who were largely responsible for the promotion of the idea and for its development in terms of a constitution and form of organization; Miss Mary Morley, the first Treasurer, Mrs. George Campbell, the Vice President, and the other members of the Executive Committee who were associated with Mrs. Tritton, the first President, and Miss Annie M. Reynolds, the first General Secretary. The character, the outlook, the faith and experience of these women were the stuff out of which the World's Y.W.C.A. was fashioned in those formative years.

The British women without exception were the product of the great evangelical movement that was of such importance to the religious and cultural development of Great Britain in the nineteenth century. The Trittons, the Kinnairds, the Morleys, the Campbells, all belonged to that remarkable group of families with large business interests and active in affairs of Empire-wide extent, which had been drawn together by the evangelical revival. These families were among the supporters of the movements for Christian evangelism of those years, and of the many philanthropic activities that were the fruit of this deep revival of personal religion. One of the striking characteristics of these able, wealthy, broad-minded, evangelical families was the encouragement given by the husbands, fathers and brothers to the activities of their womenfolk in the field of public affairs, both social and religious. Among them, the promotion of the Y.W.C.A. as well as of other missionary and philanthropic organizations might be truly described as a family project.

Lucy Smith Tritton (Mrs. J. Herbert Tritton) came to London from her home in Nottingham as a bride of eighteen. She was brought into contact with the Y.W.C.A. through her mother-in-law, Mrs. Joseph Tritton, who had been a member of that first committee formed by Lady Kinnaird in 1885, had helped to found one of the earliest hostels for girls in London, and had shared in the work of the Union Internationale des Amies de la Jeune Fille.

Though in succeeding years Mrs. Tritton had a large family of children, her interests continued many and varied. A woman of deep evangelical faith, she made her home a center for leaders of the evangelistic and missionary movements of the day, as well as for guests from many lands. She knew the continent of Europe well through frequent travel. Immensely interested in work for girls by girls, she was also interested in the current movements for social reform and in international affairs, and believed that these should have a place in the program of the Y.W.C.A. In 1889 she became Chairman of the Continental Division of the United Central Council of the Y.W.C.A. of Great Britain, and from that time on strove for the extension and strengthening of international ties among the Y.W.C.A.s of different countries. It was her effort, along with that of Miss Kinnaird and a few others, that led to the calling of the conference of 1892 to consider the formation of an international organization. She was a pioneering spirit, with a quality of far-seeing statesmanship that made her peculiarly fitted to become the first President of so new and adventurous an undertaking as the World's Young Women's Christian Association.

Emily Kinnaird, youngest daughter of Lord and Lady Kinnaird, was born in that eventful year 1855 in which her mother organized the first Y.W.C.A. in London. In her volume of *Reminiscences* she says of her parents: "They belonged to a school of thought whose conscience was awake to the evils of the time, seeking to promote a new standard of life." In her early years Miss Kinnaird was brought into contact with many of those great forces which owed their spiritual power to the revival movements of the nineteenth century. Leaders in the movement for the abolition of slavery in America, missionary leaders, and native Christian leaders from India, China, Africa—"all these," she says, "found their way to my childhood home, 2, Pall Mall East."

When Lady Kinnaird in her later years bequeathed to each of her daughters one of her own special "causes", she entrusted her beloved Y.W.C.A. to Emily. Miss Kinnaird has given to it a lifetime of enthusiastic service. She has carried many lines of activity, first in the London Association, later in the National Association of Great Britain, and then in the World's Association. She was a convinced enthusiast regarding the spiritual quality in the raising of money for good causes and was a proud and tireless and extraordinary successful "beggar" (her own descriptive word!) for the Association, local, national and world, and for its specific projects in other lands. Her special interests reached out in two directions which were of great importance for her contribution to the establishment of a world movement—toward America and toward India.

In her two visits to the United States, in 1887 and 1893, Miss Kinnaird became convinced that the American Y.W.C.A., which greatly impressed her, had something to contribute to the British organization. "In America," she says, "the Association was not, as so often here, a Bible class with a tea, a mission of the rich to the poor, or a work for girls which old people could do. It had developed there from the student Association of the colleges into the city Association with the splendid buildings planned to meet the physical, social, educational and religious needs of every girl."[1] She was keenly alive also to the possibilities inherent in the use made in the American Association of college-bred, specially trained, salaried, professional secretaries. Always, with Miss Kinnaird, to catch a vision was to become a voice proclaiming it, and she was as tireless a propagandist for the value of American methods as she was a beggar for the financial support of the Association.

Both the Association and the missionary work in which her mother had taken so large a part drew Miss Kinnaird toward India. The first of her many visits there was made in 1890-1891. From this she returned with a profound belief in the necessity of cooperation between the Associations of Great Britain and America in meeting the opportunities in India.

With a conviction that was the result of her early background and training and also of her mature experience, Miss Kinnaird entered into the task of organizing the World's Y.W.C.A. She was a member of the Committee of Three—Miss Morse and Miss Tarr of the United States and herself—charged with the drafting of the constitution. She was a member of the first Executive Committee and for many years a Vice President of the World's Association. She did valiant work in interpreting it through publications and publicity and was a vigorous supporter of those projects that promoted trained leadership and the placing of responsibility in the hands of youth. These many lines of activity have been her unceasing contribution over the half-century of life of the World's Y.W.C.A., a contribution that she is still making, for even as these pages are written she is traveling about India, speaking and writing for the Y.W.C.A.

Rebecca F. Morse was, in her background of privilege and of deep personal religion, the American counterpart of the British founders of the World's Y.W.C.A. She was a metropolitan person, her lifelong home being New York City, where her father was the founder of the weekly interdenominational religious newspaper, *The New York Observer*. She was a niece of Samuel F. B. Morse, inventor of the Morse telegraph code. She belonged to that group of evangelical Christians whose experience of religion and the fruitage of it paralleled in America, with its very different environment, that of the great evangelicals in England. Her brother, Mr. Richard C. Morse, was an outstanding leader in work for young men in the Y.M.C.A. and for many years General Secretary of its International Committee.

In the years 1879 and 1880 Miss Morse became interested in clubs for working girls in New York City, a work in which she was associated with Miss Grace H. Dodge, later the first President of the National Board of the Y.W.C.A. of the United States. This led her into Y.W.C.A. work at a time when the student Associations were just developing into a national movement. In 1890 she became the Chairman of the newly organized committee for New York State. From that time till her death in 1903 she was one of the great though personally retiring and humble-spirited leaders

Miss Mary Morley

The Hon. Emily Kinnaird

Miss Rebecca F. Morse

Miss Corabel Tarr

of the American movement. She worked in a local Association, the Harlem branch of the Y.W.C.A. of the City of New York. She carried the varied organizational and inspirational responsibilities of Chairman of the New York State Committee. She presided at conventions, led evangelistic services, and served on important national committees, such as the "Adjustment Committee" which endeavored over a period of years to find ways in which the two Y.W.C.A. organizations in America might work harmoniously together. She strove steadily and responsibly for the formation of the World's Y.W.C.A. and was a representative of the American Association upon its committee.

The quality and character of her service were recognized wherever given. Mrs. Tritton, writing of the World's Committee's sense of loss at the death of Miss Morse, said:

> When we recall the formation of the World's Y.W.C.A. and its growing work each succeeding year, we . . . know full well that without her wise judgment, her prayers and her hard work in its cause, it would probably never have existed. . . .In 1892, it was her readiness to share responsibility that gave the impetus to "go forward".[2]

Among her great contributions to the World's Y.W.C.A. was the drawing up of the constitution. Mrs. Tritton wrote in 1903: "That there has been scarcely any necessity to change a single paragraph is proof of the great care with which it was drawn up." Patience in attention to detail, judgment, wisdom, courage and perseverance and a whole-hearted consecration—these were some of the qualities that made her work with the World's Association as well as in local and national Association affairs of great significance. *The World's Quarterly* for January 1904 recalls that "she worked indefatigably to raise funds for expenses and for the support of American representatives," and adds: "We are bewildered as we think of the time and strength required to carry out all she did for the Association—organizing, developing, selecting workers, financing. She was a successful money raiser and those who knew her best attributed this success to "her own generosity and her faith and her habits of prayer."

It is said that often, when a problem arose, the Executive Committee with one accord said, "Consult Miss Morse. It is worth waiting to get her opinion." This is all the more remarkable because, except for the conferences of 1892, 1898 and 1902, all of which she attended, her responsibility as a member of the World's Committee was carried by correspondence, save for her invaluable consultations with Miss Reynolds when the latter was in the United States. Miss Reynolds spoke of her as the "American founder" of the World's Y.W.C.A. and in a very real sense she was that, for through her more than any other person except Miss Reynolds herself, the responsible participation of America in the creation and early administration of the World's Y.W.C.A. was realized.

Corabel Tarr (Mrs. Willam Boyd), the other American delegate to the 1892 conference, was the General Secretary of the American Association. Her background was that of the middle-western college community where her father, the Reverend Levi Tarr, was President of a college. After college she taught in the western states of Idaho, Washington and California. In 1889 she left teaching to become the second General Secretary of the International Committee of the Y.W.C.A., a position that she held until her marriage in October 1892. She was largely instrumental in the development of the city Associations, a characteristic feature of the American movement in those years, and was a constant interpreter of the Y.W.C.A. as a field for professional service. Through her, therefore, was brought into the new World's Association the point of view and experience of the American movement on its professional side.

These were the persons most closely and responsibly associated with the actual bringing into existence of the world organization, but there were others, the members of the first Executive Committee, and Miss Reynolds, whose influence was also formative. Of the Executive Committee members besides Mrs. Tritton and Miss Kinnaird, an outstanding contribution was made by Miss Mary Morley, who, from its organization in 1894 until 1906, when she became the President, was its able Treasurer. Like Mrs. Tritton, Miss Kinnaird and Miss Morse, Miss Morley's home background of wide contact with affairs combined with profound evangelical faith was in itself an equipment for the service she rendered. Her father, Samuel Morley, Member of Parliament for Bristol, was a great philanthropist and a warm supporter of the Y.W.C.A. from its early days. Miss Kinnaird, whose home was on a neighboring street and who worked closely with Miss Morley in the London Association, says of him:

> No appeal was too small for his attention; and it is impossible to record all the small checks this great philanthropist sent . . . and whenever there was a call for an enlarged Institute, or to open a new one, or some big central fund had to be started to extend the work of a new, unknown Association, then the check rose to £500 and £1,000 and these were not infrequent gifts.[3]

The same spirit of generous self-giving was characteristic of Miss Morley herself:

> Everyone felt she could turn to her for counsel. Whenever occasion arose for a fresh departure in the work or when fellow-workers from foreign lands appealed for help, then we gathered round Mary Morley's table, sure that neither sympathy, counsel nor money would be denied.

One who worked with her in the World's Y.W.C.A. office said:

> She was never afraid to go forward if it seemed the right thing,
> yet carefully looking into ways and means . . . a simple, humble
> child of God, waiting for his leading, and when it came, so sure
> that his way was right that perplexity ceased . . . There was no
> part of the work which did not benefit from contact with her.
> She seemed to combine in an unusual degree complete mastery
> of detail with a broad and farseeing outlook and a truly bal-
> anced judgment.[5]

With Mrs. Tritton, Miss Morley and Miss Kinnaird on the first Executive Committee were associated Mrs. George Campbell, Vice President, and
President from 1902 to 1906,[6] who had been for many years closely con-
nected with the Association work in London; Mrs. E. W. Moore, who had
been a member of the United Central Council of the Y.W.C.A. of Great
Britain from its organization in 1884 and became the Chairman of the
Traveler's Aid Committee of the World's Association and later of the
first sub-committee on the selection and training of workers; Mrs. Hatt
Noble, one of the founders of the Y.W.C.A. of Ireland; Mrs. Farmer Hall,
Lady Fairfax, Mrs. Tottenham, and Miss Minna Gollock.

At its organization, the World's Y.W.C.A. adopted from America
the plan of employing an executive officer known as the General Secretary,
with whom should rest responsibility for the administration of its policies
and plans. The functions of a General Secretary were set forth in an address on "A New Profession for Young Women" given by Mrs. Boyd
at the American Biennial Convention of 1893—just before the organization of the World's Committee. She said:

> The Secretaryship . . . has for its object the most careful study
> of young womanhood and its all-round development. To the
> Board of Managers the General Secretary, because of her life
> within the work, becomes the informant, the tactful adviser,
> confidential friend and leader; to the members she becomes an
> inspiring adviser, a true friend and counselor, leading the un-
> converted to acknowledge Jesus as their Lord and Saviour,
> helping all to see a higher meaning to womanhood. To the As-
> sociation as a whole a superintendent of its various departments,
> an executive officer, business manager and home maker; to the
> community at large an education concerning the work, and as
> no other person can possibly become, a representative of the
> entire Association.[7]

This rather formidable definition of the place of a General Secretary
in the Association required some modification when applied to a world

organization, but in its essentials it represented the task placed upon Miss Reynolds' broad and capable shoulders when she came to London in 1894.

Annie M. Reynolds was the daughter of a minister of the Congregational Church located on the outskirts of the city of New Haven in the New England state of Connecticut. She was a member of one of the first classes to attend the newly established Wellesley College for Women. She did not complete the course there, but instead went to Europe to study languages—French, German and Italian, and perhaps Spanish. Later, during her work with the World's Committee, she also studied Swedish.

Her first professional work was as a teacher of languages in a school for girls, but like so many other Christian college women, she was soon drawn into that "new profession for young women", the Y.W.C.A., as General Secretary of the city Association in Brooklyn, New York. In 1889 she became State Secretary for Iowa. She left this position in 1892 to go again to Europe. Returning, she attended some lectures at the Yale Divinity School and then joined the staff of the Y.W.C.A. of the United States and Canada as editor of their monthly magazine *The Evangel*. In 1894 she began work with the World's Committee.

Miss Reynolds brought to the World's work not only the best that America had to offer in Association experience, methods of work, and spiritual conviction, but also rare personal qualifications and gifts of temperament and disposition for her task. Her knowledge of Europe and her facility in European languages, her simple, evangelical, ethical type of Christian experience and religious expression, her practical business sense, her vigorous honesty and independence of thought, her wise and balanced judgment, all were valuable assets in her work as a pioneer in so uncharted a field. Perhaps none of these characteristics was more useful, however, than the breadth of her interest in all things human and her ever-ready humor, which carried her over many an otherwise baffling obstacle and gave a pungency to her reports, letters and speeches that made what she said remain in the memory.

These women, volunteer and professional, whose minds and hearts and hard work guided the World's Y.W.C.A. in its first formative years, built irrevocably into it the ideals, the spirit, and the point of view—religiously, culturally and socially—which they themselves embodied. Religiously, this spirit and point of view was Protestant, evangelical, interdenominational. Culturally, it was basically Anglo-Saxon, though modified by much experience of and contact with the wider world of peoples of other races. In social theory it was international, interracial and democratic, though in actual practice the exigencies of the situation often seemed to make the operation of the organization fall far short of the professed ideal. The growth of the movement over the years, its development under conditions differing widely from those in Great Britain and America, have produced many changes, some of them extremely fundamental in character, yet there remains an ineradicable element inherited from the founders, a character that is central to the basic idea of the Young Women's Christian Association.

REFERENCES

[1] Kinnaird, Emily, *Reminiscences* 1925, p. 104.

[2] *The Evangel,* November 1903, p. 5.

[3] Kinnaird, Emily, *Reminiscences,* pp. 70-71.

[4] *Ibid.,* pp. 76-77.

[5] Stevenson, E. in *The World's Quarterly,* October 1917, pp. 19-20.

[6] Mrs. Campbell was an excellent linguist. She made a great impression at the World's Conference in Paris in 1906 by welcoming the delegates in English, French, German and Italian.

[7] Fourth International Convention, Y.W.C.A.s of the United States and Canada, 1893, Report, p. 77.

Looking over the entire field, the World's Committee feels that the primary need of our National Associations is to become better acquainted with each other personally. Statistics are cold, knowledge is impersonal. We must have the sound of each other's voices in our ears, the remembrance of each other's features before our mental vision, to be able to enter fully into a comprehension of our mutual duties and difficulties.

ANNIE M. REYNOLDS. Written in 1898, before the First World's Conference.

All work which involves mutual knowledge by correspondence, difference of language, variances of standards, and habits of religious thought, requires a special grace.

ANNIE M. REYNOLDS. Report to Second World's Conferennce, Geneva, 1902.

CHAPTER 6 THE FIRST DECADE PART I: 1894-1898

THE OBJECT of the World's Young Women's Christian Association as set forth in the constitution was "the federation, development and extension of the Young Women's Christian Association in all lands." Federation and development must precede extension. The constitution further provided that active membership in the World's Association should consist of National Associations organized on the same basis as the World's Y.W.C.A. In countries without national organization but having separate Associations organized on this basis, these Associations might be affiliated in corresponding membership.

The first task before Miss Reynolds and the Executive Committee was therefore to bring existing Association work as far as possible into effective relation to the World's Association, and so to create in reality what now existed only by the avowed intention of four countries. In her first annual report Miss Reynolds said that much of her time in the first months was given to "the beginning of an extensive correspondence with the European committees as well as the colonial Associations regarding a closer linking together of all with the newly established head."

This was not a work to be done merely, or even chiefly, by correspondence. In 1895 Miss Reynolds began the series of visits to Associations near and far which remind one of the journeys of St. Paul. In these visits, by means of personal contact, meetings, addresses, conferences with leaders, reports and letters, the pioneer work was done. In the years 1895, 1896 and 1897 she visited every country save India in which the Y.W.C.A. had reached well-established proportions. In the winter and spring of 1895 she went to Germany, Denmark, Sweden and Norway, and omitted France only because her plan to go there was interrupted by "that most unwelcome scourge, the influenza." In the summer and autumn she made a six months' tour of the British Colonies, South Africa, Australasia (Tasmania, New Zealand and Australia). The great event of her visit to Australasia was the holding of an "Inter-Colonial Conference" with representatives present from Melbourne, Auckland and the branches in New South Wales. In 1896, besides visits to Scotland and Ireland, she went to France especially studying the work in Paris and in Nîmes, and to Spain, Italy and Switzerland. The summer and autumn found her in Canada at the national convention and a conference in Montreal, and in the United States, where she attended the summer conferences at Lake Geneva in the Middle West and at Northfield in the East, and held long consultations with Miss Morse. The year 1897 was spent largely at headquarters, preparing for the coming World's conference. Yet she visited many of the south of England branches, France and Italy, and again spent four months in the United States, two in vacation at her home and two attending five state conventions and visiting such important Associations as Indianapolis, Toledo and Minneapolis.

In all this visitation Miss Reynolds' first task was one of interpretation of what the World's Y.W.C.A. was, what it might become, why it was needed, what would be its relation to the Associations in different lands that should affiliate with it. At the conclusion of her tour of the British Colonies she wrote that everywhere she found a cordial spirit toward the extension of Association effort and a readiness to cooperate with it.

There had been some fear that local and national autonomy might be infringed by a world organization. Mrs. Tritton, in the first annual report of the Executive Committee, took note of this: "One word more to correct misapprehension as to methods of work adopted. We do not control National Bodies. . . . Each country brought into relationship with the World's Y.W.C.A. is absolutely free to work out its own Association in every detail on its own lines, provided it has accepted the basis."[1] While no "control" was attempted by the World's Committee, an effort was made, through interpreting the World's Y.W.C.A. as a specialized movement with a very definite field of work, to create in all national movements a common ideal of function and program. Points that called for special emphasis were its interdenominational character—"Every member of every outward and visible church is welcome to join our ranks provided she can subscribe to the basis"; and the all-round nature of its program—"Let us bear in mind also that in our Association there is provision for the cultivation of every side of our nature, spiritual, intellectual, social and physical."[2]

Questions of membership arose. It was necessary to stress that the Y.W.C.A. was not alone for girls who were already active Christians, though these, indeed, would be the ones who carried most responsibility for its development, but for all girls—"We shall neglect our opportunities and minimize results if we do not enlist in associate membership those whom we hope to win from indirect to direct connection with us."[3]

In some places there was a tendency to interpret the spiritual purpose of the Association as something opposed to a sound intellectual development of the individual. Miss Reynolds especially deplored this. One of her early reports commented upon the Association's frequent failure to appeal to or make use of young women with intellectual training or interests, and concluded: "I should not intend to urge the immediate organization of Greek or astronomical courses in our Association but I do urge the recognition of our claim to honestly carry out our constitution and do something to open the minds as well as develop the 'heart, soul and strength' of our members. The great spread of educational requirement in secular society has in itself, a suggestiveness which we should not overlook nor neglect."[4] She constantly advocated passing on to other organizations work not strictly concerned with young women. "Our work is essentially for young women. We shall do better work in our own cause, and bring less criticism upon ourselves, if we adhere strictly to this object as an Association."[5]

She stressed with vigor and often with humor the importance of youth, not only as recipients of a program prepared for them but as responsible sharers in the development of the Association. She recalled the greeting she once received from a young woman who, on being presented, exclaimed genially, "I am so glad to see you, for your pictures look so like my dear grandmother"; and the rebuke administered to her by a young Japanese who when asked her age replied, "I am very old. I am just 21." Miss Reynolds adds:

> While one would advocate a majority of elder women on the executive committee or councils in large organizations, yet we would find ourselves less likely to become narrow were the very old ones of twenty years included there also. The young woman of today will be more sympathetic and keen-sighted in her understanding of her sister's needs, than she who was the young woman of twenty years ago.[6]

Through talks, reports, letters, in season and out, with an unwavering persistence, with good humor and a tactful appreciation of the difficulties, necessities and diversities involved, Miss Reynolds laid the foundation for a common ideal regarding the Association. At the same time, she recognized the great differences existing between Associations in different countries—between those in large and wealthy lands and those in small or poor countries; those in countries where Protestantism was made up of many different denominations and those in countries like Denmark where more than ninety-five per cent of the population belonged to the one State Church. There was the difference, too, in both size and character between the Association as it developed in a Protestant environment and as it existed in a largely Roman Catholic country such as France or Italy. Miss Reynolds' first annual report expressed the conviction, borne upon her by her travels, that "the aim of the World's Association must be to encourage unity of purpose while recognizing liberally great diversity of method," and this point of view established in the first year, has been throughout its history a cardinal principle of its work.

Her extended study of the Association under varying conditions confirmed her belief that "in an interdenominational and international work on a thoroughly Christian basis the Association is keeping fully abreast of the strongest and most active spirit of the nineteenth century." But the conditions that made the opportunities before the Association so large were also producing many other movements appealing to women, and this fact offered a distinct challenge to the Y.W.C.A. "We are not the only world organization working for young women, or enlisting young women in our ranks, and the measure of our usefulness and our excuse for existence will be the amount of practical help we give to young women."[7]

A task which followed close on the heels of interpretation was that of furthering in countries ready for it the organization of National Associations that could affiliate in active membership with the World's Association. In some countries, namely Sweden and Canada, this next step came about on the initiative of the country itself, with little or no help from the World's Committee. The Canadian Associations, for some time united in organization with those of the United States, looked forward, as their work grew, to having their own separate national organization. This step was hastened by the formation of the World's Y.W.C.A. Before the close of the year 1895 the National Association of Canada had been formed and had applied for affiliation as an active member, though her official admission was not actually voted until September 1896. Sweden also began at once to remodel her organization, so that the Stockholm Committee, which until then had performed the work of a National Committee, might become technically such.

There were situations, however, in which the World's Executive Committee itself was directly instrumental in bringing national organization into being. The inter-colonial conference was a step in this direction for Australasia, but the notable illustration in these early years was Italy. When Miss Reynolds visited Italy in the spring of 1896, she found a Y.W.C.A. movement already well developed in northern Italy, largely through the initiative of Madame Schalck and Signorina Elisa Meynier.[8] She visited several of these Associations and attended a conference at which delegates from thirteen Associations in the Waldensian Valleys were present, all having come, she wrote, "in groups headed by their pastors' wives, one delegation coming five hours on foot at a pace which, to an inferior pedestrian like myself, would have meant seven for the distance covered."[9] At this conference a simple constitution for each branch was submitted, to be reported upon the following year, a resolution to form a Federation of the Associations of Northern Italy was unanimously adopted, and Turin was chosen as the location for headquarters.[10] Before the close of the year 1896, this Federation was received into active affiliation with the World's Y.W.C.A.

The following year, when Miss Reynolds again visited Italy, she and Madame Schalck began to work for the transformation of the Federation of Northern Italy into a national Italian Association. It was not an altogether simple undertaking. When Miss Reynolds presented the idea of an Association to a group of Italian young women in Rome, the head of the long-established Y.W.C.A. for British girls in that city felt that her preserves were being infringed upon. There were other difficulties too. Leaders of the Y.W.C.A. in Florence were sure that Italy was not yet ready for national organization, "there is too much distrust between the towns," and besides, "Florence would not be willing to work 'under' Turin." These objections Miss Reynolds met by calling attention to the already existing National Committee of the Y.M.C.A. and by pointing out that Madame Schalck's long experience in the Nottingham Y.W.C.A. in England qualified her to make a real contribution to the Italian Association.

Still another problem lay in the fact that the growing importance of Protestant women's organizations in Italy stimulated similar movements among Roman Catholics, and puzzling questions of relationships arose. In spite of these difficulties, however, a nation-wide conference of Italian Associations was held in the spring of 1898, with delegates present from Genoa, Rome, Naples, Milan, Pergamo, San Remo, Florence and Turin. In 1901 a second conference, held in Genoa, with representatives from nineteen Associations in attendance, elected a National Committee and set up a district organization for the country as a whole.

The World's Y.W.C.A. held its interdenominational character to be a very important principle. However, in federating already existing movements it was not always possible to apply this principle uncompromisingly, especially to Associations in countries where almost the entire population belonged to one church. The Y.W.C.A. of Denmark illustrates this situation. The Danish Y.W.C.A. was a confessional movement, a part of a youth movement for both boys and girls within the State Church, accepting as active members only those who were members of the State Church. In 1896, when the Y.W.C.A. applied for affiliation with the World's Association, this was recognized as a difficulty, and the Association was accepted as a corresponding rather than an active member. Later the Danish Association widened its constitutional requirement for membership so that it might include active members of the Associations of other lands, to whatever church they belonged, "provided they make no propaganda for their own church." With this modification, the Y.W.C.A. of Denmark was received in full affiliation at the World's Conference of 1902, although as regards its Danish members it remained on a confessional basis.

Efforts to develop Association work in the Roman Catholic countries of Spain and Portugal presented still other problems. The World's Committee was eager to continue and extend the pioneer work for Spanish girls started by the British Association with the cooperation of Mrs. Gulick.[11] Miss Reynolds visited Spain in 1896 and was impressed with the good work being done by the Y.W.C.A. in Madrid, and with a young Spanish woman, Miss Julia Castro, one of Mrs. Gulick's students who was about to take up work there. It was probably as a result of this visit that Miss Castro went to England in 1897 for a year of training in Y.W.C.A. work.

From reports which Miss Castro made to the Continental Committee and to the first World's Conference, comes a brief but vivid picture of the conditions under which Association work in Spain was carried on. She speaks of the dense ignorance among Spanish women, which nevertheless opened the way for the Association since the women longed to be educated. The work in Madrid, she said, "is necessarily of a most elementary nature," the teaching of reading and writing and of simple Bible texts, and visiting the members in their homes. Miss Reynolds had hopes, at this time, that some permanent work of a broad character might be established, for she wrote in an article about Spain contributed to *The Evangel* in October 1896: "Can we not begin in a missionary Association work directed and supported by our workers?" In 1899 the World's Executive Committee discussed the forming of a sub-committee for Spain, and three years later they reported plans looking forward to the establishment of a Spanish National Committee.

But there was another side to the picture. A Protestant organization such as the Y.W.C.A. was at an almost impossible disadvantage in Spain. Its leaders were sometimes exposed to actual persecution, and it often took great courage to enroll as a member. In spite of the great interest of the World's Committee it became necessary in 1904, after the death of Mrs. Gulick, to suspend the work in Madrid. Though for some years thereafter small sums were given to help little centers of Spanish work, it was a full quarter of a century before the World's Y.W.C.A. again began pioneer work there in earnest. In those early years it was not yet equipped either by knowledge and experience or with specially prepared leaders and the necessary financial resources to organize in a Roman Catholic country, where not even a small Protestant community offered a natural starting point.

In Portugal the situation as a field for Y.W.C.A. work was similar to that in Spain. A Young Women's Christian Association was opened in Oporto in 1897 by Miss May Cassels, daughter of an Englishman engaged in business there. The first report from Portugal to a World's Conference (Geneva 1902), written by Miss Cassels, says of this beginning:

> We began with eight or nine members and often it was very uphill work, for these people could not understand what an Association was meant for, or what good it could possibly be to them. . . . For the first two years the only class we had was a Bible class on Sunday afternoons. We had great difficulty at first in getting any more girls to join, partly because they were ashamed of being seen coming to the classes, but more especially because their companions made fun of them if they left off going to dances and worldly entertainments which are always held on Sunday in this country.[12]

This same report recorded that there was a branch in Lisbon, Lisbon and Oporto together having 246 members. In the annual report for 1904, Miss Cassels, who was now the corresponding secretary for all the branches in Portugal, wrote that there were eight branches, with a membership of about 280, and that they were considering the possibility of a national committee and planning for their first national conference. She said that many of the girls "have been and are persecuted by their families for belonging to the *Unias* but . . . with God's help they have kept firm and are bright lights shining for him in this place."[13]

These illustrations give some idea of the diversity of conditions, ideas and problems that confronted the World's Committee. But the most exciting national development of those first years, and the one that consumed most time and thought on the part of the Executive Committee, was not in

72

Miss Annie M. Reynolds

Miss Agnes G. Hill

Europe but in India. A new era opened for the Y.W.C.A. in India with the visit of Miss Kinnaird in 1892[14] and the arrival of the first full-time workers, Miss Maude Orlebar from England in 1893, and Miss Agnes G. Hill from the United States in 1895.

Miss Hill went to India to be the General Secretary for Madras, but though she gave herself with devotion and efficiency to the development of the Madras Association and soon had her sister, Miss Mary B. Hill, there working with her, her mind and heart embraced from the first the whole field of young womanhood in India. She was fresh from work in the United States and she shared the American enthusiasm for the possibilities inherent in national organization. She also came directly from the World's Committee, from whom she had received her appointment to service abroad, and she knew of their hope of creating and linking together national Associations in many lands. It is not surprising therefore to read in the minutes of the October, 1895, meeting of the World's Y.W.C.A. Committee for "Other Continents" that "important letters were read from Miss Orlebar and Miss Hill, the latter with regard to the desirability of a Y.W.C.A. national organization for the whole of India and Ceylon."

The Executive Committee had indeed considered the possibility that Miss Hill might soon leave the Madras Association, and after a year or two of preparatory travel and survey become the secretary of a national committee. Events, however, outran their cautious planning. As so often happened in the Christian enterprises of this period, it was the initiative of an individual who had faith in Miss Hill's capabilities and who was at the same time able and willing to finance the early stages of a new undertaking, that presented the World's Committee in January 1897 with the *fait accompli* of the National Y.W.C.A. of India, Burma and Ceylon.

Mr. James Stokes was an American with a deep interest in work for both young men and young women, to which he gave liberally of his time, his influence and his money. In 1896 he undertook a world tour of visitation to centers of the Y.M.C.A. On this tour he was armed with a letter from the World's Y.W.C.A. Executive Committee expressing the hope that he and his sisters, who accompanied him, would visit Y.W.C.A.s wherever they could and "thus cheer and encourage the foreign workers." Mr. Stokes reached India in December 1896. He knew of the plan for a national Y.W.C.A. some time in the future, with Miss Hill as its secretary. "But to Mr. Stokes future and present were identical, and since the Y.M.C.A. was holding a national convention in Calcutta to which ladies were invited, he believed the time might be ripe to call a women's conference at the same time, in order to form a women's national committee on that occasion. Miss Mary Hill was in Madras, why should her sister not be spared at once for the wider field?"[15]

To say that the World's Executive Committee was surprised when a cable arrived from Mr. Stokes saying, "India National Committee formed. Funds secured. Hill secretary," would be understatement. Miss Reynolds, however, when she broke the news to the astonished Committee for Other Continents gallantly explained that "Miss Hill had already received word that they were taking steps to effect an Indian national organization, thus they [Miss Hill and Mr. Stokes] were working entirely in harmony with the World's Executive Committee."

In the spring of 1897 Miss Hill went to England and expressed to the Executive Committee "the deep conviction" of the India National Committee of "the great need of unity of action for India with authority vested in an India National Committee headquarters." She added that she felt India would be able to meet all local expenses of rent, etc. but that salaries for some time must come from outside India. In this same meeting the Executive Committee passed a resolution transferring to the direction of the India National Committee "all who are at present working in connection with the Y.W.C.A. of India, Burma and Ceylon."

A reading of Executive Committee minutes for this and the following year makes clear the complicated changes and adjustments necessitated by this sudden transfer of the work of a whole country, which up to now had been almost entirely a missionary enterprise, first of the British Association and then of the World's Y.W.C.A., to a state of self-determination while yet the necessity of supplying leadership and funds remained largely with committees outside India. The report of the Standing Committee for Other Continents given at the World's Conference in June 1898 frankly admits that "for the first two years India monopolized the greater portion of time at the monthly committee meetings owing to the great progress in Y.W.C.A. work since the visit of the Honorable Misses Kinnaird" and the formation of the National Committee.[16] The generous attitude of these Committees in acknowledging the new independence while at the same time loyally continuing their responsibility for support, and patiently re-organizing all their working relationships, was an indication of the willingness and skill of the world organization in adapting to new conditions.

The question naturally arises whether in these early years the World's Association sought to extend the Y.W.C.A. into new fields. The answer to this is clear: the immediate responsibility was felt to be one of drawing together and unifying existing Associations. In the early months of 1898 the attention of the Executive Committee was drawn to the distressing conditions among girls employed in factories in Japan, but a request for consideration of this at the London Conference was refused, apparently on the ground that such consideration would be premature.

74

One bit of investigation of the possibility of opening up a new field was, however, undertaken, and that was in Russia. Here again the hand of Mr. Stokes is seen. His world tour had taken him to St. Petersburg, and on returning to London he laid before the Executive Committee a proposal for introducing Y.W.C.A. work into Russia under the patronage of the Emperor and Empress, and offered to finance a survey visit of Miss Reynolds to Russia. Although there had been some Y.W.C.A. work for German girls in Russia since 1884,[17] the Executive Committee seems not entirely to have shared Mr. Stokes' optimism about the possibility of starting work for Russian girls. Nevertheless it was voted that Miss Reynolds should make the trip at Mr. Stokes' expense, "provided she shall be entirely free to act in regard to her work there as may seem best on her arrival."[18]

On her return to London the Executive Committee heard and approved her report to Mr. Stokes, which was, in substance, as follows:

In the present condition, both political and ecclesiastical in Russia, we must recognize that work there must be done either in the Greek Church only, or in the Lutheran Church. . . . Work in the Greek Church itself can only be carried on by a member of that church. . . . The intense national pride and patriotism of Russia makes any work undertaken there by a foreigner most difficult. . . . I am therefore expressing not alone my own conviction but also that . . . of others whose acquaintance with Russian thought was the result of longer acquaintance with Russia than my own, when I say that for the present it seems most inadvisable to attempt any work there to be carried on by a foreigner. . . . That which would seem most practical . . . would be for one or two young Russians who would be nominated by the Emperor, to go abroad and study from their point of view the work of the Young Men's and Young Women's Christian Associations in other countries, France, England and America. It should be laid before their Imperial Majesties that such work should be studied with the idea of introducing it into Russia, with such modfications as might seem desirable from a Russian point of view. . . . This, therefore, is my conclusion, and I believe I am right in saying the conclusion of others, as to any present Association work in Russia for either young men or young women.[19]

This report was decisive for the World's Committee. There is no evidence that the suggestion of sending young Russians abroad to study bore fruit. Either Mr. Stokes did not make the proposal or, if he did, it was not accepted by the Emperor. It was not until after the Russo-Japanese war, in the days just preceding the World's Y.W.C.A. Conference of 1906, that the question of relations with Russia again appeared.

One other phase in the development of those early years should be mentioned. It has to do with the effect of world organization upon the National Associations that carried greatest responsibility and were most aggressive in promoting it, the Associations of Great Britain and the United States of America.

On both countries the organizing of a World Association placed an added financial burden, and the task of securing even so modest an annual budget as £600 was not easy. For the British Association it meant also the transfer of responsibility for work in many other countries which they had long carried, to the province of the World's Association, and continuing to plan its development as one unit within the new organization. For the American Association it meant entrance into an entirely new field and into cooperative relation with Associations of other lands of which they knew very little. The Association in the United States was eager to support the new venture and to take its full share in the extension of the movement but its distance from Europe and the very different conditions of life in America made it difficult both for the American and European Associations to understand one another and for the Associations in the United States to share in the month by month work of the World's Executive Committee. Miss Reynolds endeavored by every possible means—travel, visitation, attendance at conferences and conventions, letters, speeches and special reports—to interpret other types of Association work to leaders and members of the Y.W.C.A. in America, as she tried also by the same methods to interpret the American Associations to Europe and Great Britain. Only slowly, over a period of many years, were understanding and appreciation developed among the different Associations with their varying ideas of the function and program of a Y.W.C.A.

The first World's Y.W.C.A. Conference was the goal toward which all the thought and work of the first four years was directed. The character and program of the conference reflected the ideal for the movement as it had taken shape during these years. The annual report for 1897, published shortly before the conference convened and doubtless in the hands of delegates as they arrived, had on its cover the World's Y.W.C.A. motto, "Not by might nor by power but by my Spirit, saith the Lord of Hosts", in eleven different languages—English, French, German, Italian, Spanish, Swedish, Norwegian, Danish, Japanese, Chinese and Urdu. But the realities of the situation determined that one language only, English, should be the official language of the conference. A survey of the 326 delegates from the seventeen countries at the conference reveals that the overwhelming majority of those present were British.[20] This was, of course, partly because the conference was in London, but it is also indicative of the predominance of British interest in and responsibility for the World

Movement. It is noticeable, further, that almost all the nineteen delegates from India and all those representing Africa, China, Spain and Turkey were British.

The business of the conference was, in the nature of the case, largely retrospective. It heard reports by the President, Mrs. Tritton; the Treasurer, Miss Morley; the Standing Committees and the General Secretary. It ratified actions taken by them during the past four years; it adopted the constitution and the budget; and it elected the Executive Committee. There were also resolutions dealing with the date of the next World's Conference, which was set for 1901 but later changed to 1902. *The Quarterly,* publication of which had been begun in 1896, was declared to be the official organ of the World's Association. An international Week of Prayer was established, to be observed by all Associations and to be a time for securing special gifts. The date chosen for this, after much consideration, was the second week of November.[21] The Executive Committee was empowered to "select and order a suitable badge" and to publish a World's Handbook.

The real significance of the conference lay less in its formal actions than in its atmosphere of fellowship and hope for the future. Its deeply religious spirit, a spirit of prayer, of thanksgiving, and of personal consecration was expressed in the opening address of Mrs. Tritton and in the daily meditations on "The Things of the Spirit" given each morning by the Reverend G. H. C. McGregor, a minister of the Presbyterian Church of England. There was a broad and inclusive vision of the task of the Association. Among the addresses given were papers on "Women's Duties Toward the State", the "Moral and Intellectual Training of Women", "Christianity and Womanhood", and the "Y.W.C.A. in Women's Colleges". There was also a search for knowledge of one another. After the reports of the World's Committee itself, the part of the program most appreciated by the delegates probably was the large number of reports of their work given by different countries.

An interesting picture of this first conference comes from the "Introductory Sketch" published as a preface to the official report. Though signed only "one who was present", it was probably written by Miss Lucy Moor, an active worker in the Association of Great Britain from its earliest days when she was a colleague of Miss Robarts, and the author of the history of the British Y.W.C.A. entitled *Girls of Yesterday and Today* (1910). Miss Moor tells of the first afternoon's prayer-meeting which "showed us rapidly that we were met for a solemn purpose. . . . The close of the meeting," she says, "was spent in prayer and intercession. Here for the first time our ears were greeted with the sound of strange tongues, and though afterward this became a familiar delight to us, we cannot forget the sense of unity which broke over our first meeting, as we learned more fully that we of such divers nations and lands were, verily, 'all one in Christ Jesus'."

She speaks of "the interesting and somewhat mysterious ceremony of presenting our credentials to the World's Officials and of receiving in return their credentials, which authorized us not only to have voting powers and the right of discussion but provided for us also the right of free luncheon and tea each day." Referring to the World's Committee reports she says: "These reports when read were passed over to an interesting, and to some of us novel body known as the Reports Committee, who were elected by the conference for the temporary purpose of examining in an impartial way the reports of the Executive and all Standing Committees. On this Reports Committee no official of the World's Association was given a seat. . . . So much had to be reported on that it was not possible to deal fully with the future and the intensely interesting questions and developments which it contains. We got a few vistas of these as we heard some of the reports read." Regarding the adoption of the constitution, she says: "Our most animated discussion was on Thursday morning, when the World's constitution came up. It was not understood by those who were not clearly informed, and this delayed our proceedings, but with the result that we all felt we must lose no time another day, but leave constitutions to committees."

"The two resolutions," she goes on to say, "which struck us as being most pregnant were, first, the one which proposed a universal Week of Prayer for young women, and second, proposals for raising an income of £800 a year for the heavy working expenses of the World's Association. It was delightful to find how great was the difficulty to choose a Week of Prayer which suited everyone! And this for no captious reasons but only because so widespread is the Y.W.C.A. that the seasons interfere with the times."

She was full of praise for the way the conference was organized. "What can be said of all the minutiæ of this conference of ours? The skillful ever-ready Stewards with their brightness . . . the hospitality given us . . . the kindness of Lady Wells in providing two coaches so that those of us who did not know London might be driven to see the chief sights, the peaceful communion service in St. George's Church . . . and especially, perhaps, the daily prayer-meetings held before the afternoon meeting. . . . As the date of the conference recedes . . . the significance must surely remain and increase and the track of praise, along which it recedes, must run through our lives and work."[22]

From one point of view, the majority of the delegates and the setting, the conference was "very British". From another, its machinery of organization, it was "very American". The "mysterious" credentials ceremony, the interesting and novel Reports Committee, the skillful Stewards—one surmises that all these were suggested by Miss Reynolds out of her fund of experience in the United States at summer conferences and state and national conventions. But from a larger viewpoint the conference was truly a world meeting, in its depth of interest in all young women, its profoundly evangelical religious note, its deliberate consciousness of and welcome for the things that differ in different countries as well as for the things that are the same in all, as shown by the keen interest in the reports from the various Associations. The first World's Conference marked a real achievement, the realization of an idea in actual organization. It was also the starting point of a new stage in the development of this idea—a stage in which the World's Y.W.C.A. would begin as an already existing organization to deal with the future which Miss Moor felt had received so little attention in the London Conference.

REFERENCES

[1] First Annual Report, for 1895, p. 5.

[2] First Annual Report, for 1895, p. 6.

[3] First World's Y.W.C.A. Conference, 1898, Report, p. 63.

[4] Reynolds, Annie M., Second Annual Report, 1896, p. 15.

[5] First World's Y.W.C.A. Conference, 1898, Report, p. 64.

[6] First World's Y.W.C.A. Conference, 1898, Report, p. 63.

[7] Reynolds, Annie M., First Annual Report, for 1895, p. 13.

[8] See chapter 2, p. 31.

[9] *The Evangel,* August 1896, p. 4.

[10] Reynolds, Annie M., Second Annual Report, for 1896, p. 12.

[11] See chapter 2, p. 32.

[12] Second World's Y.W.C.A. Conference, 1902, Report, p. 155.

[13] World's Committee, Annual Report for 1904, pp. 15, 16.

[14] See chapter 1, p. 15.

[15] Wilson, Elizabeth, *The Story of Fifty Years of the Y.W.C.A. in India, Burma and Ceylon,* 1925, p. 28.

[16] First World's Y.W.C.A. Conference, 1898, Report p. 68.

[17] See chapter 2, pp. 33-34.

[18] Executive Committee, November 1897, Minutes.

[19] Reynolds, Annie M., Report to Mr. James Stokes, April 1897.

[20] The distribution of delegates was as follows:

Africa (Egypt-2; S. Africa-3)	5	India	19
Australasia	8	Italy	5
Canada	3	Norway	1
China	2	Russia (Finland)	6
Denmark	3	Spain	2
France	5	Sweden	13
Germany	3	Switzerland	5
Great Britain (England		Turkey in Asia	1
Scotland, Ireland)	204	United States	14
Hungary	1		——326

[21] The Y.W.C.A. of Great Britain had inaugurated a Week of Prayer, observed in February, after the evangelistic meetings held in Birmingham in 1884. This was, after 1898, merged with the World's Week of Prayer voted at the World's Conference. (See Kinnaird, Emily. *Reminiscences,* 1925, p. 111.)

[22] First World's Y.W.C.A. Conference, 1898, Report, pp. 14-19.

Today, at the opening of the twentieth century, as never before, it is increasingly true of international existence that we are all members one of another.... The nations as individuals are called upon to be responsible for each other's children and as Christian women we must bear our part in this advancing civilization.

Report of the Executive Committee to the Second World's Y.W.C.A. Conference, Geneva, 1902.

It is significant of the direction to which all thoughts and hearts have been turned in these remarkable closing days of this remarkable century that for two years this report must be dated from the Orient.... last year from Imperial India . . . this year from Imperial Japan.

ANNIE M. REYNOLDS. Annual Report for the Year 1900 (adapted).

CHAPTER 7   THE FIRST DECADE PART II:
1898-1904

THE ANNUAL reports for the two years following the London Conference reflect a feeling of great encouragement regarding the work of the World's Young Women's Christian Association. Reports from almost all countries indicated that the work was "going and growing". The affiliation of the National Association of Germany just after the London Conference, brought in new and valuable elements, a distinctive national movement with nearly 4000 branches. These German Associations were largely parochial in character, embracing a membership of approximately 85,000. Their leaders, mostly pastors and deaconesses, were specially trained in religion, in social service, and in methods of work with young people. Their extensive program was made available through an already large volume of literature prepared both for leaders and for members. The affiliation of the National Association of France in 1900 further enriched the World's Y.W.C.A. by the numerically small but nevertheless significant addition of a movement founded on democratic principles, in the framing of whose policies, local, district and national, the girl members themselves had a share.

Mrs. Tritton writes in her annual report for 1899: "The fifth report of the World's Y.W.C.A. which it is our privilege to lay before you is full of encouragement. There seems indeed only one form in which we can begin it, in the words of the beautiful Te Deum, 'We praise Thee, we bless Thee, we glorify Thee'."[1] Miss Reynolds, reporting as General Secretary, says:

> The last year has been a very active one, but the widening and practical interest in the more intelligent appreciation of Association work from the international standpoint has been most encouraging.[2]

Again, in the President's report for 1900, Mrs. Tritton remarks: "The unexpected way in which this work seems to meet the needs of today may almost be said to be a cause of surprise as well as of deep thankfulness."[3]

The office of the World's Committee, meantime, had been strengthened by the addition to its secretarial staff of Miss Ethel Stevenson, who came to act as Corresponding Secretary, responsible for carrying the increasing volume of correspondence with the National Committees and with the Corresponding Associations. Her acquaintance with the Continent, her facility in speaking German and French, and her outstanding gifts of understanding and tact were to make her of peculiar value in the development of the world fellowship.

As the World's office became more and more an accepted center for Association work and inspiration, the business of correspondence increased enormously. With the large, well-organized National Associations this correspondence was concerned especially with matters of policy of the World's Committee, but with the smaller movements and the scattered local Associations which were all that existed in many lands, the World's office became more and more the source of advice and encouragement such as Associations in highly organized countries turned for to their own national offices.

Thus the World's Committee developed a sort of double character: on the one hand, it was a center uniting National Associations for fellowship and for a common purpose; on the other hand, in carrying out its object of the "development and extension of the Y.W.C.A. in all lands," it of necessity performed for many Associations functions normally belonging to a national movement. As time went on, and especially as the large "sending countries" like the United States and Great Britain came to have workers in many far corners of the earth, this double rôle of the World's Committee was complicated by the natural tendency of workers abroad to look to their own home national office rather than to the World's office for advice and guidance.

Nowhere was the increase in "intelligent appreciation of Association work from an international standpoint" more fruitful in its practical results than in the United States. The delegates from the United States gained from the London Conference not only acquaintance with people, life and customs hitherto strange to them, but also a new vision of the significance of the international undertaking on which they had embarked. This new vision and the enthusiasm that it engendered were carried back to the home Associations in letters, reports, articles in *The Evangel*, as well as by word of mouth. Moreover, one of the delegates, Miss Elizabeth Wilson of the American national staff, remained in England for a year of study and was made a member of the Executive Committee for that period. This was an inside touch with the World's Y.W.C.A. work which no American save Miss Reynolds and Miss Morse had up to this time enjoyed. The establishing of a World's Week of Prayer also afforded a fresh opportunity to present the World's Association to the general membership of the American Associations in terms of world-wide spiritual fellowship.

But it was not the London Conference alone which contributed to a growing appreciation of the World's Y.W.C.A. by the American Associations. In 1899 the Student Departments of the American Y.M.C.A. and Y.W.C.A. became affiliated with the World's Student Christian Federation. The linking up of Christian students the world around in this organization, which had been formed in 1895, only a year after the World's Y.W.C.A., naturally carried with it for the student members of the Y.W.C.A. an enhanced sense of the value of belonging also to a world organization of Christian women, such as the World's Y.W.C.A.

The most potent factors, however, in increasing America's "intelligent appreciation" were the personal contacts which these Associations enjoyed with Miss Reynolds and with Miss Ruth Rouse of the Student Christian Movement. In 1899 Miss Reynolds made one of her most extended visits to the United States, attending the National Convention at Milwaukee and speaking on the work of the World's Association. Then, crossing the continent, she spent two and a half months visiting Associations on the Pacific coast. From 1897 to 1899, Miss Rouse spent almost two years in the United States, first as a secretary for the Student Volunteer Movement and later as a Student Secretary for the American Committee. To the American college women, lacking as most of them were in any contact whatsoever with students of other lands, the visit of this vigorous, attractive, deeply Christian and widely experienced Oxford University woman, who had already served as secretary of the British Student Movement and had traveled among students in the northern European countries, was an entrance into a new world of experience. From it, for many a student member of the Y.W.C.A. in the United States, there sprang up a permanent loyalty and commitment to the cause of Christian world fellow-ship and a lifelong sense of responsibility for those movements that pro-mote it.

In addition to these elements of encouragement, 1899 was, as the report of the Treasurer, Miss Morley, shows, one of distinctly increased though still extremely modest financial support for the World's Y.W.C.A. work. This was especially gratifying since now that the first phase of the World's Committee task, that of affiliating existing movements, was practically accomplished, the Committee was anxious to turn its attention to expansion. India was eager for a visit from Miss Reynolds and there was need to survey the needs and possibilities in Japan and China. Miss Morley's financial statement for 1899 records

> . . . the remarkable answer to earnest and united prayer for the needed funds to enable our Traveling Secretary, Miss Rey-nolds, to pay the much desired visit to India. . . . Within three weeks of the day when a final decision had to be made, an empty treasury seemed to make this a foregone conclusion. But it is nothing with our God to help, with many or with them that have no might, and so He was pleased to answer the prayers of a small company of women, separated during the summer va-cation far apart, but one in heart and desire, by sending in fully as much money as was required both for Miss Reynolds' pas-sage and for her traveling expenses while in India.[4]

Before going to the United States for the summer of 1899, Miss Rey-nolds paid a visit to the Continent, going to Hungary, where she found a work "very much in its infancy but with three branches most consecrated in spirit"; to Vienna, and to Prague. In the last-named city she found a newly organized Association, the outgrowth of the visit of a secretary of the International Committee of the Y.M.C.A. "He was making a tour in Bohemia," she writes, "and one evening after an unusually earnest gospel meeting, he asked all young men present who would like to belong to a Y.M.C.A. to rise. To his dismay there arose also seventeen young women, who manifestly could not be formed into a Y.M.C.A. but who declined to sit down until they had received the promise of being duly re-ported to those interested in young women!"[5]

On returning from the United States, and having set in order her affairs in the World's Y.W.C.A. office, Miss Reynolds sailed in early October for India. She visited Colombo and Madras and wrote her annual report for 1899 in Calcutta. She was present at the laying of the cornerstone for the new building in Bombay. From Bombay she went to Kurachee, "where the Association membership included Roman Catholics and Parsees as well as Protestants of several denominations"; to Lahore, "where the branches in the Government Medical School, the Mission Schools and the Cantonments showed the variety of the work"; to Ludhiana, Agra, Cawnpore, Lucknow, and Jhansi "with its large railway interests". "There was no place," she writes, "in which one did not hear the spirit of the Macedonian cry, never silent through the ages—'Come over and help us'."[6]

One of Miss Reynolds' concerns in India was the working out of a plan of cooperation between the National Y.W.C.A. of India and the Missionary Settlement for University Women in Bombay. The latter, started in 1897 by British university women along lines similar to the University Settlements in England, had been promoting work especially in the Parsee community and among students. As the Y.W.C.A. felt more and more keenly the need for educated Indian leadership, and as it came increasingly under the direction of American secretaries who were accustomed to a student department within the Y.W.C.A., there arose some question regarding the respective fields of these organizations with relation to women students in India. Fortunate it was that Miss Rouse, who arrived in India in 1899 to work in the Bombay Settlement and also to be a Student Secretary for the Y.W.C.A., had such a background of understanding that a plan of cooperation could be worked out. By this plan Miss Agnes de Selincourt of the Missionary Settlement for University Women was appointed Student Secretary for North India, Miss Laura Radford of the Y.W.C.A., for Bengal, while Miss Rouse herself served as a general student worker for India and Ceylon.

The trip through India impressed Miss Reynolds with the need for well-equipped, trained leaders to take advantage of the immense opportunities before the Association, both at home and abroad, as well as with the inadequacy of the methods by which in most countries Association workers were recruited. "Whether we look outside our own town or country, or go beyond the frontiers of our nation, there are the most intense appeals for more workers. . . . 'Give us more and give us of your best' is the continual cry. It is the best education, the best brain, the strongest constitution and the deepest consecration that must stand in the breach of this advance stage of the world's civilization. There is work for all, but now, when everywhere the standard of education has been so much raised, there is an especial need for those who have the higher advantages of any land to make their influence felt for Christian womanhood."[7]

Indeed, the demand for the extension of the work of the Y.W.C.A. which the existence of a world organization helped to create, and the need for leadership to meet this demand, presented the World's Committee, as the new century opened, with an acute problem. To meet it, a standing committee on the selection of workers was appointed, but this alone was not sufficient. Mrs. Tritton, in her report for 1900 emphasizes "one source of deep disappointment and dismay because it applies to every country in more or less degree. It is the absence of suitable and trained women to undertake the post of secretaries abroad and at home. . . . It has been well-nigh heart-breaking, month by month, to have the appeals from various countries entreating for helpers and to hear that no suitable ones are to be heard of. . . . We have actually had the salaries and passage money for two secretaries for India in hand for some months and yet we cannot find one lady suitable and willing to go."[8]

The reasons for this shortage of leaders were many. In Great Britain the number of university women seeking professional careers in religious and social service organizations was not large, and the tradition of the Y.W.C.A. was one of volunteer service. The British Student Christian Movement was entirely separate from the Y.M.C.A. and the Y.W.C.A., and these organizations made less appeal than the definitely student work. On the Continent the trend was almost wholly in the direction of church and missionary service for those Y.W.C.A. leaders who were desirous of doing religious work in other lands. Only in the United States and Canada had the idea of the Y.W.C.A. as a field for professional service for college and university women taken any considerable hold. To these circumstances and to the size and, comparatively speaking, the wealth of the Association in the United States, is largely due the fact that the response to the challenge for trained Y.W.C.A. leaders was, for many years, chiefly from the United States.

The opportunities before the Y.W.C.A. and the call for leadership to meet them became even more insistent when the World's Committee turned its thoughts toward the Orient. Miss Reynolds sailed from San Francisco in September 1900. "The Executive Committee," she says, "had deemed it advisable for me to undertake a journey of investigation to Japan and China, largely induced thereto by indirect suggestions or direct appeals from missionaries who had favored our considering the question of work in these countries."[9] Some small beginnings of Association work among students in these countries already existed, introduced by missionaries who had known the Association at home.[10] The moment seemed to them and to others who were aware of the rapidly changing civilization of the Orient, ripe for its extension on a larger scale.[11]

As often had happened elsewhere, the way for the Y.W.C.A. was prepared in China by the work of the Y.M.C.A. Two student Y.M.C.A.s had been organized in the 1880s. The first Y.W.C.A. secretary was Willard D. Lyon, who went to China in 1895 following the visit of Mr. and Mrs. Luther W. Wishard.[12]

In the following years the Y.M.C.A. developed rapidly under the impetus of an extraordinary group of able secretaries from Canada and

86

the United States. They brought to China the enthusiasm and flexibility of a movement which was warmly evangelistic and had freshness of approach and willingness to pioneer in new methods.[13] Moreover, from the beginning the Y.M.C.A. stressed the necessity of Chinese leadership, and concentrated much of its attention on the students, the future leaders of China. The result was that they attracted able Chinese to the secretariat and had by 1900 the beginnings of a genuine Chinese movement. The Y.M.C.A. leaders (and their wives) were quick to see the value of a Y.W.C.A. that should parallel this work for young men, and in 1899, at a conference in Shanghai, the Y.M.C.A. deliberately appointed a National Committee of women for the development of the work of the Y.W.C.A.

This Committee, in line with the established policy of the Y.M.C.A., was composed of both Chinese and foreigners. Its President was Mrs. Robert E. Lewis, the wife of a pioneer Y.M.C.A. secretary in China, but its Vice President was Miss V. Y. Tsao, a Chinese teacher who had studied abroad and whose brother was a Y.M.C.A. secretary, and its Treasurer was Miss Julia Yen. Much of the extraordinary development and usefulness of the Y.M.C.A. and the Y.W.C.A. in China in the coming years was due to the principle, established at the very beginning, of placing the leadership as far as possible in the hands of Chinese, recruiting that leadership from the Christian men and women of outstanding educational opportunity and experience. Both the Y.M.C.A. and the Y.W.C.A. in China were pioneers in affording to such young Chinese the opportunity to create and handle a Christian organization of their own.

The new National Y.W.C.A. Committee sent to the Y.W.C.A. in the United States an appeal for help, signed by women representing various groups, Chinese, English and American. This appeal the American Committee forwarded to the World's Committee. Miss Reynolds quotes at length from it in her annual report for 1901. It called particular attention to the need created by the new industrial situation among women and girls, twenty-five thousand of whom were employed in Shanghai in the modern silk and cotton factories and more than ten thousand in match factories. It also stressed the long hours, the low wages, and the almost complete lack of any welfare work. The appeal concludes: "Here is a great field, created by modernized industry, waiting for the Association."[14]

In Japan also the sudden introduction of modern industry on a large scale had created an appalling situation, especially among women and girls. In Japan, too, there was a growing number of Christian young women coming out of mission and government schools but without adequate channels through which to continue their Christian fellowship or unite for Christian service. The already overtaxed missionaries were unable to cope with these problems though gravely concerned about them. Miss

Reynolds writes of the conditions in Osaka, "the Birmingham of Japan", and in the Imperial Capital of Tokyo:

"In Osaka," she says, "besides the cotton mills, there are women employed in the following industries: copperworks, iron works, cutlery, thin plated glass wares, brass and lead works, lamp fixtures, glass, pottery, brick-making, cement, chemicals, medicine, oil, etc., also cabinet workers, lacquer ware, watches, musical instruments, writing material, bamboo ware, rattan, soap, lanterns, matches, paper, buttons, false hair, toilet articles, umbrellas, etc. etc." To this overwhelming list she adds food and drink and tobacco and "various implements such as scales, fishing tackle, etc."[15] She also adds that in Tokyo "we meet with an anomaly which is most confusing, a Women's University in the Orient. . . . This university opened in the spring of 1901 with 500 students. So eagerly had the applications come in that the examiners had been obliged to raise the entrance test, as they had not sufficient accommodation to receive the applicants. . . . There is a strong call," Miss Reynolds concludes, "to send a student secretary to Tokyo. . . . One or two promising applicants in the United States were considering this post but in both cases family reasons obliged them to withdraw. This post, so unique in its possibilities is still empty."[16]

Partly, no doubt, as a result of Miss Reynolds' visit in the early months of 1901, the Women's Missionary Conference which met in Tokyo and included representatives from all the missions in Tokyo and Yokohama "as well as others interested in missions" sent to the World's Committee in the closing months of the same year the following appeal:

Whereas, under the new industrial conditions in Japan there is a large class of factory and other working women, almost entirely untouched by present Christian effort and,

Whereas the Christian graduates and ex-students of Mission Schools and the graduates and undergraduates of Government Schools are not as yet banded together in any interdenominational movement for personal and institutional work for the betterment of the social and spiritual condition of their fellow women,

Resolved, that the Women's Conference of Tokyo and Yokohama express its appreciation of the work and methods of the Y.W.C.A. and its conviction that there is a great and growing need for the work of the Y.W.C.A. in Japan and,

Resolved, that the Women's Conference of Tokyo and Yokohama urge upon the World's Committee of the Young Women's Christian Association the importance of sending as soon as possible, secretaries to organize the work of the Young Women's Christian Association both in cities and in schools.[17]

These appeals from missionaries and others in both China and Japan raised for the World's Committee the whole question of an aggressive program of expansion involving leadership and funds on a far larger scale than anything yet attempted. Miss Reynolds' report of her tour of investigation in the Orient closes with this summary of the situation:

These are the questions which have presented themselves to the Committee during this last year and which are by no means easy to solve in a single negative or a complaisant affirmative. They have not yet felt that they could assume the responsibility of taking a step fraught with so many and so grave responsibilities. Indeed, the final decision must be deferred until the World's Conference.[18]

When, therefore, the second World's Y.W.C.A. Conference convened in Geneva, Switzerland, in July 1902, the extent and character of the missionary program of the Y.W.C.A. as a world organization was the most significant question before it. All the National Associations acknowledged and cultivated missionary responsibility, but often this responsibility was expressed wholly in terms of support given to the regular church missionary societies.[19] Only in India were workers, sent out by the Y.W.C.A.s of Great Britain and the United States, definitely building the Y.W.C.A. as an independent interdenominational organization. Now came urgent appeals for the extension of this program to Japan and China. They touched the very heart of the aim of the World's Association. In submitting these appeals to the conference for its "earnest consideration and discussion" the Executive Committee said:

We would remind the conference that in matters of foreign policy, as well as in national affairs, the World's Association has no power to legislate. . . . We also recall to the conference the third reason for our existence as an international Association . . . "to help young women in Christian countries to realize more closely their responsibilities toward young women in non-Christian lands." The national reports will tell us something of what each country is attempting to do in missionary support, but we may safely classify the missionary help given by our Associations of the different countries under two heads:

1. Associations give direct to some Missionary Society representing the church with which many of their members are connected.

2. Some Associations have learned of the support of the secretaries doing missionary work in India, the only country where we are at present privileged to have secretaries, and give regularly and systematically to them, as the members' substitute in proclaiming Christ's name.

We bring before you today the calls of China and Japan, which can hardly be considered as having any Association work at all, and we ask you how it is your wish that they should be answered.[20]

"We have groped our way," said Miss Reynolds in her conference report, "in our own work from the local to the larger union, and we have grown up to our national work and lastly our World's organization, and in *'l'union qui fait la force'* we are called to go forward to greater advance in our work. . . . I am expressing only my own individual opinion of the opportunities as well as our responsibilities toward them, as I saw them in my visit to Japan and China, but I do most deeply believe that this is a direct call from God to us and one which we do not well to neglect."[21]

In spite of the conviction expressed by Miss Reynolds, and probably fully shared by the Executive Committee, the recommendation of the Committee was meticulously true to the fundamental policy of recognizing and encouraging unity of purpose with great diversity of method. They proposed:

> . . . an increased recognition and development of the responsibilities of the young women of Christian lands toward those in non-Christian lands by those methods which, on the careful consideration of the National Committees, may be deemed best in furtherance of the cause of our Master, whether it be by the support of missionaries working under missionary societies, or by direct connection with the support of secretaries sent out to do Association work in foreign countries.[22]

This recommendation was unanimously adopted by the conference, with the following addition:

> . . . that the Association work be undertaken only in those countries to which we have been called by the resident missionaries, recognizing that such work may be a valuable link to unite all National Associations, and to create a center of interdenominational work in the field. As at home we strive to supplement, not to supplant, church work, so our desire in the mission field is only to supplement, in no wise to supplant or encroach upon the scope of the missionary societies.[23]

The decision that the World's Y.W.C.A. should approve and sponsor the development of the Association in countries regarded as foreign mission fields was of great importance for the future. Its effect was to define the responsibility of the World's Committee as that of promoting the Young Women's Christian Association as such, while allowing those National Associations that chose to do so to continue to interpret their missionary responsibility in terms of church missions. The Associations that continued to do this were of course those in which the Association program was practically synonymous with the youth program of the church. But as the conditions, educational, industrial and economic, which had led to the development of the Association as an independent interdenominational agency in countries like Great Britain and the United States were reproduced more and more widely in the countries of the world, the call for a definitely Y.W.C.A. program to supplement the work of church missions became more insistent. Since the conference resolution presupposed that the expansion of the Association which would result from it would be the work of the National Committees that chose to undertake it, rather than of the World's Committee acting for all Associations, its immediate practical result was to authorize the National Associations of the United States and Canada, already deeply interested in Japan and China, to recruit and send out secretaries to these countries.

The missionary policy of the Y.W.C.A. was the central subject of consideration at the Geneva Conference, and the resolution regarding this was the climax of the conference deliberations, fittingly followed by the singing of the Doxology. It was a smaller conference than that of 1898, 175 delegates as against 326 at London, but with a better distributed international representation. The German Association, it is true, sent but one visiting and no voting delegate, which seems to show that in spite of the sympathetic attitude of its official leaders the movement in Germany was not yet fired with understanding and enthusiasm for the World's Association. The continental representation as a whole, however, was considerably larger than in 1898, and included twenty-three from Italy and fourteen from France. This, along with a larger delegation from the United States (twenty-eight as against fourteen), made a better balance in conference personnel. At London only the English language was used. At Geneva the primary language was French, with English as a second. Miss Reynolds refers to this fact as "marking a new epoch in the history of the World's Y.W.C.A."[24]

Among the recommendations adopted was one establishing a four-year period instead of three as previously recommended, between world conferences. Another important resolution provided for an interim meeting of the World's Committee in London in 1904 "to discuss all matters of Association interest." To this meeting the National Associations were to be allowed to send proxies if their regular delegates were unable to attend, and the meeting was to be "of sufficient duration to consider the serious problems of each country, to note the extent to which the recommendations of this conference are being carried out, and to forecast the needs of the next conference."[25]

Other resolutions reaffirmed the aim of the Association "to seek to meet the needs of the mind and body as well as the aim of ultimate spiritual welfare," and dealt with the matter of trained leadership.

> We recommend each National Association to place clearly before itself a high ideal of Association aims and methods, and that this can only be reached by efficient, educated, well-trained workers who shall be in themselves the best exponents of Association standards. While the day may be for most countries remote when a training school for Y.W.C.A. secretaries may be opened for those who shall make the secretaryship their life profession, as women make medicine or other sciences, yet this ideal may still be upheld. We want the best women to do the best work, and that work on Christian lines.[26]

More important, perhaps, than its pronouncements was the influence of the conference in making the delegates conscious of their responsibility for the World's Association. Writing a year later, Miss Reynolds compares Geneva with London:

> The delegates at London all had a certain air of strangeness and uncertainty both as to their duties and as to their privileges. . . . At Geneva, the delegates felt that it was their conference, and one in which they were responsible for the decisions. . . . There was a readiness to serve on the conference committees and to assume the duties of such committees quite different from the reluctant manner so manifest in London.[27]

The following year Miss Reynolds gave notice of her resignation from the position of General Secretary, to take effect in the summer of 1904, at the close of ten years of service. Other changes also were taking place. At Geneva Mrs. Tritton had retired as President and was succeeded by Mrs. George W. Campbell, who since 1898 had been one of the Vice Presidents of the World's Association. In 1903 came the death of Miss Morse, whose wisdom and untiring effort and persistent pressure on her colleagues had been so large a factor in the creation of the World's Association, and in the early months of 1904, that of Mrs. Hatt Noble, President of the Association in Ireland, another charter member of the Executive Committee.

Two things rounded out the work of the first decade. Miss Reynolds wrote a brief history of the World's Y.W.C.A. to date. She called it *Ten Years' Record*. Among the matters she deemed it important to record regarding this formative decade is the fact that the number of the National Associations affiliated with the World Movement had reached twelve, and that the first Y.W.C.A. secretaries had gone out to Japan and China, Theresa Morrison to Japan in 1903, supported by the Associations of California, Oregon and Washington, and Martha Berninger, formerly a

Mrs. George Campbell

missionary in China, to open Y.W.C.A. work among the industrial girls of Shanghai, her support guaranteed by the city Associations of Detroit and Grand Rapids, Michigan, and the student Associations of the State of Missouri.

The other closing event of the decade was the meeting of the World's Committee in London, June 28 to July 1, 1904, as had been provided for at the Geneva Conference. Besides the members of the Executive Committee and the British World's Committee members, active members of the Committee were present from Denmark, Sweden, France, Italy, Hungary and India, while corresponding members were there from New South Wales, South Africa and Portugal. At the third World's Conference in Paris in 1906, it was reported that this meeting in London "did much to draw us closer together and to help in the understanding of one another's difficulties."[28]

Thus the first decade when it closed could present a modest but substantial record of accomplishment, of National Associations affiliated, of acquaintance and understanding cultivated, of new fields surveyed and work in them begun, and of organization set up which made provision for continuity of consultation and discussion between the varied elements of which the world movement was composed.

REFERENCES

[1] Annual Report for 1899, p. 5.

[2] *Ibid.*, p. 9.

[3] Annual Report for 1900, p. 5.

[4] Annual Report for 1899, pp. 22-23.

[5] Annual Report for 1899, p. 10.

[6] Annual Report for 1900, p. 11.

[7] Annual Report for 1899, pp. 13-14.

[8] Annual Report for 1900, pp. 5, 6.

[9] Annual Report for 1901, p. 5.

[10] See Chapter 3, pp. 45-46.

[11] In 1890 there began a chain of events which precipitated the rapid crumbling of inherited Chinese culture, a revolution without precedent in Chinese history. First the war with Japan and the defeat of China. Then the threatened partition by ambitious European powers, the acquiring of extra-territorial rights, the Boxer uprising of 1900 followed by the imposition of the Boxer indemnity, the Russo-Japanese war of 1904-1905 with Japan again the victor. In the face of all this China set about adopting western culture. . . . Chinese culture was fluid as it had not been since before the advent of Christ. The time was most favorable for the spread of Christianity. To a greater degree than in any other major civilized land, there was an opportunity to build Christianity into the warp and woof of the emerging civilization—the China that was to be (Latourette, Kenneth S., *History of the Expansion of Christianity,* Vol. VI. p. 260 ff.).

REFERENCES

[12] See Chapter 3, pp. 46-47.

[13] See Latourette, Kenneth S. *History of the Expansion of Christianity,* Vol. VI, pp. 341, 342.

[14] Annual Report for 1901, p. 6.

[15] *Ibid.,* pp. 9, 10.

[16] Annual Report for 1901, p. 11.

[17] *Ibid.,* p. 9.

[18] Annual Report for 1901, p. 12.

[19] See Chapter 2, p. 28.

[20] Second World's Y.W.C.A. Conference, 1902, Report, pp. 33-35.

[21] *Ibid.,* pp. 47, 48.

[22] *Ibid.,* p. 37.

[23] *Ibid.,* p. 21.

[24] Second World's Y.W.C.A. Conference, 1902, Report, p. 15.

[25] *Ibid.,* p. 19.

[26] *Ibid.,* p. 37.

[27] Annual Report for 1903, p. 15.

[28] This 1904 meeting was the first of the regular biennial meetings of the World's Committee which it became the custom to hold. In years of a World Conference, the Committee met at the place where the conference was held, and had two sessions, one before and one following the conference. From 1904 to 1914 the biennial meetings between conferences were held in England. No meetings were held during the first World War. From 1920 to 1930 they were held on the continent of Europe (1920, 1922), in the United States (1924), and in England (1926).

*At no time in the history of the World's Association
has the World's Committee been confronted with so
many open doors and such vast opportunities for
service. . . .The time is one of crisis; opportunities
await us now, but we know not how long they may
last.*

Report of World's Committee, Fourth World's Y.W.C.A.
Conference, 1910.

CHAPTER 8 THE ERA OF EXPANSION

AFTER Miss Reynolds' resignation in 1904,
the Executive Committee turned again to the United States for a woman
who should succeed her in the exacting and many-sided task of administering a still new and somewhat experimental world organization of women.
And again the American movement supplied a woman of exceptional qualities of mind and spirit, equipped with an experience in Christian work
both at home and abroad that fitted her in a peculiar manner for the leadership of the World's Young Women's Christian Association in the years
immediately ahead.

Clarissa Hale Spencer typified in her own background, upbringing
and experience much that was best and most characteristic of American
life in the later years of the nineteenth century. Writing of her after her
death in 1926, a member of the World's Committee said, "For much that
was sound and strong in Clarissa Spencer's character we are indebted
to the sturdy pioneer stock from which she sprang." Her grandfather, born
in New England, as a young man trekked across the Allegheny mountains
"driving a two horse team" through Ohio and Indiana, and settled as a
farmer in Illinois. Some years later he moved, as did so many of these young
pioneers, still further west, finding his permanent home on the east bank
of the Mississippi river, where he was one of the first settlers in what became, in time, the present city of Rock Island.

Living first in a deserted Indian wigwam and then in a log cabin, he
was one of those who helped to establish the first Methodist Church in
Rock Island. One of his sons entered the ministry, and it was in a Methodist parsonage that Clarissa, the eldest child and only daughter, spent, as
she herself said, "a free and happy childhood". When she was fifteen her
father was called to the position of Secretary of the Board of Extension

of the Methodist Church, and the family moved to Philadelphia. Her first year of college was at Wellesley, but she was compelled by illness to stay at home the following year, and when she could again resume her education, instead of returning to Wellesley she entered the newly established Women's College of Baltimore, now Goucher College, which graduated its first class the year she entered. Here she took her B.A. degree in 1895.

It was during her three years at Goucher that Clarissa "found herself" and gained her vision of a life of Christian adventure and service. College education for women was still, in itself, an adventure. Christian movements such as the Y.M.C.A. and the Y.W.C.A. were spreading rapidly in the colleges and universities and the Student Volunteer Movement, with its appeal to students to pledge their lives, God willing, to the work of Christian evangelism in other lands, was in full swing. Into this atmosphere of Christian idealism Clarissa was quickly drawn. She helped to organize the college Y.W.C.A. and became its first president. Here, too, she faced the struggle of the use she should make of her own life. She was musically gifted, and music, next to the deeply affectionate relationship she had with her father, had been up to this time the strongest influence in her life. But even stronger was the call to some form of definitely religious work. She became a student volunteer, and spent her first year out of college as a traveling secretary for that movement, visiting especially the colleges in the South and passing on to other students the challenge to which she herself had responded.

In 1896, two years after the organization of the World's Y.W.C.A. and one year after the birth of the World's Student Christian Federation,[1] she was sent to Japan by the Board of Foreign Missions of the Methodist Church. Here she spent five years. At first she was in charge of the five day-schools which the Methodist Church operated in Tokyo. Later she was the head of their Bible Women's Training School in Yokohama. She proved herself an adept at languages, completing the four-year course of study in Japanese in three years, and she revealed what was to be a permanent characteristic of all her work, her strong evangelistic emphasis.

Her father's death in 1901 made it necessary for her to return home, and here she turned naturally to the Young Women's Christian Association as a field in which she might continue her Christian service. In 1902 she attended a summer training course of the American Committee, a course attended also by Mabel Cratty, who in 1906 was to become the General Secretary of the American movement, and who from that time until her death in 1928 was a wise and far-seeing counselor of the world's Y.W.C.A. After the completion of this brief course of training she became the State Secretary for Ohio. It was from this position that she went to London to become the General Secretary of the World's Committee.

In addition to her valuable equipment of character and experience Miss Spencer brought to the World's Committee qualities of intellect and heart that were of deep significance for her work. Intellectually she was both sound and progressive. Throughout the sixteen years of her connection with the World's Association she was an invaluable interpreter of both the old and the new forces stirring in the life of the world, and particularly in the life of women, in the closing days of the old century and the opening years of the new. Her academic training had imbued her with the best ideals in American education of religion, scholarship, freedom and responsibility. She was well acquainted with one of the great nations of the Orient, in which the chief geographical expansion of the Y.W.C.A. in the next few years was to be made. Her recent experience in the Association in the United States assured her understanding of that movement.

Added to these qualifications and her so necessary facility in languages, Miss Spencer brought rare spiritual qualities—a humble, teachable spirit, a sensitive sympathetic response to all that was good and beautiful in places, persons and nations, and a delightfully engaging and never-failing sense of humor. These qualities were all of inestimable value in the intricate and delicate work of building a world-wide fellowship out of the varied elements that made up the Y.W.C.A.

In a way, the work of the second decade repeats the pattern of the first. The time of the General Secretary was again given largely to the task of being a peripatetic interpreter of the idea and the ideals of the World's Y.W.C.A. She traveled almost incessantly, impressing upon the larger, more developed movements their responsibility for the work of the World's Y.W.C.A. and interpreting to them the Associations in lands where conditions were so different from their own. She carried to the newer and smaller Associations suggestions for their growth drawn from her contact with the older organizations; helped to frame constitutions and organize national committees where this was a natural next step. She gave counsel, encouragement and friendship to the little groups of women who were pioneering in remote and difficult places.

These long periods of travel and visitation alternated with months spent at headquarters, usually in preparation for a World's Conference, of which there were three in this decade—Paris 1906, Berlin 1910, and Stockholm 1914. Besides these primary responsibilities there was the continued necessity of keeping in close touch with the work of the Young Men's Christian Association, the World's Student Christian Federation, the Student Volunteer Movement, and with organizations such as the Union Internationale des Amies de la Jeune Fille through attendance at their conferences in many parts of the world.

Superficially Miss Spencer's diary for the years 1904-1914 might read much like that of Miss Reynolds for the first decade. The year 1905 found her at the sixteenth World's Conference of the Y.M.C.A. in Paris and the sixth Conference of the World's Student Christian Federation at Zeist, Holland, where for the first time a special session of women students was held; at the national conference of the French Y.W.C.A., and in a prolonged visit to the tiny Association in Portugal. The following year was given largely to the preparation and holding of the third World's Y.W.C.A. Conference in Paris, but the summer following this meeting found her attending conferences of the Associations in the United States and Canada, and in the autumn she visited the Associations in Holland, Belgium and France. In 1907-1908 she made a world tour, going first to the World's Student Christian Federation Conference in Tokyo in April 1907 and then visiting Japan, China, the British Colonies in Australasia, and India, returning to London in time for the biennial meeting of the World's Committee in May 1908. Following this meeting she was off again to the Continent, and to Ireland, and then back to attend the national biennial conference of the Associations of Great Britain. A tour of the northern European countries in 1909 was followed by a survey of work among young women in Russia, the first official touch of the World's Y.W.C.A. with that country since Miss Reynolds' visit in 1898. The summer of 1909 was once more given to conference work in America.

In her report to the Berlin Conference (1910) Miss Spencer wrote:
Since the Paris Conference four years ago I have spent only about a year and a half at headquarters, the remaining months, apart from holidays, being given to visitation. I have had the great privilege of seeing something of the Y.W.C.A. in Germany, France, Holland, Belgium, Denmark, Sweden, Finland, Russia, Japan, China, India, Burma, Ceylon, the Straits Settlements, Egypt, Australasia, Canada, Great Britain and the United States of America; traveling in all over 75,000 miles and being as far north as Jacobstadt in Finland (4° below the Arctic Circle) and as far south as Invercargell, New Zealand (46° below the Equator).[2]

The four years from Berlin to Stockholm tell a similar story. In 1911 she was in France, in northern and then in southeastern Europe, where for the first time visits from the World's Y.W.C.A. were made to Bulgaria and Turkey. She attended the World's Student Christian Federation Conference in Constantinople. In 1912, after the biennial meeting of the World's Committee, held this time at the Swanwick conference center in England, she went to South Africa, and returned to Europe to visit Switzerland, Germany and Russia. The year 1913 once more included a lengthy visit to the United States, with attendance at the Lake Mohonk conference of the World's Student Christian Federation, while the winter of 1913-1914 was spent largely at headquarters, preparing for the coming conference at Stockholm.

This formidable record by no means tells the whole tale of World's Y.W.C.A. travel in this decade. Miss Spencer's diary for these years must be supplemented, as Miss Reynolds' was not, by the official travel log of other staff and members of the World's Committee. Miss Ethel Stevenson, who came to the staff in 1900, and Miss Ethel Knight, who came in 1908 to carry some of the increasing volume of headquarters work, also did considerable visitation. Miss Stevenson represented the World's Committee at French, German and British conferences, as well as at Student Volunteer Movement and World's Student Christian Federation meetings, while her visit to Berlin in preparation for the 1910 conference laid the foundation for her invaluable understanding and appreciation of the German movement.

Meanwhile, the World's Committee was represented at conferences in Holland, Ireland and Germany and at the Union Internationale des Amies de la Jeune Fille at Bâle by Miss Knight. The Honorable Mrs. Fraser, a member of the World's Executive Committee, and Miss Knight together held meetings for the promotion of the Y.W.C.A. in Austria, Belgium and Bohemia. Mrs. E. W. Moore went to the United States to represent the World's Y.W.C.A. at the 1905 biennial convention of the American Association. In 1911 Mrs. Tritton, who had again become President of the World's Association, visited the United States and Canada, attending the biennial convention of the American Associations in Indianapolis. Here she was accompanied by Miss Grace Tottenham of the Executive Committee, Miss Stevenson of the World's Y.W.C.A. staff, and Mademoiselle Bidgrain of France.

At Berlin, in 1910, the conference had urged an increase in the traveling staff. Owing to the difficulty of finding the right person, this had not been achieved at the time of the Stockholm meeting in 1914, though it was possible to announce at that time that Baroness Olga Meyendorff of Russia would begin work with the World's Committee as a traveling secretary in the autumn of that year. In the report of the Executive Committee to the conference, however, there appears a long list of committee members "who have most generously given their time and services to this work of visitation." The list is impressive: Mrs. Tritton, Mrs. Head, the Honorable Emily Kinnaird, Miss Brown-Douglas, the Honorable Mrs. Alistair Fraser, Miss Gabb, Miss Nugent, Lady Procter, Miss Picton-Turberville, Miss Tritton, Miss Tottenham, Miss Andersen (of Denmark,), Mademoiselle Bidgrain (France), Pastor Burckhardt, Fräulein Müller (Germany), Miss Kawai (Japan), Mrs. John R. Mott, Mrs. Thomas Gladding and Miss Reynolds (of the United States). "These members," says the report, "together with Miss Spencer, Miss Stevenson and Miss Knight, have visited the following countries: Austria, Australasia, Bulgaria, Canada, China, Egypt, France, Germany, Great Britain, Holland, Hungary, India, Italy, Japan, Norway, Portugal, Russia, Spain, South Africa, Sweden, Switzerland, the Turkish Empire and the United States."[3]

All this is indicative of the normal, wholesome growth in extent and volume of World's Y.W.C.A. work, and of the constant cultivation required to keep the connection with the World's Committee, once it was established, vital and growing in significance. At two points this record of travel and visitation is of special significance—in its emphasis on the Orient, and in the interest shown in Russia and the countries of southeastern Europe, especially Bulgaria and Turkey. The new contacts in these two parts of the world represented not only normal expansion but the introduction of new factors into the life of the World Movement destined to have a radical influence upon it.

After the Geneva Conference in 1902, the Associations in North America had taken up vigorously the task of helping to lay the foundations of Y.W.C.A. work in Japan and China. Late in 1904 Canada sent one of its finest and most experienced workers, Miss Caroline Macdonald, Secretary for the City Department of the National Council, to Japan. In 1905 she became the Secretary of the Japanese National Committee. In 1905, also, the United States sent Miss Estelle Paddock to China. In 1906 both the Japanese and the Chinese National Associations were welcomed into active affiliation with the World's Y.W.C.A.

Both countries looked forward to rapid expansion of the Association to meet the extraordinary opportunities before them, and for this they desired trained leadership from abroad on a large scale. To this appeal the Associations of Canada and the United States, particularly that of the United States, responded eagerly. Miss Spencer, in a report of her summer spent in those two countries in 1906, largely attending summer conferences, writes:

> Another development of the American work is the number of really splendid young women considering the secretaryship of the Y.W.C.A. as a life work. This was especially true in regard to the young women offering for our Association work in mission lands. Japan and India were the two countries for which special appeals were made, but South America and China received some attention also. Judging from the experiences of this summer, I believe that an increasing number of young women of broad culture, deep spirituality and real leadership will offer themselves for Association work in other lands.[4]

Miss Clarissa H. Spencer

Miss Caroline Macdonald

It was in the light of these developments that Miss Spencer made her visit to Japan and China in 1907. Her carefully written letters to the Executive Committee, published under the title "To Tokyo, Shanghai and Beyond", are informing in regard to the religious, economic, social and educational conditions affecting women in the Orient, as well as the progress already made by the Y.W.C.A. They analyzed the opportunities that the Association faced and the needs that must be met if these opportunities were to be taken advantage of. Regarding the Y.W.C.A. in Japan she wrote:

> It is very inspiring to remember what has been accomplished in Japan during the seven years since Miss Reynolds' visit.[5] First let us thank God for the company of girls who have found Christ through the Y.W.C.A. . . . Then consider too, the fact that a strong representative National Committee has been organized of women, both foreign and Japanese, with whom we can harmoniously work and whose judgment we can trust. With the Committee I should like to couple the names of Miss Macdonald and Miss Fisher [secretaries], both doing such excellent work. . . . There are eleven Associations actually in existence in Japan. Four of these are called 'city Associations', but the members are really students, mostly from secular schools. The other seven are branches actually in schools. . . . A monthly magazine, *Young Women of Japan,* is published. The second summer conference will be held very soon, the World's Week of Prayer is observed, and a hostel has been rented in Tokyo. . . . This is a splendid record of work accomplished . . . yet we need to fear lest we are not fully awake to the marvelous opportunities God has given us in Japan. . . . How great is the need just now for specialized work, how desirable are all forms of interdenominational effort and how necessary it is that as far as possible the Japanese should lead while the foreigners must more and more take the place of helpers and advisors working by prayer and personal influence. . . . Then the political social and educational conditions in Japan make our work well-nigh imperative. . . . This is the open door no man can shut which Christ has set before us.

> But as our opportunities are great so are our needs. First we need four or five foreign secretaries *at once* to reinforce Miss Macdonald. . . . Miss Macdonald has expressed herself . . . as desirous of having two British college women as a part of the secretarial staff. American secretaries are also needed. Then there is the need for Japanese secretaries. . . . There is need too, for money, that more hostels may be erected, as they are needed in Tokyo and elsewhere; and, above all, there is need for money

for a central building in Tokyo that can serve both as national and local Headquarters. We need to pray that as our work becomes popular it may be kept spiritual; that all organization and the social and educational elements may not hinder its continuing to be a soul-winning agency; that the Japanese women who will more and more lead it may be women filled with the Holy Spirit and taught by Him.[6]

At the close of her reports on China, which include letters on such subjects as "Mission and Gentry Schools", "Mill Women in North China", "The Morrison Missionary Centenary", the "New Woman of China", "Higher Education for Women in Tientsin", she sums up the status, needs and opportunities of the Association thus:

There are student branches of the Y.W.C.A. in the following places: Weihsien, Hangchow, Soochow, Hingua, Foochow. In Hong Kong there is both a European and a Chinese branch; in Shanghai there is no branch but work has been carried on among the women and girls working in the cotton mills. Three secretaries have been sent to China: Miss Berninger, who has been doing the mill work and who has returned home; Miss Paddock, the National Secretary, and Miss Coppock, who is to be the General Secretary of Shanghai. . . . An appeal was made to Great Britain and America for several secretaries to be sent out as soon as possible for language study and for work. . . . A larger number of foreign secretaries will be needed for China than for Japan. They should not only be thoroughly spiritual, but also refined and cultured women with the power of leadership. Where possible they should be college women and certainly they should be linguists, unless going out solely for English work. As to methods of work, I do not see why the methods used in Great Britain and America should not be used in China with some modifications. . . . But we must make our work as Chinese as possible, bringing Chinese women on to the committees as fast as they are ready for the work.[7]

In these reports the purpose and attitude of the World's Y.W.C.A. in regard to work planted under its auspices in "missionary lands" are clearly set forth. It is assumed that its basic purpose will be evangelistic, the increase, through its efforts, of the number of intelligent, devoted Christian young women in these lands. But the necessity of something more than evangelism is also recognized. It was the educational and the industrial situation in both Japan and China that had led to the appeal of the missionaries ten years before. Miss Spencer saw the opportunity of the Association in the Orient as one that would necessarily lead to organization, and to institutional equipment on a large scale, and would require leadership capable of dealing with great social, economic and religious problems. She also saw the Association primarily as a field of service for the Christian women of the Orient, and the task of the "foreign" secretary as first and foremost that of giving aid, advice, and encouragement where needed, but always stepping aside as soon as Chinese and Japanese leadership was available. The reports indicate clearly, however, the need of help on a considerable scale, both of leadership and of money, in the initial stages of the development of independent National Associations.

In the long run, the membership of National Associations in these Oriental lands would bring into the World's Association new gifts, new and enriching varieties of experience. The more immediate result, however, was to press upon the World's Committee new questions about the relationship of the World's Committee to the National Associations affiliated with it. The great opportunity for the Association in the Orient had already stirred the imagination and the missionary enthusiasm of the Associations of Canada and the United States. The coming years were to see an extraordinary development of this interest and a great increase in missionary activity as a result of it. What was to be the relationship of these secretaries, drawn in the main from the ranks of the local Associations in the United States and supported by money given by the members of local Associations, to the National Association of the country to which they went and to the World's Committee in London? The whole question of the respective functions of National Committees and the World's Committee in the promotion of Association work in new fields was raised in a quite new way by the expansion of the Association in the Orient. The formation of policy in this realm became one of the major issues of this decade.

An even more fundamental issue was raised by the advance of the Association in eastern and southeastern Europe. There had been some Y.W.C.A. work among German young women in Russia since 1884[8], and in 1898 Miss Reynolds had investigated the possibility of starting work for Russian girls.[9] The matter was brought again before the Executive Committee in the autumn of 1905, when a request was received from the St. Petersburg Association for affiliation with the World's Committee as a corresponding member. The work of this Association was among German-speaking Lutherans and its constitution was not entirely in line with World's Committee policy, since it made no provision for membership of the girls themselves. The Executive Committee, for these reasons, suggested that Baroness Nicolay, the President of the St. Petersburg Association, should become the "correspondent for Russia" rather than the Association itself a corresponding member of the World's Association. She was urged to attend the Paris Conference and "to invite ladies from other branches to come as visiting delegates." While Baroness Nicolay herself did not come to Paris, she did secure the attendance of two representatives from Russia, Princess Mary and Princess Sophie Lieven, and she herself wrote the report of work in Russia which was presented at the conference.[10] Moreover, in 1907 she spent some time in London, where, she says, she "soon felt at home at the headquarters at 26 George Street, and was most kindly cared for by Miss Ethel Knight, Miss Kinnaird, Miss Boyd, Mrs. Tritton and others."

These contacts were the first steps on the part of the World's Y.W.C.A. toward a serious facing of its responsibility for helping to develop the Association among Russian women. The matter was discussed by the Executive Committee several times during the year 1908 and in the early months of 1909. The Honorable Mrs. Fraser and Miss Spencer, after a tour through the northern European countries and the Baltic States, went to Russia "to make a thorough investigation into the needs of young Russian women, especially those of the Greek church."[11]

In her report to the Berlin Conference in 1910 Miss Spencer says of this visit to Russia:

> . . . we visited both St. Petersburg and Moscow, spending most of our time, however, in the former city. We spoke both to German and to Swedish branches, explained our work at draw- ing-room meetings and elsewhere, addressed a Feminist Club, and saw a little of student work. Some of my time I devoted to a study of conditions in Russia. . . . I visited churches, a nunnery, a woman's prison, schools for girls, a cotton factory where many women and girls were employed, hospitals and various other institutions, including homes for girls.[12]

Meantime the Executive Committee was being asked to open Y.W.C.A. work in Bulgaria. The first intimation of this was in November 1906, when Miss Spencer reported that an American missionary in Turkey, Miss Ellen Stone, had stated that there was great need of work among Bulgarian women, because, since Bulgaria had become a free state, educa- tion was making rapid progress among women as well as men. She said there were already several hundred women students at the University of Sofia, and that a fully qualified secretary was urgently needed.[13]

A year and a half passed before further consideration was given to the opportunity in Bulgaria, perhaps owing to the fact that during this period Miss Spencer was making her world tour and the Executive Com- mittee had not the facilities for looking further into the situation. In 1909, however, Miss Rouse visited Bulgaria for the work of the World's Student Christian Federation and at the same time investigated Y.W.C.A. possibilities for the World's Committee. Late in the year 1910 Mrs. Nedelkoff, a Bulgarian lady who was anxious to help in forming a Y.W.C.A. in Sofia, came to London, met the World's Executive Committee, and gave them an account of the need of organized work among the women students coming in from country districts to attend the university.

As a result of this meeting, various plans by which the World's Committee might be of help were discussed, and the suggestion was made that "a foyer or small hostel be started by the Bulgarian ladies themselves without, at present, any official connection with the World's Y.W.C.A." The Committee at the same time pledged itself to raise £150 a year "unofficially" for this work, "on the condition that the secretary who should have charge of the work should be sent for at least a term to Switzerland to gain an insight into the work carried on there by the World's Student Christian Federation for women students; and that the name of the Y.W.C.A. should not be attached to this effort."[14] Meantime, plans were made for Miss Spencer to visit the Levant, including Bulgaria and Turkey, in the spring of 1911 and to attend the biennial conference of the W.S.C.F. in Constantinople in June of that year.

The pressure to undertake work in these predominantly Eastern Orthodox countries forced the World's Y.W.C.A. to face the whole question of its relation to work for young women other than Protestant. It is true that its statement of basis was not an exclusively Protestant one, but there was a general acceptance of the Y.W.C.A. as a definitely Protestant organization. This was natural, considering the environment within which the movement had its rise. It had now to consider whether and on what basis its work could be extended in a culture dominated by another of the great Christian confessions. It was recognized by the Committee that a still more momentous problem lay just beyond the immediate horizon, for the sending of Miss Emma Jean Batty of the United States to Buenos Aires, Argentina, in 1906 was the beginning of a potentially extensive spread of the Association in the midst of a predominantly Roman Catholic culture. In the years under discussion, however, the immediate question that the World's Association faced was its relation with the Eastern Orthodox churches, though it did this with full realization of the larger implications of any action that might be taken.[15]

Thus the normal development of the work of the Association had brought the World's Y.W.C.A. face to face with important questions of policy vital to the structure and character of a world movement: its relation as a world body to the constituent National Associations that composed it, and its nature as a religious movement defined in terms of basis of membership and statement of purpose. A third equally significant question arose in the field of program. How far should the program be related to "the larger whole of the present social order" as well as to the individual?

It was the changing conditions of society, affecting the life of women, that had produced the Y.W.C.A. in the first place. It was the consciousness that both the dangers and the advantages of these changes were to an ever-increasing extent world wide that had drawn the various National Associations together into a world organization. But it was only slowly that the vastness of these changes and the newness of the tasks and responsibilities they might impose on all Christian groups were realized.

In every country the early history of the Y.W.C.A. was one of endeavoring to provide the safeguards, the comforts, and the practical services for young women that new conditions obviously made necessary, and in addition, and above all, through the contacts and opportunities thus presented, to make possible for young women a quickened spiritual life. Until the turn of the century, the distinguishing mark of the Association was the rapid spread of work along these lines. But increasingly the leaders were compelled by circumstances to think in new categories, to face new questions. Was a ministry to individuals, as far as they could be reached, an adequate fulfillment of Christian responsibility, or was it demanded of a Christian woman's organization that it should also use its influence to change those social conditions and oppose those social forces which it recognized as harmful to young women?

This was especially true in highly industrialized countries such as the United States and Great Britain, where a great variety of movements, religious, educational and political, organized for social reform, had existed for many years. It was also true in the countries of the Far East, where the sudden transformation of a medieval society into one dominated by modern industry created conditions even more appalling than those in western lands. The appeal for workers sent by missionaries and leaders in the Orient to the World's Y.W.C.A. had been based on the double need to develop and direct the increasing number of women students and to begin work for the army of girls in industry. To begin Y.W.C.A. work in Shanghai with a center for industrial girls before there was an established organization behind and underneath it, may well have been a mistake, but to recognize the challenge to the Y.W.C.A. presented by industrialization on a large scale and to feel responsibility for entering the field was an authentic Christian insight.

Within the Y.W.C.A. of Great Britain a "Factory Helpers' Union" had been started as early as 1886, and this had gradually developed into a "Federation of Working Girls' Clubs" which in 1909 had a membership of 120 clubs. Bible classes and evening prayers were the central feature of these club programs but their magazine *The Girls' Club Journal* "contained articles on the laws affecting women, on educational work, and reviews of books on social problems." In reply to a questionnaire from the World's Committee, the Y.W.C.A. of Great Britain said:

> A new phase of work has been begun in the London Division in cooperating with other agencies which exist for improving the industrial conditions of women workers. As a first step it was the means last year of issuing a leaflet giving a short and simple summary of the Factory Acts as they affect women, and the same has been printed on a card and hung up in the London institutes and club rooms.

The British National Conference of 1909 also passed the following resolutions:

> In view of the fact that existing social conditions are militating against the full development of the Christian life among young women in this country, the conference, while affirming that it is not within the scope of the Association to connect itself with party politics as such, calls for:
>
> 1. A wider knowledge on social subjects, including existing legislation.
> 2. A greater sense of individual responsibility as members of the community.
> 3. A more sympathetic attitude toward well-considered movements for the amelioration of the conditions under which women live and work.
>
> This conference recommends that the British National Council consider the appointment of Social Service Referees who shall have cognizance of the existing work of the Association, helping the development of such work and providing a center for information relating to social subjects.[16]

In the United States the growing social concern of the Y.W.C.A. found characteristic expression in an effort to extend the work of the city Associations to groups of girls who hitherto had seldom come to the activities in the Associations' central buildings, especially to those employed in factories. To do this, some Associations began to employ special "extension" or "industrial" secretaries, who visited the factories, organized clubs or other activities among the girls in a given center or occupation, and often carried on their program in the factory rather than in the Y.W.C.A. building. The first conference of such secretaries to discuss their special program and problems was held in Chicago in 1901, with an attendance of nine. At the second conference, in 1903, there were nineteen secretaries present, and when the announcement of "the regular biennial conference of Industrial and Extension Secretaries" for 1905 was made, it was accompanied by a directory of these secretaries listing thirty-five who gave full time to extension work in factories and a considerable number of others who gave part time to this phase of the work.[17] In 1905 also *The Evangel* published an article on "Women in the Industrial World" by Dr. Annie Marion MacLean, Professor of Sociology at the University of Chicago, which gave statistics regarding women in industry in the United States, summarized protective legislation affecting women, the effects of trade unions, the ameliorating forces in legislation and in the effort of enlightened employers, and then discussed the possible rôle of the Y.W.C.A. in the industrial world.

The work thus begun in the study of the new industrial world of women and the practical local experience in working within this world was greatly stimulated in the American Associations by the reorganization that brought about a united national movement in 1906. One of the early acts of the new National Board was to set up an Industrial Department. To this department the National Board called as Executive Secretary Miss Florence Simms, a woman of strong Christian faith and the enthusiasm and devotion of a crusader. As a local and later a territorial secretary, she had struggled with the problem of how to reach and help girls in industry. She had made for herself the discovery that it could be done only when she came to them not to impose some ready-made program of her own but to meet them on their own level, with a full knowledge and understanding of their peculiar environment, the conditions under which they worked, their wages, their home life, and the personal problems resulting from all these.

As her knowledge and understanding in this field increased she became deeply concerned over the evils and injustices in the industrial system, and profoundly convinced of the duty as well as the power of Christian groups and organizations to strive actively for the redemption of society. From this concern came a growing conviction "that the Y.W.C.A. should openly declare itself for social righteousness and constitute itself one of the organs of social reclamation. . . . We must stand together, she said, as a body for certain things, human things, things that make for the larger life of human beings."[18]

In 1907, at the convention that formally adopted the constitution of the new National Association, the statement of purpose for which the organization was formed, i.e. "to unite in one body the Young Women's Christian Associations of the United States; to establish, develop and unify such Associations; to advance the physical, social, intellectual, moral and spiritual interests of young women; to participate in the work of the World's Y.W.C.A.," was further defined by this addition: "The ultimate purpose of all its efforts shall be to seek to bring young women to such a knowledge of Jesus Christ as Saviour and Lord, as shall mean for the individual young woman fullness of life and development of character, and *shall make the organization as a whole an effective agency in bringing in the kingdom of God among young women."*[19] By this statement the Young Women's Christian Association of the United States officially declared its responsibility as a Christian organization to be twofold, involving both a program for the individual young woman and a program aiming to bring the influence of the "organization as a whole" to bear on those social issues that helped or hindered the bringing in of the kingdom of God.

In view of their growing interest in the promulgation of the Association in the Orient, with its acutely critical issues of social change, it was inevitable that both the American and the British Associations should urge that the World's Y.W.C.A. also go on record as similarly recognizing a twofold Christian task. Miss Spencer interprets the openings before the World's Y.W.C.A. as immediate and urgent, offering an opportunity that may pass if it is not seized. "God has given us as members of the World's Y.W.C.A. a great day of opportunity for serving him and the young women of this generation. But no one of us can tell how long or how short may be the hours of this day. As we see the unrest and uncertainty in the Orient and the great and increasing social problems in the West, our duty certainly is to faithfully and earnestly employ every moment that may be granted to us."[20] At the Berlin Conference two years later the questions thus raised were of intense interest and concern.

To understand the character of the World's Y.W.C.A. as it was in 1914, on the verge of the first World War, it is necessary to look more in detail at these three major issues of the immediately preceding years and at their effect upon the movement as a whole.

REFERENCES

[1] The World's Student Christian Federation was organized at Vadstena, Sweden, in 1895.

[2] Fourth World's Y.W.C.A. Conference, 1910, Report, p. 70.

[3] Fifth World's Y.W.C.A. Conference, 1914, Report, p. 258.

[4] Spencer, Clarissa H., Report of visit to United States and Canada, June-September 1906.

[5] See Chapter 7, pp. 86-87.

[6] Chapter 2, pp. 33-35.

[7] *Ibid.*, pp. 127-128.

[8] Chapter II, pp. 44, 45.

[9] See Chapter 6, pp. 74-75.

[10] See Chapter 2, p. 33.

[11] Executive Committee, December 10, 1908, Minutes.

[12] Fourth World's Y.W.C.A. Conference, 1910, Report, pp. 74, 75.

[13] Executive Committee, November 8, 1906, Minutes.

[14] Executive Committee, November 17, 1910, Minutes.

[15] "The Executive Committee agreed to obtain all possible information regarding the position of the Greek Orthodox Church with regard to the World's Y.W.C.A. and also to ascertain from Miss Batty, the American secretary of the Association in Buenos Aires, what was the attitude there towards members of the Roman Catholic Church" (Executive Committee, Minutes, May 1909). Later, however, the Committee decided that one step at a time was enough, and as their immediate responsibility was toward Russia and Bulgaria they would "for the present" continue discussion to the Eastern Church (Executive Committee Minutes, January 19, 1911).

[16] Fourth World's Y.W.C.A. Conference, 1910, Report, p. 142.

[17] *The Evangel,* November 1905, pp. 18, 19.

[18] Roberts, Richard. *Florence Simms,* 1927, p. 187.

[19] Italics ours [Ed.].

[20] Annual Report for 1908, p. 19.

One very important action taken by the World's Committee at this meeting [the biennial meeting of 1912] was the careful consideration of the sphere and scope of the World's Committee and the National Committees in affiliation with it and their relationship one to the other. The World's Committee was empowered by the World's Conference held in Paris in 1906 to study this matter. The scheme which has finally been evolved is the result of much careful thought and consultation. While realizing that with the growth of our work it must always be subject to further alteration and amplification, we believe it is the best plan of cooperation between our different bodies, local, national and world-wide, which has yet been found.

Report of World's Committee to Fifth World's Y.W.C.A. Conference, 1914.

CHAPTER 9   MAJOR ISSUES: 1904-1914 (CONTINUED) FUNCTIONS OF THE WORLD'S COMMITTEE AND OF THE NATIONAL ASSOCIATIONS IN THE WORLD TASK OF THE ASSOCIATION

THE EXPANSION of Young Women's Christian Association work in the Orient through the efforts of the World's Committee and the National Associations of Great Britain, the United States and Canada, raised questions of policy in regard to the respective functions of the World's Committee and the National Committees engaged in the world enterprise. The consideration of these questions began with Miss Spencer's arrival in London in 1904, and was a major concern of the entire decade, culminating in the adoption in 1914, at Stockholm, of a statement of policy known as the "Scheme of Relationships". This statement defined in detail the "sphere and scope" of the World's Committee and the National Committees in the promotion of the Association in lands that required help in leadership or money from outside.

The provisional constitution drawn up in 1894 had declared the object of the World's Association to be "the union" (changed in 1898 to "federation"), development and *extension*[1] of the Y.W.C.A. in all lands." The methods of this extension were not defined, but that the World's

Committee should be the administrative body for the promotion of whatever program of extension might develop was assumed. This is evident from the fact that the work in other lands hitherto carried by the National Association of Great Britain was at once turned over to the World's Y.W.C.A., its two committees responsible for developing work on the continent of Europe and in countries outside Europe becoming standing committees of the World's Committee, "for the European Continent" and "for Other Continents" respectively.

In its first annual report, the last-named committee introduces its statement by saying: "At the close of the year 1894, the organization of the World's Y.W.C.A. having taken definite form, the ladies who had been connected with the Extra-European Council [of the British National Council] became members instead of a Standing Committee for Other Continents. . . . The work of this committee is to deal with the affairs of the World's Y.W.C.A. in all countries outside the European continent."[2] This transfer of a considerable volume of work from the Y.W.C.A. of Great Britain to the World's Y.W.C.A. seemed at the time a natural and on the whole a simple proceeding. The urge for an international organization had come, in the first instance, from the more far-sighted members of these two British committees that had been the first to see the need and the value of it. The women who made up the World's Executive Committee were, almost without exception, the women who had helped to initiate the foreign work of the British movement, and many of them still continued to serve in various capacities on the British National Council.

Moreover, in inheriting the work of the British Association in other lands, the World's Y.W.C.A. inherited also, as the report just quoted shows, the personnel responsible for directing it. The practical working of these committees in the early years of the world organization was much as before, only in a larger setting. Since the British workers in other countries at this period were many of them "voluntary secretaries" going out at their own expense, and since, where this was not the case, the funds for their support continued to be raised by appeals to those friends in Great Britain who had previously supported this work of the British Association, the financial burden upon the new organization was not at first great.[3]

Unlike the British Association, the American movement had, in 1894, no responsibility for Association work outside the United States and Canada. Its energies up to this time had been almost wholly concerned with the urgent needs and unbounded opportunities for expansion and development within their own two countries. There was missionary consciousness and interest, but it had so far expressed itself entirely in gifts to the missionary enterprises of the churches. Their share in organizing the

112

World's Y.W.C.A. and in sending Agnes Hill to India, supported by Associations in the United States but appointed by the World's Committee, at almost the same moment that the World's Y.W.C.A. came into existence, was the first definite move of the American Associations to assume responsibility for the development of the Y.W.C.A. in other countries. The relation, therefore, of the World's Committee to the American Committee was quite different from its relation to the National Council of Great Britain. In anticipation of its increasing share in a world-wide program, the American movement organized an "American Department of the World's Y.W.C.A." A report of the activities of this department and its financial statement were included as a part of the annual report of the World's Committee in the early years.

When the provisional constitution was presented to the first World's Conference for formal adoption in 1898, its by-laws were amended to include a standing committee to be called the "Secretarial Committee" or the "Committee for the Selection of Workers". The work of this committee was defined as "the selection and training of all workers to be sent out under the World's Committee."[4] By the year 1905, however, the World's Committee was facing a different situation from that with which it had hitherto dealt. In the years from 1900 to 1905, nine young women from the Y.W.C.A. in the United States had gone out to India, China and Japan, while from Canada, Miss Macdonald had gone to Japan. Moreover, the formation in 1906 of one united movement out of the two national movements formerly existing in the United States gave increased impetus to the world program of the American Associations. The time had come for a large expansion in this direction.

In the Y.W.C.A. of Great Britain, also, these years saw a great increase of missionary activity. The report of the World's Committee to the Paris Conference in 1906 states:

> Your Committee has not only endeavored to organize work in these mission lands and newer countries, but has also supplied secretaries. . . . During the past four years, twelve secretaries from Great Britain, six from the United States, and one from Canada have been sent out. Of this number, nine have been sent to India, two to China, two to Japan, two to Egypt, and four to South Africa.[5]

This outpouring of life from the British and American Associations into Association work in the Orient and Africa raised acutely the question of procedure and relative functions between the World's Committee and the National Committees involved. This was especially true with relation to the United States. The London headquarters of the World's Y.W.C.A. were a long way from the actual Association centers in America. The support of American secretaries abroad must come from America, as the support of British workers had come from Great Britain, but whereas to the British, giving to a committee of the World's Y.W.C.A. was practically no different from giving to the British National Council, to the American Association it would have been difficult to interpret and to administer. The matters of distance and expense also made it impossible for the World's Committee to function effectively in the selection or the training of American secretaries for work abroad.

In the United States it was felt that the missionary program should be the concern of the members of the local Associations, and that its support should come, as far as possible, from small gifts from many Association members rather than from large gifts from a few individual donors. As Miss Hill's case proved—for her salary was raised by business girls of the Toledo Association of which she had been General Secretary—this could be accomplished if the Association members had a warm feeling of personal contact and continuing responsibility. The National Committee, with its knowledge of and close touch with the local Associations, was in a position to cultivate this personal contact and keep it vital. It was doubtful if this could be done at all if the chief official relationship of the American secretary in the foreign field was with the World's Committee. Moreover, there was no precedent in the policies of other organizations such as church missionary societies, for sending funds to be administered by a world, rather than by a national body.

Added to such practical difficulties as these was the fact that in spite of its constitutional provisions, the World's Committee was not, either in organization or committee personnel, set up to handle the selection, training and equipment of workers recruited in considerable numbers from different countries to go out to distant lands, nor to carry detailed advisory and administrative relations with them in the field. To do this in a period of large and rapid expansion such as that opening before the World's Association would have necessitated the development of the executive functions of the World's Y.W.C.A. on a greatly increased scale, a large increase in its staff and budget, and a complete reorganization of the personnel of its executive and standing committees, now almost wholly British.

The available records furnish little information about the thought and discussion that must have gone on during the early years of the century about this problem. In the minutes and reports there is no evidence that a fundamental reorganization of the World's Association to make possible its carrying the administration of this growing program was ever suggested, much less seriously considered. Even had it been thought desirable, it would have been deemed wholly impracticable. The solution of the problem was sought rather in the modification of the by-laws of the World's Y.W.C.A. and in a redefinition of the function of the World's Committee with relation to the promotion of work in countries asking help from outside.

It seems probable that Miss Spencer had discussed the matter fully with American leaders before coming to London, and felt that some action with regard to it should be taken at the Paris Conference in 1906. At the Executive Committee meeting in January 1905 she and Mrs. Tritton presented the following resolution:

> In view of the conference to be held (D. V.) in 1906, the following suggestion is made for the consideration of committees sending representatives: The development of the missionary work done by the Associations in connection with the World's Y.W.C.A. is one of the most joyful signs of its progress. But the time seems to have arrived when the reconsideration and perhaps the readjustment of the Constitution in regard to this branch is desirable. The necessity arises, if this department is to deepen, for the closest possible union between National Associations and their representatives in other lands. Might it not be greatly to the advantage of all if the selection, the equipment, the financing and the personal correspondence regarding all home affairs connected with these, were entirely under the control of their National Councils? The national secretaries alone, if such are provided by any other country, would still be financed and in direct correspondence with the World's Executive Committee. The arrangement by which all control of local affairs in a foreign land is placed in the hands of the National Committee would, of course still hold good.[6]

The minutes of the Executive Committee testify to much discussion of this proposal to transfer to National Committees most of the functions heretofore exercised by the World's Committee with relation to secretaries in the field, but details of these discussions are lacking. At the meeting of the Executive Committee in February 1905, "a letter was read from Miss Reynolds regarding the resolution, and after consideration and discussion several amendments were made." At the March meeting, "letters having been read from Mrs. N. W. Campbell and Mrs. Thomas Gladding [American members] the resolution, with some amendments which added to its clearness, but in no way changed the sense, was adopted." The minutes of the April meeting (1905) say that "a scheme of relationship between the World's Y.W.C.A. Committee and the different countries was presented by Miss Spencer but has not yet been fully discussed." No outline of this scheme accompanies the minutes and the subject does not appear again until the Paris Conference, May 1906. At that conference the following recommendation was presented by the Executive Committee:

> Some Association work has been begun in the mission field, and
> much more is being planned as a result of the recommendation
> adopted by the Conference of 1902.[7]. . . . This aggressive work
> brings about new relationships and necessitates the formation
> of policy hitherto unnecessary. The Committee feel unable to
> bring to the conference recommendations bearing on these new
> relationships, without having an opportunity for consultation
> with all parts of the field. Amongst the important points to be
> considered are:
>
> 1. The sphere and scope of National Committees in the field.
> 2. The sphere and scope at home of National Committees send-
>   ing secretaries to the field.
> 3. The sphere and scope of the World's Committee in the light
>   of these developments.
>
> The World's Committee are carefully considering these points
> and would ask authority of the conference to formulate and
> test a policy which would be brought before the World's
> Committee meeting in 1908 for final acceptance.

This resolution, with the addition to (1) of the words "i.e. in lands
that are not entirely self-supporting" was unanimously adopted.[8] That
an alteration of World's Committee policy in practice had already begun
even before the Paris Conference is revealed in the Committee's report
on secretaries sent out to mission lands, which says: "The Secretarial
Committee in Great Britain and the American Department Committee
in the United States have been responsible for the selection of these
workers."[9]

Interesting sidelights on some of the elements in the situation which
troubled the World's Y.W.C.A. leaders come from the very frank comments on the point of view of the American Association in a personal
letter written by a World's Committee member in 1906, during a
prolonged visit to the United States. She says:

> There is evidently a strong feeling over here that there should
> not only be a territorial division of the World's work but that
> the American Committee should control as fully as the World's
> Committee does the work in those countries which they ought
> to claim. This means that America should be the headquarters
> for the work in China, Japan, the Philippines, the West Indies
> and North and South America. . . . The country is so large and
> the work so well developed that it is as much as they can do to
> grasp their own work. It is difficult for them to enter into the

traditions and past history which make the special difficulties of work in European countries.[10]

At the meeting of the World's Committee that followed the Paris Conference, the Scheme of Relationships worked out by the Executive Committee was discussed and adopted for purposes of "experiment and testing". This scheme, in brief, recognized the National Committee in the field as the authoritative body for deciding all questions of national policy. It recognized the secretary working abroad as the representative of the National Committee which sent her out, placing upon that Committee the entire responsibility for her support and the conditions of her service, but providing for consultation between the National Committees sending out secretaries and the World's Committee, in order that there might be "as far as possible" a unification of the standard of salaries, etc. The function of the World's Committee was defined as the development and organization of National Committees in unorganized fields; acting as an advisory council to aid National Committees in formulating policy and plans; ratification of the appointment and recall of secretaries sent out by National Committees; and the maintenance of a proper balance in all parts of the World's Y.W.C.A. work, to which end it should "sit as final council on debatable questions."

In the United States those functions assigned to the National Committee were carried by the Foreign Department of the National Board, which, after the reorganization of the national work in 1906, took the place of the American Department of the World's Y.W.C.A. In Great Britain and a little later in Canada and Australia also, Foreign Departments were organized, and the British National Council took back that portion of its work that had been handed over to the World's Committee twelve years earlier, which was in so-called mission lands. Reports of the British and American Foreign Departments appear for the first time in the annual report of the World's Committee for 1907. The report of the British Department says: "In presenting our first report of the Foreign Department we are glad to say that it is now thoroughly organized. During the short time since its formation it has, of necessity, been obliged to devote most of its energies to taking over the British secretaries abroad hitherto financed and equipped by the World's Executive Committee."[11]

The report of the Foreign Department of the Y.W.C.A. in the United States also stresses the foundation nature of the work of the year: "The department aimed, in cooperation with the World's Committee, to send out picked women of the first class who shall be ready for positions of leadership"; to see that "every secretary who is sent by the Foreign Department to the foreign field, shall have had, in addition

question of the Scheme of Relationships required a great deal of consideration, a sub-committee should be appointed to deal with it fully and bring a recommendation to the biennial meeting." She asked that this sub-committee consider:

1. The sphere and scope of the World's Committee.
2. The sphere and scope of National Committees and the relation of National to local Committees.
3. The revision of the By-Laws to bring them up to date.

It was further agreed that the present Scheme of Relationships should remain in force till 1912.[16]

At the meeting of the World's Committee preceding the Berlin Conference, the by-laws had already been amended by dropping out the Standing Committee for the Selection of Workers and putting in its place an Extension Committee, the duties of which were defined as: "To develop the existing Associations in unorganized countries, study new fields with reference to the extension of the work, and assist in the forming of national organizations where practicable.[17] A succinct statement of the procedure as it had developed in practice up to this date appears in an address given before the Berlin Conference by Miss Michi Kawai, of Japan, on "The Place of the Y.W.C.A. in the Missionary Awakening".[18] Miss Kawai says:

. . . our Foreign Departments have come into existence to meet, as far as possible, the demands for help from non-Christian lands, which are constantly increasing. . . . The Foreign Department has the responsibility for the selection, equipment and financing of the secretaries sent to mission lands, the appointment of such secretaries being ratified by the World's Committee. The Foreign Department further undertakes to raise and remit to the National Committee in the field the funds necessary to sustain the work of their representatives until the National Committee in the field is able to become entirely self-supporting. The allocation of the World's workers is always left to the committee in the field.[18]

Under this system there were, in 1910, fifty-two World's Y.W.C.A. workers sent out by the National Committees of Great Britain (twenty-eight), Canada (two), the United States (twenty-one), and Australia (one). Of this number, twenty-eight were located in India, Burma and Ceylon, three in Egypt, six in South Africa, one in West Africa, nine in China, four in Japan and one in Argentina. This number was to grow to seventy in the next quadrennium.

The sub-committee on the Scheme of Relationships, appointed in pursuance of the resolution offered by Miss Dodge in Berlin, was chaired by Miss Reynolds, and made its report at the biennial meeting of the

119

World's Committee at Swanwick, England, in 1912.[20] At this time the whole scheme was carefully considered, paragraph by paragraph, and revised for presentation at the Stockholm Conference in 1914. The Committee's sense of achievement in the matter is reflected in the final words of its report on this item of business: "It was proposed by Frau Ufer (Germany), seconded by Miss Taylor (U.S.), and carried unanimously, that the whole Scheme of Relationships as it now stands be adopted and acted upon until 1914, when a report shall be submitted to the Quadrennial Conference. The Doxology was then sung and the Committee adjourned." [21]

At Stockholm, after further discussion at the meeting of the World's Committee which preceded the conference, it was reported to the conference that:

> After eight years of careful consideration of the best basis of work and cooperation between the World's Committee and the National Committees affiliated with it, the World's Committee asks that this conference authorize it to adopt the scheme which has been considered and accepted at the biennial meeting in Stockholm, 1914, with power to make such alterations as to meet any emergencies or developments.[22]

The sheme adopted defined, first—the sphere and scope of the World's Committee (1) in unorganized lands, (2) in countries having National Associations, (3) in countries where two or more National Associations are concerned; second—the sphere and scope of National Committees (1) in countries not self-supporting, (2) in countries where the National Committee has a Foreign Department. The function of the World's Committee is declared to be "the promotion of a well-balanced development of the Y.W.C.A. throughout the world." This it should endeavor to achieve (1) in unorganized lands by organizing National Associations "when requested to do so . . . such requests coming from a responsible body of workers"; (2) in countries having National Associations by "guiding as far as possible, the National Committees in the development of their work on lines in harmony with the general policy of the World's Y.W.C.A. as well as appropriate to the needs of the countries in which they exist."

In order to assure a close relationship between the World's and the National Associations, World's Committee members were to be members of their respective National Committees, and their duties were to be attendance at World's Committee meetings and representation of the World's Committee and promotion of its interests in their own countries. In the case of countries where the National Committee was not self-supporting, the World's Committee was, in addition, to be consulted regarding the appointment of a national secretary and to ratify that appointment. It was also to receive all appeals from such countries for secretaries, building funds, etc., and if it approved, to forward these appeals to National Committees. In case of questions involving two or more National Committees, the World's Committee was to be the final court of appeal in all matters.

The function of the National Committees in countries that were not self-supporting was defined as that of responsibility for "the assignment, change of location, specialized training . . . and general welfare of secretaries sent to them from various Foreign Departments." The function of National Committees having Foreign Departments was to "aid the work in lands that are not self-supporting by selecting, training and equipping secretaries and securing their salary and secretarial expenses if necessary." The problem of varying standards, customs and procedures in countries that might be sending out secretaries to other lands was recognized in the provision that "in order to secure as far as possible uniform action and a high standard of efficiency, each Foreign Department shall consult with the World's Committee with reference to their regulations for foreign secretaries."

The policies adopted at Stockholm in 1914, after almost a decade of consideration, were chiefly a formulation of those practices which had come into use almost spontaneously under the stress of existing circumstances. They did much to regulate and regularize these practices and to define the channels through which the influence of the World's Association might play upon and modify in the direction of world unity the missionary activity of "sending" Associations, and give guidance and organizational help to new movements. A factor working for a unified world movement existed, too, in the common Christian point of view and purpose required of all national movements affiliated with the World's Committee. The remarkable increase in concern for the planting and growth of the Y.W.C.A. in all lands and for all young women was indeed, as was said at the Paris Conference, "one of the World's Committee's chief causes for gratitude as well as for satisfaction."

It should not be overlooked, however, that in formulating a policy for promoting this development in the only way that seemed possible at the time, i.e., by placing the responsibility and the control and direction of that program almost completely in the hands of the National Associations, the World's Committee surrendered a large part of its authority to direct and control the movement as it developed in new lands, and was creating difficulties as well as seizing an opportunity.

The recognition of the principle of national sovereignty in the contribution of the National Associations to other countries, and the definition of function of the World's Association in terms of a consultative relationship made it inevitable that the type of Association work promoted in these and the following years should reflect the pattern *of the National Committee sending out secretaries, rather than the pattern of a world movement combining the best features of various different national movements. The expansion of the Association in this period did little toward creating a world type of Y.W.C.A. out of the differing ideas, viewpoints, methods and experience of the Association movements in the British Empire, on the continent of Europe and in the New World. On the contrary, in China and Japan, where by far the largest contribution in trained personnel and money came from the United States, it fostered a distinctly American type of Association. In Africa, where practically all the workers sent out were from Great Britain, it resulted in an Association along distinctly British lines, while in India the two types of work developed side by side.

The fears of some World's Committee members that the responsibility for the extension of the Associations might be territorially divided between the World's Committee and the American Association, were, in theory at least, avoided. But the aggressive promotion of work in other lands by the Y.W.C.A. in the United States, together with its large resources and the natural tendency of American secretaries abroad to look for guidance to the Association whose representatives they were, tended in effect to make a division of responsibility between London and New York. In the years immediately following 1914, the moral and spiritual unifying power of the world fellowship might well have done much to offset this tendency and to make the function of the World's Y.W.C.A. realistic, even with regard to the American foreign program, had not the first world war immediately disrupted the processes of consultation and cooperation. On the other hand, the definitions of function arrived at enabled the National Associations having Foreign Departments to act as agents of the World's Y.W.C.A., in accordance with an agreed policy, in a period in which the World's Committee itself, because of the war, was unable to expand its functions.

REFERENCES

[1] Italics ours [Ed.].

[2] First Annual Report, for 1895, p. 19.

[3] When the constitution was adopted at the first World's Conference in 1898, a Committee for Corresponding Associations was substituted for the standing Committee for Other Continents. The budgets of the Committee for the European Continent and the Committee for Other Continents were not included in the general budget of £600 for which the British and American Associations made themselves responsible from 1894-

REFERENCES

1898. These two committees continued, as they had done within the British movement, to raise and spend their own funds. Their financial statements, however, appear as a part of the annual finance statement of the World's Committee.

[4] Appendix 1, By-Laws, Article III, Section 2 (e), p. 273.

[5] Third World's Y.W.C.A. Conference, 1906, Report, pp. 25-26.

[6] World's Y.W.C.A. Executive Committee, January 19, 1905, Minutes.

[7] See Chapter 7, p. 90.

[8] Third World's Y.W.C.A. Conference, 1906, Report, p. 28.

[9] *Ibid.*, p. 26.

[10] Miss Una M. Saunders, Letter to Miss Ruth Rouse, February 1906.

[11] Annual Report for 1907, p. 21.

[12] Annual Report for 1907, p. 19.

[13] Executive Committee, May 3, 1906, Minutes.

[14] *Ibid.*, December 13, 1906.

[15] Miss Grace H. Dodge, President of the National Board of the United States.

[16] World's Committee Meeting, Berlin 1910, Minutes, pp. 10-11.

[17] Fourth World's Y.W.C.A. Conference, 1910, Report, p. 9.

[18] Miss Kawai later became the National General Secretary of Japan.

[19] Fourth World's Y.W.C.A. Conference, 1910, Report, pp. 189-190.

[20] The Swanwick Conference Estate, Derbyshire.

[21] World's Committee Meeting, 1912, Minutes, p. 10.

[22] Fifth World's Y.W.C.A. Conference, 1914, Report, p. 30.

Progress in the Association, she said, was to be judged by the degree to which it was achieving "the working together of ever-enlarging and more inclusive groups of women for ever-receding goals."
MARGARET E. BURTON: Biography of Mabel Cratty.

CHAPTER 10 MAJOR ISSUES: 1904-14 (CONTINUED) — 2. THE RELATION OF THE WORLD'S Y.W.C.A. TO SOCIAL ISSUES — 3. THE ECUMENICAL POSITION OF THE WORLD'S Y.W.C.A.

THE fourth World's Conference, held in Berlin in July 1910, was a turning point in the history of the World's Young Women's Christian Association. Up to this time the chief concern had necessarily been the building up of a world organization, unifying and developing the work brought together in 1894. Along with this had gone the investigation of new fields for expansion and the solid beginnings of occupation of some of them. At Berlin the World's Association was conscious of itself as a well-established organization, prepared to take its place among other organizations and make its distinctive contribution with realism and courage.

This new feeling of assurance regarding its place and work finds expression in many documents of the period. The official report of the conference says: "While the Association may still be in its first stages in some countries, one realized from the outset of the meetings at Berlin that the World's Y.W.C.A. as a whole had passed the stage of fighting a way for itself among social agencies."[1] Miss Reynolds, writing for *The Association Monthly,* official magazine of the Y.W.C.A. in the United States, reports: "The Berlin Conference established conclusively the fact that the World's Y.W.C.A. is not a hope, as some of us have long striven to believe, not an aspiration for the optimistic, but a fact and a power to be reckoned with and depended upon in the world's social, religious and missionary progress."[2]

Many of the National Associations represented at Berlin testified to the progress evidenced in the World's Association and the influence of that conference on their own work. Reporting two years later to the

124

biennial meeting of the World's Committee, the British report says: "The British Association has come to look back to the World's Y.W.C.A. Conference in Berlin two years ago as an epoch-making time."[3] The report from France says: "The Berlin Conference has certainly given a new impetus to our work,"[4] and the report from Germany: "The fourth World's Conference was not to become only a highly valued remembrance, but rather a spring of life for all the Y.W.C.A.s in all the countries of the world . . . [it] has enlarged our horizon, has made us look more toward other countries."[5] Miss Harriet Taylor, Executive Secretary of the Foreign Department of the National Board of the Associations in the United States, reported that it was "impossible for anyone who had been at the conference in Geneva and Paris not to recognize the wonderful development that has taken place in all parts of the World's work."[6]

That which made so deep an impression at Berlin was the endeavor of the World's Y.W.C.A. to analyze itself and to assess its powers and responsibilities in the light of its fundamental aims and purposes in relation to a world situation marked by profound and accelerating change. The subject chosen for the conference was "The Place of the Y.W.C.A. in the Social, the Evangelistic, and the Missionary Awakening". Preparation was made for conference discussion by means of papers on each of the three phases of this subject, sent out in advance to the conference delegates. These papers were compiled by international commissions, and contained not only information about the program of the Associations affiliated with the World's Y.W.C.A. but also material gathered from other sources—people and books.

The chairman of these international commissions were: for The Place of the Y.W.C.A. in the Evangelistic Awakening, Fräulein Elizabeth von Woelwarth-Lauterburg of Germany; for The Place of the Y.W.C.A. in the Missionary Awakening, Miss Michi Kawai of Japan; for The Place of the Y.W.C.A. in the Social Awakening, Miss Florence Simms of the United States. At the conference these reports were summarized by their chairmen and supplemented by a series of addresses.

The addresses on Evangelism were given by Dr. John R. Mott and Miss Ruth Rouse of the World's Student Christian Federation, by Mademoiselle Anne of France, and by Pasteur Le Seur of the *Berliner Stadt* Mission. Dr. Mott, whose address was the opening one of the conference, stressed the ripeness of the time for a deepened evangelistic emphasis, because of the plastic character of the non-Christian nations, the rising tide of nationalism and the new vitality being manifested by non-Christian religions. He challenged the Y.W.C.A. in this field as "the most comprehensive Christian organization among women in the world" and as one presenting "an attractive type of Christianity with

125

ethical and social power." Addresses on the Missionary Awakening were
given by M. Daniel Couvé, Secretary of *Missions Evangéliques de Paris,*
and by Pastor Doktor Julius Richter, historian of modern missions, as
well as by the national Y.W.C.A. secretaries of India, China, and Japan,
Miss Ethel Hunter (Mrs. C. de J. Luxmoore), Miss Estelle Paddock, and
Miss Caroline Macdonald. The addresses on the Social Awakening were
given by Professor Seeberg of the University of Berlin, who spoke on
"The Social Problem of Today and Its Call to Christian Women"; Miss
Constance Smith of the Christian Social Union of Great Britain, who
appealed for the study of social conditions; and M. Elie Gounelle of
Paris, editor of *Le Christianisme Social,* who spoke on the essential char-
acteristics of Christian socialism.

The Relation of the World's Y.W.C.A. to Social Issues

Against the background of these addresses and reports the delegates
discussed the place of the Y.W.C.A. in the world of the day, and
reaffirmed their evangelistic and missionary purpose in the light of new
opportunities and new needs. The most significant action of the conference, however, because it represented very largely the breaking of
new ground, was taken as a result of the discussion of the social
and industrial awakening. A series of resolutions was adopted, recognizing the relation of the teachings of Jesus to social life as well as to the
life of the individual, and calling upon the leaders of the Association
for a "thorough and systematic study of the social significance of these
teachings." Present social and industrial conditions, it was declared, "mili-
tate against the highest development of Christian womanhood," and leaders
and members of the Y.W.C.A. were urged "as a definite duty", to study
the social and industrial problems of the day:

"(a) by investigation of the physical and economic requirements of
    working women,
"(b) by study of the means of amelioration which legislation and
    private endeavor offer for the conditions under which women live
    and work,
"(c) by a careful examination of organizations among working
    women."

Other resolutions urged the extension of Association work beyond
its own membership with special adaptation to the peculiar needs of
various groups of working women, and also to adolescent girls; an
enlarged program of recreation, education and religious training; and
a special effort to lead women of leisure to study the conditions of
working women and to take up service for them. Following the conference, all these resolutions were sent to each National Committee, and

126

all Associations were invited to adopt them as a statement of their own policy.'

These resolutions embodied the convictions already reached and put into practice in the Associations of Great Britain, the United States, and the Orient. A trend in the same direction was apparent in certain other countries, though in a less marked degree, but for some Associations these resolutions implied a type of work so different from any they had hitherto undertaken as to seem revolutionary. There had been, indeed, a steady educational process carried on by the World's Committee through the pages of *The World's Quarterly*. Beginning in July 1904, with an article on the Matsuyama Factory Girls' Home in Japan, there had been a succession of articles touching on industrial conditions as they affect young women, and on the relation of the Y.W.C.A. to industrial problems. Such titles as the following appeared from 1904 to 1910: "The Social Question: the Mission of This Generation"; "The Social Question: Temperance Reform"; "Immigration in Canada"; "The Industrial Life of Belgian Women"; "Christian Social Work and Social Democracy in Germany"; "The Life of Scottish Fisher Girls"; "The Industrial Problem in Japan"; "The Social Problem as It Affects the Y.W.C.A. of Great Britain"; "American Y.W.C.A. Work in Factories"; "Work in the Cotton Mill Villages of the South (U.S.)"; "Mill Work of the Bombay Association"; and a series on "The Y.W.C.A. and Factory Girls". Among the letters written by Miss Spencer during her tour of the Orient in 1907, those on "Factory Women in Osaka" and "Mill Women of North China" further underlined the need for work with industrial girls which the missionaries had stressed as early as 1899, when they first appealed to the World's Y.W.C.A.

It had been, therefore, because of indications from many quarters of the globe that "the great and increasing social problems" were of urgent concern to women and therefore to a world organization of Christian women, that the World's Committee had appointed the International Commission with Miss Florence Simms as the chairman and including Association leaders and social experts from Sweden, France, Great Britain and other countries, to prepare for the Berlin Conference a report on "The Place of the Y.W.C.A. in the Social and Industrial Awakening". Miss Simms described the work of the commission and its outcome in these words:

> The World's Committee of the Y.W.C.A. sent to all the countries a questionnaire asking what the Associations of each country had done to meet the social and industrial situation. One of the questions was, "What do you believe about the possibility of the social teachings of Christ being applied to the

127

social order of today?" . . . The answers began to pour in. It was England that had seen ahead of any other country. It was the English women who had first gotten together at the labor conference in Manchester and decided that Christianity had really something very definite to say and do in the face of the industrial situation, and it was a very splendid French woman who was the leading spirit among us and who said that what had been visioned in England must be done the world over. At the meeting in Berlin the charter for the development of the work of Y.W.C.A. in its industrial life was agreed upon.[8]

As the Geneva Conference, eight years earlier, had aroused the member Associations of the World's Y.W.C.A. to commit themselves to the expansion of the Association geographically in "unoccupied" lands, so the Berlin Conference secured their commitment to another pioneer task, that of attempting to understand the problems of the new social frontier and bring to bear upon them the united power of the Association. It is difficult now to realize how courageous a pioneer step this was. The responsibility of Christian organizations in matters involving questions of legislation and labor organization was by no means generally accepted in 1910. As the British resolutions of 1909[9] indicated, it was by many regarded as becoming connected with party politics and hence most unsuitable. Especially for a woman's organization, in those days before woman's suffrage, to take such a step was looked upon as very doubtful wisdom, a turning of the attention to secular issues, with the consequent danger of making the program in this field a substitute for the religious emphasis which was the fundamental purpose of the Y.W.C.A. On the other hand, many were already aware that it was the Christian religion itself that was calling the Y.W.C.A. to a program for social right- eousness as well as to one for individual evangelism and personal service. Those leaders saw the new emphasis not as a competitor with or a substitute for the old but as an extension of it, demanded by the crying need of the times. In this conviction they felt that they were upheld by the teachings of the great prophets of Israel and of Jesus himself. Miss Rouse, speaking at Berlin to those who feared as well as to those who approved the new trend, strongly emphasized the pos- sibility and the necessity of a message that stressed both personal evangelism and social responsibility.

The effect of the Berlin resolutions was widespread. As was natural, it was greatest and most immediate in the countries already deeply con- cerned with social issues. In the Y.W.C.A. of those countries the reso- lutions gave direction and added weight to an enlarged program of education which included Bible study on the social teachings of the

128

prophets and of Jesus, as well as study of industrial conditions. This study, going hand in hand with the extension and adaptation of the Association program to industrial girls, was bound to lead to a stand on such matters as a minimum wage and night work for women. This was particularly true in countries like the United States, in which the government was not yet committed to a fundamental program of social legislation and where, therefore, the creation of public opinion on these matters was of vital importance. But in almost every country some result was seen, some increased consciousness of the responsibility of Christian women toward those hard-pressed by the industrial system, a responsibility not only for providing services that would soften or counteract its worst effects, but for endeavoring to bring about changes in the system which would, in the end, make such services unnecessary.

The policy to be promoted henceforth by the World's Committee is summed up in a general statement of the Executive Committee on "the present position of the Association and some lines of advance in the near future."

> The problems of industrial life need to be studied, and the many evils surrounding women's life and work, such as bad housing, sweated labor, the living-in system, excessive hours, etc., understood and grappled with. Existing legislation should be known and made known to the workers themselves, and everywhere it should be the aim of the Christian worker to seek to realize both sides of the many perplexing problems of modern industrial life, in order to bring about a better understanding between employer and employee, that both may be helped to fulfill faithfully their duties to each other.
>
> The Association may do something to lighten the burden of working women by educating public opinion, making their condition and needs known, and by helping them to understand and take advantage of the laws already existing for their benefit.
>
> This, in general terms, outlines the position of the World's Y.W.C.A. at the present time, and defines the policy aimed at by the World's Committee.[10]

The Ecumenical Position of the World's Y.W.C.A.

Important as were the issues of organizational relationships and social emphasis for the future of the World's Y.W.C.A., the most far-reaching of all the adjustments to a changing world made in these years was the revision of the constitutional statement of Basis and the new definition set up of the Aim and Principles of the organization. In these changes the Y.W.C.A. recognized its obligation to take part in the developing ecumenical movement within Christianity. It was true to the genius of the Y.W.C.A. that it was moved to make these changes not by the logic of abstract argument but by the impulse to respond to appeals from leaders in countries of Greek Orthodox and Roman Catholic culture to extend the work of the Association to their young women and to receive them into the world fellowship.

In the nineteenth century, Association work in these countries had been almost wholly for the small groups of Protestant young women, often largely foreign. In the early years of the twentieth century the increase of religious liberty in eastern orthodox lands, especially in Russia and Bulgaria, had opened the door for work among young women of the Orthodox Church, while in South America the way seemed clear for a developing movement in a Roman Catholic environment. The kind of fellowship and the type of activity that the Protestant Christian youth organizations had promoted were proving their power of appeal to wider circles, even in some cases to non-Christian youth. At a meeting of the World's Executive Committee in December 1908, Dr. Mott, who was there as a guest for the purpose of consulting with the Committee on its relation to non-Protestant bodies, said: "It is a very difficult question, especially in Russia. . . . It is a question on which both Associations will soon have to form a definite policy, in view of the development of work also in Turkey, Japan and Latin America." He cited the case of a Y.M.C.A. in the Near East where "Protestants are outnumbered by members of the Greek Orthodox, Armenian, Coptic, Roman Catholic and other churches."[11] By their interest in and concern for the welfare of all youth in all lands, and by the proved adaptability of their program to meet the needs of youth wherever spiritual aspiration was united with the impulse to practical service, both the Y.M.C.A. and the Y.W.C.A. were now finding themselves caught up in a movement reaching out toward an ecumenical fellowship.

In this new outreach a trail already had been blazed by the World's Student Christian Federation. The fact that there was, in many countries, a close relationship between the Student Movement and the Y.M.C.A. and the Y.W.C.A., and that leadership for the Association in all lands increasingly was drawn from the Student Movement, made it natural and, indeed, inevitable that the Associations too should seek to become more ecumenical. As the early days of the Association had been marked by an insistence on its interdenominational character as an expression of evangelical Protestantism, so these years of the early twentieth century were characterized by a determination to make the Association a still wider fellowship, at the same time retaining at its center the warmth and vigor of the evangelical experience of Christianity which was recognized as its spiritual mainspring.

Following the discussion with Dr. Mott in December 1908, the matter was kept constantly before the Executive Committee by the developing situation in Russia and Bulgaria. In 1910, when Miss Spencer was setting forth with Miss Rouse for her tour of the Levant and her attendance at the World's Student Christian Federation conference in Constantinople, it was deemed essential that some guidance should be given her as to the basis on which work in eastern orthodox countries might become affiliated with the World's Committee. At the meeting of the Executive Committee on December 15, 1910, a statement was presented by a "Special Purposes Committee", which, after consideration by each committee member, was amended and adopted at the meeting in January 1911, on the understanding that it was "not a pronouncement for public use, but drawn up provisionally only, in view of Miss Spencer's visit to the Levant, to help her as regards a broad outline of the general views of the Committee." [12]

This statement was as follows:

The Y.W.C.A., being an interdenominational Association of young women consisting of members of the various branches of the church of Christ, warmly welcomes as fellow laborers those of the Greek Orthodox or other Christian churches who can sign the Basis and work in accordance with its teaching, on the condition, however, that no questions involving ecclesiastical difference be raised.

The Basis as given in the constitution was further interpreted as follows:

The Y.W.C.A. is interdenominational in its membership and methods of work:

1. a) *Associate*: All young women are welcomed to its meetings and accepted as associates irrespective of creed or religious denomination.
   b) *Full member*: Only those who with sincere hearts can sign the Basis can be full members of the Associations.
2. Associations are recognized as belonging to the Y.W.C.A. which are prepared to work on these lines.

The religious teaching of the Y.W.C.A. is on those cardinal and foundation doctrines of the faith, about which all sections of the church are in accord. All matters of religious or denominational controversy are to be avoided, the sole object of the teacher in Association work being to attract her hearers to the love and service of the Lord Jesus Christ, and their edification in the faith as taught by the Word of God. [13]

In Bulgaria, where a committee composed of three Greek Orthodox, two Roman Catholic, and four Protestant members had been formed "to draw up a constitution and to work up interest in the Association" [14] there was, writes Miss Spencer, "an unwillingness on the part of some to adopt the Basis of the World's Y.W.C.A. and a desire to have one of a somewhat different character." [15] The basis which they suggested would allow them to accept as active members "all women belonging to any of the Christian churches, who fully sympathize with the aims of the Association, who believe that Christianity is the only basis for the moral training of young women, and who, by signing the constitution, promise to work actively to promote its aims." [16] The difficulty in the minds of those on the Ladies' Committee in Sofia who were not wholly in sympathy with the World's Y.W.C.A. basis, was, it appears, mainly a theological one, a hesitation about asking personal commitment to a doctrinal position as a qualification for active membership. This is significant, for it is the point at which difficulty was to arise in other countries in the coming years. The reply made by the Executive Committee to the suggestion if the Bulgarian Committee was, that "while the Basis which the Ladies' Committee wished to adopt would be suitable for the work of starting a hostel, it would not be sufficient for the Y.W.C.A." [17] On this account, the Executive Committee urged that for the time being the work in Bulgaria be confined to hostel work, without the use of the name Y.W.C.A.

From this point on, until the World's Conference in 1914, the question of a constitutional statement by which National Associations affiliated with the World's Committee would be firmly united in their commitment to evangelical Christianity and yet the individual be given liberty for personal interpretation of that faith, was one to which special and continuous thought was given, not only by the Special Purposes Committee and the Executive Committee but by various National Committees and by the World's Committee itself at its 1912 and 1914 biennial meetings. Several leading theologians of different denominations in Great Britain were asked for advice regarding the wording of the basis, and a new statement, framed in consultation with them, was submitted to a representative of the Greek Orthodox Church.

As a result of this discussion and consultation, the World's Committee recommended to the Stockholm Conference in 1914 the substitution for the Article on "Basis" in the constitution, of three new Articles, entitled "Basis", "Aim", and "Principles". The first of these defines the faith upon which the World's Y.W.C.A. rests. The second declares the aim of the World's Y.W.C.A. to be to "organize, develop and unite National Associations which accept the World's basis or one in conformity with it." The third declares the desire to be representative of all sections of the Christian Church in so far as they accept its basis, and to include in the field of its activities young women without distinction of creed. [18]

The effect of this revision was to reaffirm in unmistakable but entirely non-sectarian terms the commitment of the World's Y.W.C.A. to the historic Christian faith, yet at the same time, by placing responsibility for assent to this basis upon each National Association rather than upon each individual member of every Association, to open the membership and even the leadership of the Association to women who might be unable to give full assent to the particular wording of the Basis. It was also to make unmistakably clear the desire to make of the Association an ecumenical fellowship.

The World's Y.W.C.A. in this momentous decade reached, as it were, mature stature. By study, consultation, and experimentation it altered its organizational structure to meet the exigencies and needs of a period of large expansion; it revised and enlarged its conception of its fundamental task in view of a changing social situation; it reinterpreted its basis of membership in terms that would enable it to become a truly ecumenical fellowship.

REFERENCES

[1] Fourth World's Y.W.C.A. Conference, 1910, Report, p. 31.

[2] *The Association Monthly,* August, 1910, p. 285.

[3] World's Y.W.C.A. Committee Meeting, Swanwick, 1912, Reports, p. 5.

[4] *Ibid.,* p. 14.

[5] *Ibid.,* pp. 17, 19.

[6] Foreign Department, National Board, Y.W.C.A.s of the U.S.A., Report, September 1910.

[7] For full text of resolutions and discussion see Fourth World's Y.W.C.A. Conference, 1910, Report, pp. 89-91.

[8] Roberts, Richard, *Florence Simms,* pp. 190, 191.

[9] See Chapter 8, p. 106.

[10] Annual Report for 1910, p. 14.

[11] World's Executive Committee, December 17, 1908, Minutes.

[12] Executive Committee, January 19, 1911, Minutes, p. 1.

[13] Executive Committee, January 19, 1911, Minutes, p. 1, 2.

[14] *Ibid.,* March 16, 1911, p. 6.

[15] *Ibid.,* March 16, 1911, p. 5.

[16] *Ibid.,* July 10, 1911, p. 6.

[17] Executive Committee, July 10, 1911, Minutes, p. 6.

[18] Constitution, Articles II, III, and IV, Appendix II, p. 275.

*We must face present social conditions with courage
and without fear. . . . As an Association we must
help to form a right public opinion on these matters.
The Association in its earlier periods, and in its
humility, worked quietly behind the scenes, laying
the splendid foundation on the spiritual side which
has resulted in the present growth. The same foundation remains today, but the time has come for the
Association to be recognized as a real power by the
governments of nations. Are we a strong power,
making for righteousness by the Grace of God?*

MR. J. HERBERT TRITTON. Opening Address, Fifth World's
Y.W.C.A. Conference, 1914.

CHAPTER 11 AT THE END OF AN ERA

IMPORTANT as were the changes introduced
by the expansion of the Young Women's Christian Association in
the Orient, its increasing sense of social responsibility, and the contacts
with Russia and southeastern Europe, these do not tell the whole story
of the World's Young Women's Christian Association in that period of
development of program and of policy which came to an end in 1914.
Requests for the extension of Association work came to the Executive
Committee from many quarters besides the Orient; increasing travel of
young women for study or employment presented new needs for which
the World's Y.W.C.A. as well as National Committees felt concern; it
was necessary to frame policies in regard to relations with other organizations, particularly the Y.M.C.A. and the World's Student Christian Federation. Throughout the period also there was a growing sense of the responsibility of the Y.W.C.A. as a woman's movement, and a desire to
see more clearly the function of such a movement in relation to national
and world problems.

Of the requests for further extension of the Association, the most
pressing were those from Portugal, from the Near East, and from Africa,
including South Africa, Egypt, and East and West Africa. In Portugal,
the work that had been begun by Miss May Cassels in 1897 was small but
vigorous.[1] The Executive Committee of the World's Y.W.C.A., keenly
alive to the significance of a vital Association in a Roman Catholic environment, sent Miss Spencer for an extensive visit to that country. A National

134

Association was formed and affiliated with the World's Association. The acceptance of this small National Association early in the year 1906 led Miss Spencer, in her report to the Paris Conference, to use Portugal as an illustration of one of her favorite themes—the value of the exchange of experience between the diverse movements within the World's Association. After stressing the great contribution made to the Portuguese work by leaders from Great Britain, she adds:

> But not only is Portugal a recipient. She is also a giver, and from her various experiences our World's Association may learn many valuable lessons. In the first place, Portugal can help solve the question of how to adapt the Y.W.C.A. to the needs of a country where the number of Protestants is very small. . . . In the second place, Portugal can demonstrate in a marvelous way what the Association can do for the full development of womanhood. The Association is one of the few organizations for Portuguese women and has the advantage of being peculiarly suited to their needs.[2]

Nevertheless, here, as previously in Spain, the problem of leadership proved insuperable. The Executive Committee, its minutes show, struggled over a long period to find the urgently needed French-speaking national secretary who would go to Portugal to work with Miss Cassels. The National Committee of France made a donation toward the support of such a secretary, but the right person could not be found, and the work in Portugal for many years failed to grow.

In the Near East, the Y.W.C.A. as a student group in mission schools and as a center for fellowship for young women from other countries had been known since the turn of the century. At about that time, a Y.W.C.A. in a mission school in Marash, Turkey in Asia, wrote to the World's Committee asking for affiliation in these words: "A branch may be easily lost, but when it is joined to a large and strong trunk it is more safe."[3] An article in *The World's Quarterly* for October 1901 reports on a branch in Constantinople, telling of a Bible reading and tea, and commenting on the visitors in the city from other branches and on "the many lively young women who find friends here." In 1908 the World's Executive Committee received a letter from Miss Harriet Taylor, Secretary of the Foreign Department of the Association in the United States, saying that Miss Frances Gage, who had been a missionary in Marsovan, Turkey, and was now a Y.W.C.A. secretary in the United States, had written her about the possibility of returning to Turkey as a Y.W.C.A. secretary.[4]

It was, however, the World's Student Christian Federation conference held in Constantinople in 1911 which brought the question of work in the Near East definitely before the Executive Committee. Preliminary to this conference, various meetings of representatives of Christian movements in the Near East had been held. Regarding these Miss Spencer wrote to the Executive Committee:

> These discussions showed that there was a field of service for the Y.W.C.A. in Syria and Palestine especially when it could unite in itself the various Christian activities of the girls' schools. There is even greater need of the Y.W.C.A. for girls who have left school, both for Protestants and for oriental Christians.

The result of these deliberations, Miss Spencer continues,

> . . . was the appointment of a Promoting Committee for men's and women's work in the whole of the Turkish Empire, to be composed of missionaries, church dignitaries, laymen and women, both European and native. Its function is to develop and amalgamate both student and city branches of the Y.M.C.A. and the Y.W.C.A., to work toward the formation of a National Committee, and to devise a suitable basis for active membership.[5]

The Executive Secretary of this Promoting Committee, Mr. E. O. Jacob of the Y.M.C.A., corresponded with the Executive Committee during the years from 1911 to 1914 about the opportunities for Y.W.C.A. work in Turkey, the need of an experienced secretary "preferably an American", and the possibility of affiliating the women's section of the Promoting Committee with the World's Y.W.C.A.[6]

In all this discussion the World's Committee was also in consultation with the Foreign Department of the Y.W.C.A. in the United States. Miss Gage returned in 1913 to Turkey at the request of Anatolia College, Marsovan, to make an investigation of women's work, and that same year the Foreign Department of the United States sent Miss Anna Welles to Constantinople. Early in 1914 Miss Gage was appointed National Secretary for Turkey. At the Stockholm Conference in 1914, two representatives of this new work, Mrs. Ravendal and Miss Welles, were present. The report given there shows the status of the work at that time:

> During the last four years the Y.W.C.A. in the Turkish Empire has made steady progress. In the spring of 1911 the visit of Miss Rouse, Miss Spencer and Dr. Mott gave a great impetus to the work. At the conclusion of their meetings in Beyrout a small committee was formed of English, American and Syrian ladies, with the object of extending Association work throughout Syria and Palestine. This Committee has recently become affiliated with the "Union of Christian Societies in the Turkish Empire". As in most eastern countries, the great majority of our members have been educated in the mission schools. . . . We

are only beginning to organize our work systematically; it has hitherto consisted of isolated gatherings, chiefly in connection with mission stations. . . .

Our latest development [the report concludes] is the appointment of Miss Frances Gage as traveling secretary for Turkey and Miss Anna Welles for special student work in Constantinople, and we are now looking forward to the possibility of the consolidation of the work generally. In common with the rest of the world, the women of the Turkish Empire are sharing in the "Woman's Movement". The Missionary Societies alone cannot cope with the new conditions and demands.[7]

The work thus begun in the Turkish Empire was chiefly for Greek, Syrian and Armenian young women. Work among Turkish girls was not at this time envisaged. The report given at Stockholm says: "The greater proportion of members are Syrian, but we have also British, American, Dutch and Greek. Among the *attenders* are Moslems, Jews, Druzes, Maronites and members of the various branches of the Eastern Church."

In Africa, the World's Committee faced three separate and widely different situations—South Africa, the colonial territories of European countries in East and West Africa, and Egypt. South Africa had been a field of Association work ever since the first Y.W.C.A. was opened in Cape Town by British women in 1884. In this decade, and under the guidance of the World's Committee, marked progress was made. A National Association was formed and affiliated with the World's Y.W.C.A. in 1905. Miss Spencer, Miss Emily Kinnaird, and Madame Alfred Bertrand, a member of the Italian National Committee, all visited South Africa between 1904 and 1910. These visits not only helped to consolidate and set forward the work already carried on for English and Dutch girls, but led to undertaking the first real work attempted among native girls. Regarding Miss Kinnaird's visit in 1908 and that of Madame Bertrand in 1909, it was reported:

That the Association has extended its borders during the last eighteen or twenty months is very greatly due to her [Miss Kinnaird's] visit and enthusiastic interest in the work and power to inspire others with interest also. . . . Another result of Miss Kinnaird's visit in 1908 was the first impulse toward starting branches of the Y.W.C.A. among native and colored girls, but nothing was done until 1909, when Madame Bertrand, wife of the well-known traveler, Captain Bertrand, and herself a member of the National Council of the Y.W.C.A. of Italy, visited South Africa with her husband. Madame Bertrand stayed at several mission stations in Basutoland and Griqualand East, talked over the matter with the wives of the [French] missionaries, and induced several of these ladies to organize branches among the Christian girls in their stations and to seek affiliation with us through our National Secretary. Our National Council then took up the matter, appointed a small sub-committee for native and colored work, and a national secretary for this department in particular.[8]

It is interesting to note that in this same period the recently formed National Board of the Associations in the United States was recognizing the responsibility for Negro young women by calling to its national staff two Negro Secretaries, one, Mrs. Addie Hunton, in 1907, for student work in Negro schools, the other, Miss Eva D. Bowles, in 1908, for work in city Associations. These secretaries were charged not only with the development of Negro branches of the Y.W.C.A. but with cooperation in making plans for joint consideration by white and colored groups together within the Association, of problems in which both were concerned.

The need of young women of the colored races was brought before the World's Committee not alone in connection with the long-established Associations of South Africa. The Executive Committee was again and again urged to start work among native young women in East and West Africa. As was true in the preceding decade with regard to starting work in China and Japan, these requests came in the first instance from missionaries. In 1906 the Committee for Corresponding Associations reports:

The West Coast of Africa is now earnestly desiring to form Associations. Missionaries of the Church Missionary Society, Wesleyan and other societies have urged the need of starting work amongst native Christian women and girls all along the Coast.[9]

The report then refers especially to the opportunities in two towns in Nigeria—Abeokuta and Lagos.

The following year, Miss Rankilor, a missionary of the Church Missionary Society in West Africa, returned after a visit to England "as a World's worker, to work under the Y.W.C.A. and the Church Missionary Society."[10] The annual report for 1908 contains a report of progress in West Africa and speaks especially of the Week of Prayer services at Abeokuta. These were arranged by a members' committee and were held in six different churches during the week, with an average attendance of upward of two hundred. Miss Rankilor's report concludes: "All my work was to write a short paper in Yoruba, explaining what the Association was and for whom, which was read at each meeting. It was the Abeokuta Week of Prayer, arranged, conducted and attended by Abeokutans."[11]

In 1911, problems of the developing work in Nigeria were frequently on the Executive Committee agenda. That same year Bishop Tucker of Uganda discussed with the Committee the possibility of forming an Asso-

138

ciation in that country, but since native girls married very young, the judgment of women missionaries was, in the end, that a Mother's Union was the more immediate need. In 1913 a guest at one Executive Committee meeting was Deaconess Meier, a German missionary from Togoland, West Africa. She gave an account of her work there, "where there were several Associations in charge of missionaries" which she was anxious should be affiliated with the World's Y.W.C.A. This year saw also a second secretary sent out to Nigeria by the British Foreign Department, and much discussion of the needs of Kenya, East Africa, particularly its leading city of Nairobi.[12] From Jamaica, in the British West Indies, came urgent requests also for work among colored young women. The concern of the World's Committee with the development of work among native girls in Africa and elsewhere is summed up in the report of the Executive Committee for 1912:

> Each year God seems to press the needs of some portion of his great harvest field. One year it was the Far East, another the Near East, this year the great Dark Continent of Africa has been repeatedly brought to our notice. From Onitsha and Abeokuta on the West Coast, with the urgent call of missionaries to help in building up the Christian women and girls in the face of temptations which surround them, alas, as much from the presence of the white races as from their heathen environment; from Nairobi on the East, promising to become the Johannesburg of that part of Africa, and from South Africa, needing secretaries for work among both colored and white races, come appeals for workers, while closely akin is that from Jamaica.[13]

Work in the mission fields of Africa brought before the World's Committee the question of the relationship of the Association to the church in primitive communities, and the Executive Committee sent out a letter asking for information about "the Association working in countries where the church is still in its infancy." Replies from Nigeria and from South African leaders gave assurance that "the Association has proved very helpful and in no way a hindrance to the church" and that it "in no way tended to lessen the responsibility for church membership."[14] Many different missionary societies were at work in Africa and the Executive Committee of the World's Y.W.C.A., noting that sometimes a request for Association work came from some of the missionaries while others were not heard from, reaffirmed the policy which in earlier years had been established in regard to work in the Orient, namely, that Y.W.C.A. work should be started only at the unanimous request of the missionaries.

In Egypt also there were interesting developments in these years. Though the first recorded Y.W.C.A. is the one opened in Alexandria in

1876, the real impetus to the growth during this decade came from the opening of work in Cairo in 1902, under the leadership of a young English-woman, Miss Rosa E. Margerison. Miss Margerison was educated at Queen's College, London, one of the first colleges founded in England for the higher education of women. "In 1902, she read in the *Times* an appeal issued by the Y.W.C.A. for workers among women and girls in Egypt. She volunteered her services as an honorary worker and was accepted, and from this time on she never faltered in this work of the Master's to which she had set her hand."[15]

In the beginning things were most discouraging. She had to struggle almost alone; there was no committee; many old British residents in Cairo insisted that the Y.W.C.A. was not wanted; there were financial difficulties; the not-too-suitable flat in which she began was besieged with exacting visitors, and among her difficulties she records "not least the perplexing Arabic language." But Miss Margerison was a person of courageous daring and of humor. By 1910 the cramped quarters of her little flat had been replaced by a palatial old residence known now as Connaught House, the hostel was filled with girls, religious and social work had been developed, an employment bureau had been opened and was being used by all nationalities. The house was a center for a varied educational program of Bible, language and other classes, and lectures, as well as for many clubs. The international character of the work was manifest in the twenty different nationalities found among the residents and in the different clubs. Moreover, by 1914 the staff was international, including British, Swiss, German, French and Austrian workers. The German member, Fräulein Hanna Burckhardt, daughter of Pastor Burckhardt, President of the National Association of Germany, was the first secretary sent out by the recently organized Foreign Department of the German National Committee. Work in Alexandria was reopened, "where there is a large sphere of work as yet untouched by any agency among the young shop girls of all nationalities."[16]

The record of expansion during this decade is the record of work undertaken largely by Great Britain and the United States. But the policy of the World's Committee to encourage the development of Foreign Departments in order that each national movement might share in this expansion, was beginning to bear fruit. Canada had long had such a department, and its representative in Japan. Australia sent its first worker, Miss Nina Brentnall, to India in 1909. Germany sent Fräulein Burckhardt to Egypt in 1913. Though no secretaries were sent out by the French Association, the French National Committee was prepared to contribute toward the support of a French-speaking secretary in Portugal. There was good reason at Stockholm, in 1914, to feel that the so diverse movements making up the World's Y.W.C.A. were coming together in the shared responsibility of a common task.

A reading of Executive Committee minutes for these years brings to light the fact that the World's Committee was in far more intimate and influential relationship to the work of the British Foreign Department in Europe and in Africa, than to the work of the Foreign Department of the United States in the Orient and South America. The location of the World's headquarters in London and the interlocking personnel of the World's Executive Committee and the British National Council largely account for this. The result was that in some lands the workers, though closely related to the British Council, felt at the same time in vital, practical touch with the World's Committee as well, while the workers in other countries looked toward and relied upon the National Board in New York and had little consciousness of relation to the World's Executive Committee in London.

The international character of the hostel in Cairo illustrated a situation that presented a particular and practical problem for the World's Y.W.C.A. in this period. That problem was the increasing number of young women resident for longer or shorter periods, either as students or as employees in business concerns, in countries other than their own. In two cities of Europe, Paris and Rome, it was a problem with which the World's Y.W.C.A. as well as the Y.W.C.A. leaders in these cities endeavored to deal. Indeed, such a responsibility was recognized by the World's Committee in 1900, when it established in Paris an International Home for the young women from many countries who came to the city in connection with the Paris Exhibition.

This, however, was a temporary project. At the Geneva Conference in 1902, the desirability of international homes in Paris and Rome was brought to the attention of the delegates, and in the year 1903, Miss Reynolds made a visit to Paris, during which she was greatly impressed by the needs of American students in the Latin Quarter and of British young women employed in the city. The opening of a hostel to meet these needs was made possible in 1904 by the gift of 5,000 francs a year for two years from Mrs. J. J. Hoff, an American, the wife of a business man in Paris. Mrs. Hoff, who had formerly been President of the Y.W.C.A. in the city of Detroit, became deeply interested in this project in Paris. Under her chairmanship of the committee that sponsored it, and with her generous financial support and the guidance of experienced Association workers whom she recruited from the United States, there developed a British-American Y.W.C.A. in Paris which carried on a large and varied program. Its finances and program were entirely in the hands of the special committee in Paris, but its General Secretary was regarded in some sense as a World's Committee worker, and her appointment was ratified by the World's Executive Committee.

With the development of an International Home in Rome the World's Executive Committee had a much more intimate connection. A gift of 200,000 lira from Miss Helen Gould of New York City made possible the purchase of property for this Home. Many perplexing problems arose, however, over the relation to the project of the Italian National Committee, the Committee of the Y.W.C.A. in Rome, the special International Home Committee, and an Advisory Committee of gentlemen in Rome whose duty it was to deal with a Trust Company in London, created by the World's Y.W.C.A. and holding the property in its name. Between 1907 and 1911, the Executive Committee gave more time and thought to the problems of the International Home in Rome than to almost any other single piece of work. In the course of these years, several of its members made special visits to Rome in order to advise with the various committees. Eventually, though only after a three months' special visit by Miss Reynolds, whom the Executive Committee called in for the purpose, the Home became a recognized part of the work of the Italian National Committee, carried on by it under a special committee.

The significance for the World's Y.W.C.A. of the international centers in Paris and Rome lay in the struggle to arrive at a general policy in relation to such projects, at that time so much needed in continental countries where the National Committees were not as yet able to cope with the problem. Since these Homes were especially concerned with students, the question of their relation with the World's Student Christian Federation was also involved. As time went on, National Committees and local Associations more and more took work for the foreign young women within their countries as a normal part of their programs, and the World's Committee ceased to carry responsibility for it.

In the field of relationships with other international organizations, particularly the World's Y.M.C.A. and the World's Student Christian Federation, the decade was one of important policy making. Here, as elsewhere, policy was developed not out of theoretical discussion but through dealing with practical situations as they arose. The World's Y.W.C.A. was greatly influenced by the policy and program of its older, larger, and more experienced brother-organization, the Y.M.C.A. The similarities in the needs of youth of both sexes and the common Christian basis and aim of the two Associations made close relation and cooperation natural on a world scale as well as on the local and national scale. At the same time, the World's Y.W.C.A., like the national and local Associations in most countries, held the firm conviction that it had a special call to develop a work for and with young women by women. Two factors tended constantly to reinforce this conviction: the revolutionary changes in the life of women, far more revolutionary than in the life of men in the same period, which called for specialized consideration; the Y.W.C.A.'s growing consciousness of itself as a woman's movement, and of the need of women themselves to gain experience and skill in the administration of organizational affairs.

This latter need, together with the fact that women were in almost all organizational fields a minority group, at a disadvantage as far as the opportunity for carrying responsibility and exercising leadership was concerned, has been throughout the years an important factor in Y.M.C.A. and Y.W.C.A. relationships. To the mind of the generous, kindly brother organization, a relationship that approached closely to amalgamation often seemed desirable, whether the field was local, national or world. It seemed natural also that in such a joint organization the chief positions of leadership should be occupied by men. But the last hundred years have been for women years in which they were growing to maturity in public life and action. In almost every country their experience has shown that to attain this they must be "on their own" in a very real and final sense. For all these reasons the relations between the Y.M.C.A. and the Y.W.C.A. over the years have reflected both the patent need of close partnership in youth programs, and the equally patent need, from the women's point of view, of maintaining a freedom and independence which they instinctively felt would be endangered by anything that blurred the separateness of the two movements.

The actual situations out of which the World's Y.W.C.A. developed its policy with relation to the Y.M.C.A. were various in kind. A question of local cooperation in Italy, laid before the Executive Committee by Madame Schalck[17] and discussed at the meeting of the World's Committee that preceded the Paris Conference, raised the question of "affiliation between the Y.M.C.A. and the Y.W.C.A."[18] The fact that in Norway, in 1905, the work for young women hitherto carried by three separate national organizations was united in one National Christian Association working with both boys and girls, raised the issue of the basis on which the young women members of a joint Y.M.C.A. and Y.W.C.A. could be related to the World's Y.W.C.A.

In July 1907 a meeting of Y.M.C.A. and Y.W.C.A. representatives of National Committees was held in London "to discuss the advantages and disadvantages of joint meetings in local Associations and the question of cooperation between committees of the two organizations."[19] Among the Y.W.C.A. representatives present at this meeting were Madame Schalck (Italy), Frau Ufer (Germany), Miss Mellin (Sweden), and

143

Lady Procter representing the National Committee of India. After discussion, this meeting approved the following statement regarding cooperation:

In view of the number and acivity of secular agencies at work among young people, and a strong feeling of the importance of cooperation in the present day, it is increasingly necessary that societies whose name is Christian and whose aim and methods are identical should cooperate as far as possible. Spiritual work for young men and young women is indeed their very *raison d'être,* and unitedly they should manifest a strong testimony to the claims of Christ on the young men and young women of each generation. The methods by which Y.M.C.A.s and Y.W.C.A.s can cooperate has been a subject of careful thought and prayer by the World's Y.W.C.A. Committee since their conference in Paris in 1906, and they have thought it well to ask the opinion of National Committees in their federation.

It is suggested that regular communication between the World's Y.M.C.A. and Y.W.C.A. Committees is desirable in order that each should know the contemplated forward movements of the other, so as to obtain information as to the scope for fresh work in new lands, and the conditions to be met on the field. This inter-communication might be effected (1) by meetings like the present, (2) by occasional attendance of the respective General Secretaries of the two World's Committees at conferences, and (3) by each World's Committee furnishing to the other such parts of the General Secretary's reports as bear on the other's work, with contemplated developments or difficulties in the field.

The minutes of the same meeting record further, that:

The World's Committee of the Y.W.C.A. desire to express their warmest gratitude to Mr. Sarasin Warnery, the President, and to the International Committee of the Y.M.C.A. for the sympathy and kindness shown to them in the formal conference and in the informal gatherings of the past week. They are greatly encouraged by the mutual consultations and friendly discussions which took place, and believe that the cooperation already begun between the two Associations will result in an increase of blessing and furtherance of God's work among young men and young women in all parts of the world.[20]

The point of view of the World's Y.W.C.A. is clear: consultation and frequent interchange regarding plans, problems, and experience are urgently desired; organizational unity of any kind is not to be thought of. It is also evident from the record that the Y.M.C.A. made considerable concession to the Y.W.C.A. in this matter. In practice, however, the relationship was not so easily settled. When, in 1908, Mrs. E. W. Moore is asked to represent the Y.W.C.A. at the Plenary Meeting of the World's Y.M.C.A., Mr. Warnery asks for the advice of the Y.W.C.A. Executive Committee regarding the affiliation to each World Movement of "mixed Associations", that is, Associations such as the one in Norway, including both men and women, "as the World's Y.M.C.A. is undecided what action to take."

The Executive Committee discussed this matter, and Mrs. Moore replies to Mr. Warnery that:

> The Executive Committee of the World's Y.W.C.A. has had under consideration the subject of mixed Associations, with no separate meetings of young men and young women. They have always maintained that such Associations do not fulfill the Y.M.C.A. and the Y.W.C.A. ideals, but they earnestly desire to promote any work on Association lines which will advance the moral, physical and spiritual welfare of young women. Their policy hitherto has been to suggest to such mixed Associations the advantages to be derived from separate meetings, where, necessarily, more frank treatment of many subjects can be adopted. The Executive Committee have not been authorized either by the World's Conference or by the biennial World's Committee meeting to formulate any fresh policy and are therefore unable to make any further pronouncement on the subject.[21]

When Mrs. Moore reported the discussion at the Y.M.C.A. Plenary Meeting, she presented three resolutions which the Y.M.C.A. was suggesting as the basis of future policy on the part of both organizations:

1. The World's Committee of Y.M.C.A. recognizes the difficulties which in certain countries have led to the formation of mixed Associations of Y.M.C.A., but they can neither recommend the formation of such nor cooperate in the foundation of such societies.
2. The National Alliances of countries belonging to the World's Alliance of Y.M.C.A. may, if circumstances do not allow the formation of separate Associations for young men only, admit the male sections of mixed Associations, provided these have adopted the Paris basis.
3. The World's Committee of the Y.M.C.A. recommends to the National Councils of the Y.M.C.A. in such countries as are concerned, to work to the effect that women members of mixed Associations in their respective nations should be induced to join the national organization of the Y.W.C.A. in their own country.[22]

That the World's Y.W.C.A. felt that these resolutions represented a considerable yielding on the part of the Y.M.C.A. to a point of view that it did not altogether share is indicated by the recommendation that a letter be sent to the Y.M.C.A. "expressing the sympathy of the Executive Committee with the conciliatory spirit of the resolutions." The Y.M.C.A. was perhaps moved to some inward impatience by the further information, conveyed in the same letter, that "no action could be taken by the Executive Committee until the next World's Conference," that is, until 1910. Meantime, the Executive Committee voted with characteristic caution "to send the resolutions to their National Committees with a request for opinion."[23]

In the following December, Dr. Mott met with the Executive Committee and had laid before him letters from Finland and Sweden which showed "strong anti-feeling to the advisibility of mixed Associations." Also discussed with him was the application of the Young People's Union of Norway for affiliation with the World's Y.W.C.A., to which the Executive Committee had replied that it "could only affiliate them if they had a separate organization for their women's department."[24] At this meeting Dr. Mott advised the Executive Committee to send to the next international meeting of the Y.M.C.A. a resolution emphasizing the importance of having separate men's and women's departments in mixed Associations. Thus a policy that provided for cooperation but discouraged any trend toward amalgamation was at length established.

One practical field in which, during these years, there was cooperation between the World's Y.M.C.A. and the World's Y.W.C.A. was the preparation of the program for the World's Week of Prayer. The value of a common approach to this Week, both in time and in material used, had long been recognized, and the custom of having the program prepared in alternate years by each Association had been established. This plan had proved very rewarding in many ways, providing as it did a united expression of the deepest common purpose of the two organizations, but it was not always easy to carry out. In the summer of 1908 the Y.M.C.A. sent word that it could not use the topic selected that year by the Y.W.C.A., as it did not translate well. Denmark and Germany, however, both requested that the topics for the Y.M.C.A. and the Y.W.C.A. be the same, since they often had joint meetings. After discussion, the Executive Committee of the Y.W.C.A. decided to adopt the topic chosen by the Y.M.C.A. Two years later the Y.M.C.A. again was "unable to adopt the Week of Prayer topics chosen by the Y.W.C.A." and chose its own subject "with special reference to the international conference."

Sometimes also the Y.W.C.A. had difficulty in using the material furnished by the Y.M.C.A. In July 1912 the Executive Committee commented on the fact that the material had not yet come from the Y.M.C.A.

and expressed the desire "that every effort should be made to make use of the subjects prepared by the Y.M.C.A." The minutes of November 7, 1912, record that the "scripture topic received from the World's Y.M.C.A. had been considerably revised and amplified," and the Committee voted to ask that when next someone from the World's Y.M.C.A. was in London, he should confer with the World's Y.W.C.A. about the topic for 1913. The result of this conference was the decision that, since the Y.M.C.A. used the Week of Prayer for purposes of demonstration and appeal as well as for prayer, each Association should make its own choice of subject and scripture, but would include in the program a prayer for both Asociations.[25]

Similar yet also different factors were influential in determining the basis of relationship of the World's Y.W.C.A. with the World's Student Christian Federation. In Great Britain and on the Continent, as well as in the Dominions, the Student Christian Movement was quite separate from the Y.M.C.A. and the Y.W.C.A., and composed of both men and women. In the United States, however, the student work for men was a part of the Y.M.C.A. and that for women, of the Y.W.C.A.

In each country there was strong championship of the particular system there in use. The British pattern was praised for its recognition of equality and cooperation between men and women and for the significance of an entirely distinct Student Movement in which men and women together faced the problems, individual and social, of a new age. The American pattern was upheld by those who thought that it afforded more opportunity for the development of leadership on the part of women, and for dealing with the problems and interests of the woman movement. It was felt by believers in the American system that it was a great advantage to both the Y.M.C.A. and the Y.W.C.A. to have within their organizations the vital, progressive student groups from which came the leadership for other parts of the work, and conversely, that membership in the Association gave the students valuable and realistic contacts with workers in business and industry.

To those reared in the independent student movements, the connection with the Y.M.C.A. and the Y.W.C.A. often seemed inhibiting. The relationship it involved with the all-too-often conservative group of city board members at times limited the democratic control of the movement by the students themselves and the freedom to pioneer of the naturally more daring student group. It also tended to impress upon the student work an institutionalism similar to that which was demanded by the needs of the city work. In reality, the different types of student work were a natural development from the different social pattern as a whole which pertained in Europe and in America.

The World's Student Christian Federation, from its beginning, included both types of student organizations. In those countries where the students were a part of the Y.M.C.A. and the Y.W.CA., the Student Departments united in a joint Student Y.M.C.A.-Y.W.C.A. for purposes of affiliation with the World's Student Christian Federation. Thus these student movements had a double relationship—Y.W.C.A. students were a part of the World's Y.W.C.A.; jointly with the student Y.M.C.A. they were an integral part of the World's Student Christian Federation.

The tension created within the two World Movements by these organizational differences in national movements, and the effort it cost to accomplish their integration, are revealed by a number of instances in these years. The relation of the two organizations was discussed at the Paris Conference in 1906, where Miss Hermione Baart de la Faille of Holland, and several British leaders of the World's Student Christian Federation were present as fraternal delegates. The conference approved the following recommendation regarding cooperation: "In view of the fact that student work in some lands is affiliated with the W.S.C.F. as well as with the World's Y.W.C.A., the World's Committee recommends that all National Committees cooperate with the W.S.C.F."[26] The satisfaction felt by the World's Student Christian Federation over this recognition, by the conference, of responsibility to cooperate with them is revealed in a letter from Miss Margaret Bretherton, a Student Secretary, to Miss Rouse, Secretary of the World's Student Christian Federation:

> The conference as a whole, from the Federation point of view, was exceedingly satisfactory. . . . The World's Committee and, I think, all of the American leaders at any rate, understand what the Federation is and what its relations are and ought to be with the Y.W.C.A. in different countries. . . . The American delegation was . . . very understanding concerning the reasons why student work and the Y.W.C.A. cannot, in every country, be organically united.[27]

The practical problems of relationship between the Y.W.C.A. and the World's Student Christian Federation arose, as did the Y.W.C.A. internal problems of organization, especially out of the work on the foreign field, for here British and American workers each tended to reproduce their own ideas of student organization and relationships. In Japan and China the pattern was distinctly American, and this was largely unchallenged, since both the missionary and the Association leadership in these countries was predominantly American. But in India, where both British and American secretaries for student work were employed by the Student Department of the India National Committee, and where the Missionary Settlement of University Women carried on work for students in Bombay, considerable adjustment was necessary. Miss Rouse, who had worked a year in the Missionary Settlement and had been also a traveling secretary for student work in the United States, was the moving spirit in bringing about a co-operative plan of student work in India, in which the responsibility was carried jointly by the "Settlers" and the American secretaries. Although this relationship was eventually dissolved, it was a significant step in the development of student work on the foreign field.

But the differences in viewpoint and the shortcomings of the American type of organization were keenly felt by British workers. Miss Bretherton, who went out from England to do student work in Madras under the Y.W.C.A., writes frankly to Miss Rouse of her difficulties:

> I can't help feeling that the India National Committee doesn't really understand the ideals of the Student Movement and thinks only of the Y.W.C.A. and the formation of the Y.W.C.A. branches among students, which doesn't seem to me to be the thing needful, or rather, it should be looked upon as only a means to an end. Also, I've a feeling that the India National Committee thinks I have too many Student Movement ideas and too few Y. W. ones. . . . I think it should be much more recognized that the student work, in the nature of the work and of the members, ought to be the first part of the Y.W.C.A. to show signs of leadership and self-government. . . . I do not feel that student work in the East should be separated from the Y.M. and the Y.W., but I do think it should be much more specialized within each, having its own national student committee as soon as possible. . . . I don't see even why the student work shouldn't have its own name (Student Union or Student Movement with the addition 'affiliated with the Y.M.C.A. and Y.W.C.A.').[28]

The World's Committee, having tried and failed in 1899 to secure Miss Rouse as a Student Secretary on the World's staff, did not itself develop a Student Department, but through the close cooperation of its staff with the staff of the World's Student Christian Federation the work of the two organizations was correlated in such a way that the experience of each was available to the other. In this it was immeasurably helped by the fact that Miss Rouse, Secretary of the World's Student Christian Federation, was also a member of the World's Y.W.C.A. Executive Committee and by her thorough understanding of and sympathy with both movements helped to make the cooperation fruitful. The close connection during the same years of Dr. John R. Mott with the World's Student Christian Federation and the Young Men's Christian Association established the same kind of understanding between the W.S.C.F. and the World's

Y.M.C.A. Out of the intimate relationship of Miss Rouse, Dr. Mott and Miss Spencer, there developed a relationship between the World's Y.M.C.A., the World's Y.W.C.A. and the World's Student Christian Federation which succeeded in large measure in utilizing for the good of the whole the advantages of the varying types of student work.

In June 1914 the fifth World's Y.W.C.A. Conference met at Stockholm, with an attendance of over 800 delegates coming from twenty-three countries. The Y.W.C.A.'s growing consciousness of itself as a woman's movement was embodied in the conference theme, "The Unfolding of the True Plan for Woman in God's Purpose for the World". The World's Committee, in its report to the conference, said:

> We are in the midst of a widespread agitation concerning women, which has been called the "Woman's Movement" and which has greatly grown during the past four years. In some countries it has reached an acute stage, in others it is just in its beginnings. But it is a movement of which we form a part, and it brings to us questions which we as a World's Y.W.C.A. must face and do our utmost to help solve. . . . The modern woman can only find her full satisfaction, her complete liberty and her truest service in discipleship to Jesus Christ, and as his followers we would seek to learn afresh how to bring his gospel to bear more powerfully and effectively upon her problems and her needs. . . . We believe that God has brought the World's Y.W.C.A. to this point in its development that we, its members, may take our full share in helping to solve the problems of the adjustment of modern womanhood to the new environment of the twentieth century.[29]

Addresses by leaders from both within and without the Y.W.C.A. in many countries were given on various phases of the conference theme, such as "The Christian Ideal for Women", "Spiritual Impulses Underlying the Woman's Movement", "The Position of Women as Affected by Christianity in the East", "Women in Family Life, in Community and National Life, in Church Life", and on "Training of Women for Public Life". The sense of these matters was embodied in three resolutions:

> This conference desires to record its conviction that although the economic pressure of the present day has forced so large a number of women out of the home sphere, home life is of vital importance for the extension of the Kingdom of God and for the well-being of the nation. . . .
>
> In view of the great need of a Christian standard of national righteousness in all parts of the world and the increasing influence and power exerted by women in the State, this confer-

ence urges national and local Associations to place before their members the duty of good citizenship, to endeavor to fit them more adequately for loyal and efficient service to the State, and to urge both leaders and members, as a matter of Christian conviction, to avail themselves of opportunities of civic and national service. . . .

Whereas a greater share in the work of the church is devolving upon women, this conference recommends to national and local committees the careful and intelligent preparation of their members for the responsibilities and privileges of church life, in order that as Christian women they may make their peculiar contribution to the church and serve it efficiently.[30]

These resolutions, together with the constitutional revision of the statement of basis and aim,[31] the Scheme of Relationships[32] adopted at this conference, and the resolutions relating to social and industrial problems adopted at Berlin,[33] record the development of the World's Y.W.C.A. since its organization twenty years earlier, with regard to its conception of its purpose, its function in relation to its constituent national movements, and its field of effort. These changes, however, were not alterations in fundamental purpose but adaptations in the expression of that purpose in order to meet new circumstances. The pattern of organization and the leadership were still largely Anglo-Saxon. Yet some not inconsiderable steps had been taken in the direction of an organization more truly international, interracial and interconfessional in character. The biennial meetings of the World's Committee, in which members from actively affiliated National Associations took a vital part, increasingly furnished the directives for the Executive Committee and determined the content of World's Y.W.C.A. conference agendas. The conferences themselves had ceased to be largely a means of acquaintance and exchange of national reports, and had become meetings in which broad lines of world policy recommended by the World's Committee were debated and voted upon.

It was with profound regret that the Stockholm Conference accepted the resignation, because of illness, of the President, Mrs. Tritton, but in the Honorable Mrs. Montague Waldegrave, whom they elected to succeed her, they knew that the same traditions of deep evangelical faith and broad international outlook would continue.

Though by no means unaware of the national tensions and the disturbing tendencies in the life of the times, the fifth World's Y.W.C.A. Conference came to its close with no suspicion of how utterly new and how immensely tragic the environment of the twentieth century would become, even before some of the delegates from more distant lands should reach their homes. But when the outbreak of war separated the governments of some of the nations whose women had experienced so profound a comradeship at Stockholm, it was found that this fellowship in Christ and in work for his Kingdom was stronger than the barriers raised by suffering and war.

REFERENCES

[1] See Chapter 6, p. 72.

[2] Third World's Y.W.C.A. Conference, 1906, Report.

[3] Wilson, Elizabeth. *World Cooperation of the Y.W.C.A.s of the U.S.A.*, 1929, p. 17.

[4] World's Executive Committee, November 12, 1908, Minutes.

[5] Wilson, Elizabeth. *World Cooperation*, pp. 42, 43.

[6] World's Executive Committee, July 10, 1911, Minutes.

[7] Fifth World's Y.W.C.A. Conference, 1914, Report, pp. 304-5.

[8] Fourth World's Y.W.C.A. Conference, 1910, Report, pp. 215, 216.

[9] World's Y.W.C.A. Annual Report for 1906, p. 21.

[10] *Ibid.*, 1907, p. 15.

[11] *Ibid.*, 1908, p. 26.

[12] This led, just after the close of this decade, to the sending out to Nairobi, as General Secretary, of Miss Maude Saunders, whose two sisters were already deep in the work of the Association—Miss Grace Saunders in Sofia, Bulgaria, and Miss Una Saunders, formerly a member of the World's Executive Committee and at this time the General Secretary of the National Dominion Council of Canada.

[13] Annual Report for 1912, pp. 14, 15.

[14] Executive Committee, March 16, 1911, Minutes.

[15] Paine, E. *Rosa E. Margerison; a Pioneer of Y.W.C.A. Work in Egypt and Palestine.*

[16] Fifth World's Y.W.C.A. Conference, 1914, Report, p. 279.

[17] Executive Committee, January 11, 1906, Minutes.

[18] *Ibid.*, February 8, 1906.

[19] Executive Committee, February 14, 1907, Minutes.

[20] Executive Committee, July 18, 1907, Minutes.

[21] *Ibid.*, July 16, 1908.

[22] Executive Committee, October 8, 1908, Minutes.

[23] *Ibid.*

[24] In 1912 the Y.W.C.A. of Norway, having achieved independent organization within the Christian Youth Association, was received in corresponding membership in the World's Association. Its basis of membership, however, was Lutheran, not interdenominational.

[25] Later, when more frequent consultation was possible, the former custom was renewed.

[26] Third World's Y.W.C.A. Conference. 1906, Report, p. 45.

[27] Letter of June 1, 1906.

[28] Letter of April 10, 1910.

[29] Fifth World's Y.W.C.A. Conference, 1914, Report, pp. 263, 264.

[30] Fifth World's Y.W.C.A. Conference, 1914, Report, pp. 20, 24, 25.

[31] See Chapter 10, p. 131.

[32] See Chapter 9, p. 117.

[33] Chapter 10, p. 125.

[34] *Ibid.*, p. 133.

*The history of the Association up to 1920 has fallen
into three well-defined periods: a period of organization and extension, 1894-1904, under its first General
Secretary, Miss Reynolds; a period under her successor, Miss Clarissa Spencer, of closer linking up of
National Associations, the developing of work on a
world basis, Trinitarian and profoundly evangelical
in doctrine, intended to meet the needs of members
in all parts of the Christian Church; an agreed system of work done by the National Associations outside their own boundaries, and the beginnings of
study of many of the interests that have become so
important in later years. This period came to a rather
brilliant climax at the Stockholm Conference of 1914.
The war, following immediately after, brought about
the third period, covering the years 1914 to 1920,
when some National Associations grew immensely
in numbers and activities but the World's Y.W.C.A.
as a whole was obliged to mark time.*
NIVEN, CHARLOTTE T. *A Fifteen Years' Survey*, 1935.

CHAPTER 12   WAR AND THE WORLD'S Y.W.C.A.:
1914-1920

THE STOCKHOLM Conference in 1914," says
a report written some years later, "raised hopes of a period of expansion on all sides."[1] The outbreak of war barely six weeks after the
close of that conference seemed to give a shattering blow to those high ex-
pectations. In its unpreparedness for this emergency the World's Young
Women's Christian Association shared the common experience of other
social and religious organizations. It is true that at the conference of the
World's Student Christian Federation at Lake Mohonk, New York, in
1913, a few delegates, chiefly those from Germany, were very pessimistic
with regard to international relations and even stressed the possibility of
war. But so widespread was the conviction that the nations had passed
beyond this method of settling their differences that these warnings had
little effect.

The impact of the war upon the World's Y.W.C.A. was immediate and
drastic. The possibilities of international contact through travel were suddenly greatly restricted. Communication, even by correspondence, became

in some cases difficult, in others impossible. All plans for future meetings of the World's Committee had to be held in abeyance, since a meeting which some active members were prevented by war from attending was unthinkable. The location of the World's headquarters in one of the chief belligerent countries and the almost entirely British personnel of the Executive Committee and the staff further limited the Committee's ability to function as the representative body of a world organization under war conditions.

In 1913 Miss Spencer had offered her resignation, to take effect in 1914, following the precedent set by Miss Reynolds of a ten-year term of office for the General Secretary. No successor had been secured, however, and the Executive Committee now asked her to continue "for the duration". Following the Stockholm Conference she had gone to the United States, and the National Board of the United States proposed, in view of the curtailment of the World's Y.W.C.A. work, that she should remain there and serve on its national staff. This proposal the Executive Committee accepted, with the understanding that she should be free to return to the World's staff whenever conditions should permit. Miss Knight, and later Miss Gladys Bretherton were lent to the British Y.W.C.A. for short periods to help in the emergency work thrust upon that Association by the war. The coming of Baroness Olga Meyendorff, who was to have begun work as a traveling secretary in the autumn of 1914, was postponed. Miss Rickard, the World's Y.W.C.A. worker in St. Petersburg, since it was impossible for her to return to Russia, was also lent to the British Association, the World's Committee continuing for six months to pay her salary. The Executive Committee felt that its main task during the war must be to maintain the links between the Associations on both sides of the conflict, and to gather and disseminate as much news as possible about the Associations and about those tendencies and events that particularly affected the life of women.

One act of fellowship, however, it was possible to arrange and carry through during the war. It had been agreed before the war came that Miss Spencer should spend the Christmas season of 1914 in Berlin with the leaders of the German Association. Early in December its President Pastor Thiele, and Fräulein Zarnack, the General Secretary, sent an urgent plea that this promised visit be not given up, since it would now have very special value. The Executive Committee accordingly arranged for her release from her work in the United States for this purpose. She reached Berlin on Christmas Eve, 1914, having been escorted through the Netherlands by friends from the Dutch Association, and met at the German border by leaders of the German movement. She spent two weeks in Berlin, and after stopping a few days in Copenhagen for conference with

Danish leaders, she reported to the World's Executive Committee in London before returning to New York. By this visit Miss Spencer was able personally to carry to the German Association assurances of the unbroken bond of fellowship and love of the World's Y.W.C.A. She also learned at first hand of the thoughts and feelings of the German leaders, and was able to interpret these to the Executive Committee.

With this important exception, the work of the Executive Committee from 1914 to 1918 consisted largely of correspondence with such Associations as could be reached in this way, and the continued publication of *The Women's International Quarterly,* in which appeared inspirational articles, articles bearing on questions affecting women, and news of the Associations. In a sense it was truly a period of "marking time", yet it was more than that. The minutes of the regularly held monthly meetings of the Executive Committee show that there came up for consideration and decision many matters of concern to Associations whose work was continuing comparatively unhampered, or to those that because of war were facing grave new conditions.

There were continuing problems regarding Bulgaria, where in spite of difficulties and uncertainties, Miss Grace Saunders remained at her post until early in 1916. Egypt, where wartime conditions immediately increased the scope and the importance of Y.W.C.A. activities, was frequently on the agenda. There was much correspondence with the Y.W.C.A. of Norway about its constitution, a correspondence that led in 1916 to the adoption by that Association of an interdenominational basis, and the return of this charter member of the World's Y.W.C.A. to active affiliation with the World's Committee. There was long consideration given to India, where the changes in the life of women brought about by the war gave the Y.W.C.A. an unprecedented opportunity. The minutes record that the Executive Committee especially deplored the fact that work in India was so largely confined to the "extremely small Eurasian group" and expressed anew its conviction that the India Association should concentrate on vernacular work. The question of a separate national organization for Malaya was again and again before the Committee, though it was finally decided that the time was not opportune for this.

There was some agitation for the formation of a sub-committee for the continent of Europe, composed of leaders from various European Associations, with offices in a neutral country. The Executive Committee laid this proposal before the National Committee for advice. Although some Associations frankly favored the idea, others were doubtful and some were definitely opposed. It was finally agreed that little would be gained by such a move. The discussion, however, pointed up the growing conviction that the Executive Committee should be a more representative international group. It also raised the question whether London should continue to be the location of the headquarters of the World's Association.

As the war went on, the Executive Committee became acutely aware of the needs of the masses of young women in every country with whom the Association had no touch, who were exposed to the strains and pressures of war under new and bewildering conditions. This led it to consider more definitely than hitherto the responsibility of the Association for *all* girls and not only, as some Associations assumed, for the comparatively small group of their own members. The matter was presented both in *The Women's International Quarterly* and in a letter sent to National Associations. This letter, after noting the new position that women would undoubtedly hold after the war, said:

> We are unable to resist the impression that this change in the position of women and girls constitutes the great opportunity of our Association and yet our great problem. . . . Our Associations with their present organization and program seem to present little attraction to some of the girls who are most in need of its influence. Must we not in a new way try to show these girls that Christ is the Lord of all life? Your Executive Committee is specially concerned at the time over the problem of recreation.[2]

The letter then proceeds with utmost care and tact to raise the question of policy in regard to "certain forms of amusement, such as the dance and the drama, which are increasing in influence and popularity in nearly all communities," and to suggest the opportunity which the Association has for "educating young people in taste and discrimination" in such amusements. "Could we use more courageously the advantage we have in the possession of hostels and clubrooms to allow of greater freedom of intercourse between young men and young women, even, possibly of their dancing and acting together under good conditions?"[3]

An article in the same number of *The Quarterly*, entitled "An Agonizing Problem", probably represents the reaction of Association leaders in many countries to this letter. It takes the stand that the introduction of dancing and dramatics for girls and boys together would imperil the very foundations of the Association's work, though it suggests that much more might be done with rhythmic gymnastics, sports and music, especially singing, to make the program of wider appeal.

The minutes of the Executive Committee add many further details to the picture of what was happening in the World Movement in these war years. They record the use of the World's Y.W.C.A. scholarship at the National Training School in New York by candidates from Switzerland, France, Norway, China and New Zealand; the sending out of the first

156

foreign secretary by the newly organized Foreign Department of Sweden; the great increase in the calls for trained leadership in India, China and South America; and the appointment of a large number of secretaries to foreign service.

The records, however, fail to suggest the extent and importance of the changes wrought in the Y.W.C.A. during and immediately following the years of war. Developments were taking place in Great Britain, in China, in Europe, in the United States and in the countries of South America, of which we get only fleeting glimpses in Executive Committee minutes, yet which made the World Movement that came together at Champéry, Switzerland, in 1920 for its first peacetime gathering something new and different from that which had met at Stockholm on the eve of war. It was these developments that made it possible to record later that "the hopes of a period of expansion raised at Stockholm were more than fulfilled during the difficult period of the war."[4]

In Great Britain, on the outbreak of the war, the Y.W.C.A. was plunged at once into greatly enlarged activities along quite new lines. Within five days came a call to help the great numbers of girls of foreign nationality, particularly German and Austrian, who were stranded in England. "Hundreds of such . . . were housed, fed and comforted, their permits and passports arranged for and themselves finally seen off in special trains provided by the government."[5] Then came the rush of Belgian refugees into England, and the opening of a club for the women and girls among them. Clubs were also opened in the neighborhood of military training camps, where British girls could meet their soldier friends.

The greatest expansion came, however, when the Association undertook to serve the thousands of women and girls at work in munition factories. Between June 1915 and February 1919 the Y.W.C.A. Munition Workers Welfare Committee started one hundred centers (51 canteens, 40 clubs and 9 hostels), and in addition took over the management of a government colony of 700 girls working on dangerous war material.[6] Later a similar service for women government clerks was undertaken. In 1917, when the girls of the Women's Army Auxiliary Corps (the WAACS) were sent abroad to replace men in various services, the Y.W.C.A. followed them to France, opening there forty-three clubs and recreation centers for their use. The extent of the increase in Y.W.C.A. activities is vividly reflected in the budget of the National Council, the income of which in 1913 was under £6,000, but rose in 1916 to £104,000 and in 1918 to more than £269,000.

Much of this emergency work came to a close with the end of the war, but there was left a permanent enlargement of the constituency of the Association, with an increased sense of responsibility born of contacts made in war time, for all the girls of the nation. These things had a profound effect on both the policy and the program of the Y.W.C.A. of Great Britain after the war. It was perhaps this experience of the British Association that influenced the World's Executive Committee to write its letter to National Associations urging wider outreach through recreation.

On the other side of the world, the Y.W.C.A. of China, for entirely different reasons, experienced an amazing growth during these years. The era of expansion for this National Association, of which the years 1914 to 1918 were the center, began in 1911, with the revolution that established the Chinese Republic. Its climax was reached in 1923, in the first national Y.W.C.A. convention. In this twelve-year period the Y.W.C.A. grew from a small group of some twenty student Associations, one city Association, one Chinese secretary and eight foreign secretaries, into a vigorous national movement of more than eighty student Associations, twelve city Associations, fifty-one Chinese and eighty-seven foreign secretaries.[7]

This remarkable development was the result of a cooperative enterprise of Chinese and Western women under circumstances unique in the history of the Young Women's Christian Association. The time was propitious for the creation of an organization such as the Y.W.C.A. in China. The vision of it had been present in both East and West ever since the China Y.M.C.A. had organized a National Committee of Women in 1899 and the American Association had sent out Estelle Paddock to be its General Secretary in 1905.

Growth at first had been slow, but with the revolution came the sudden opening up of opportunity. The new freedom and the spirit of reform found expression particularly in youth organizations, among women as well as men. There was an eagerness to adopt Western ways and methods and a desire to receive help from abroad. Moreover, it was a time favorable to the spread of Christian influence. Many of the revolutionary leaders had been educated in Christian schools and colleges. Dr. Sun Yat Sen himself was a member of the Christian Church. In America the Y.W.C.A. was ready to respond to the challenge. In the years 1912 and 1913, ten new secretaries went out to China. By 1914 Great Britain had sent out two secretaries. More important perhaps than the number of secretaries at this critical juncture, was their quality, for this call appealed strongly to young women of exceptional intellectual and spiritual qualifications.

Among the foreign secretaries in China at this time was Miss Grace Coppock, who had gone to Shanghai in 1906, fresh from her studies at the University of Nebraska, to be the General Secretary of the first Chinese city Association. One of her fundamental convictions regarding her task was shown very early. At the close of her period of language study, although the Shanghai Committee insisted that there was no Chinese woman prepared to be a Y.W.C.A. secretary, she refused to begin her work until a Chinese young woman, Miss Mary Ting, had been appointed as her associate. In 1913, just as the possibilities of expansion were being clearly seen, Miss Coppock became the General Secretary of the National Committee, and her vision and faith in the Y.W.C.A. and in the possibilities of Chinese womanhood contributed in large measure to the achievements of the next few years.

At the Stockholm Conference in 1914 Miss Coppock put the challenge of China squarely and vigorously before the conference, stressing especially the opportunity among the large number of women students, the vast majority of whom were not in mission schools but in government or private institutions, with no touch with Christianity. She told of the successful evangelistic work carried on among students by the Y.M.C.A. and of the great readiness of women students for this same message. "The mission body of China has asked us to take the responsibility of bringing Christianity to these students. Whether we prove equal to the task depends upon the Church of the West."

The report of the China National Committee to the Stockholm Conference reveals that the policy of placing authority as rapidly as possible in Chinese hands had so far developed that while

> four years ago but half the Board of Directors of the Shanghai Association were Chinese, the other half being British and American, today all the Directors are Chinese women, taking full responsibility for the Association, raising a heavy budget, and planning to purchase land for a permanent building site.[8]

The demands of the new era on the limited number of women of modern education were so many that it was no easy task to find these leaders for the Association. Yet in 1919 it was possible to make the announcement that the Executive Committee of the National Association was composed entirely of Chinese women. In the following year Miss Ting Shu-ching, one of the three members of the first graduating class of Peking Union College for Women, became the General Secretary of the Association in Peking, the first Chinese woman to hold such a position in the Y.W.C.A.

If the Y.W.C.A. was to take advantage of the extraordinary opportunities before it in these years, much help must come from outside China, both to initiate the new work and to train Chinese leaders. The China National Committee was fully conscious of this. In 1917, it decided "that no less than thirty-six new foreign secretaries are needed immediately and that Miss Coppock must go to America at once to recruit them." This she did. The record continues:

Great was the excitement when within the course of the year nineteen actually appeared. The number steadily increased until it reached its climax in 1920, when twenty-six new workers landed in China.[9]

These new workers, making the total eighty-seven in 1923, were most of them from the United States, fruit of several recruiting trips by Miss Coppock, but they came also from Great Britain, Sweden, Canada, Australia and Norway. Thus another goal of the China Association was achieved —that its foreign workers should not come from one country only, but should form a truly international staff, bringing to the Association the variety of experience within the World Movement. The China Association has, it is true, been largely patterned after that of the United States, but to a large degree it has been the product of Chinese thinking and planning for the peculiar needs of China, consciously seeking the gifts of spirit and experience from all the older Associations.

After 1920, the post-war problems of the world, and particularly the decreased amount in the budget of the Association in the United States available for foreign work, led to a marked decrease in the number of foreign secretaries going to China. Changing conditions in China were also a factor. But the foundations had been firmly laid. Chinese leadership, both volunteer and professional, while far from sufficient for all the needs, was able to take over. An indigenous movement had been created, still needing and desiring much help from the West but making its own decisions regarding the kind of service required from abroad, and ready to take an independent and active part in the councils of the World Movement.

Compared with the strides made by the Y.W.C.A. in China, advance in South America during these years was meager, yet it was of importance in determining the character of the post-war World Movement. Until 1918, Buenos Aires, Argentina, and an early center in Georgetown, British Guiann, were the only Y.W.C.A.'s on the continent of South America. However a Congress of Christian Work in Latin America which was held in Panama in 1916, had stimulated fresh interest in the possibilities there. Miss Spencer, Miss Rouse, representing both the World's Y.W.C.A. Executive Committee and the World's Student Christian Federation, and Mrs. John R Mott, representing the Foreign Department of the National Board if the United States, were all present at this conference, as was Miss Elisa Cortez of the Association in Buenos Aires.

Following the meeting at Panama, Miss Rouse visited South America in the interests of the W.S.C.F. and studied also the work of the Y.W.C.A. in Buenos Aires. This visit proved to be the beginning of an effort on the part of the Association in the United States to enlarge the work in South

Miss Grace Coppock

Miss Ting Shu-ching

America. In 1917 one, in 1918 three, and in 1919 seven American secretaries were sent to the sister continent. Miss Emma Jean Batty, who had been in Buenos Aires since 1906, went to Brazil to open work in Rio de Janeiro. In 1919 Miss Elizabeth MacFarland was appointed Continental Secretary, and a start was made in the development of a plan for the continent as a whole. By the time of the Champéry meeting of the World's Y.W.C.A. in 1920, Association work had been organized in five cities in four South American countries—Buenos Aires, Argentina; Rio de Janeiro, Brazil; Santiago and Valparaiso, Chile; Montevideo, Uruguay.

This expansion was important for the future of the World's Y.W.C.A. not only because it brought another continent into the world fellowship, but because membership in the Latin American Associations was composed largely of young women of Roman Catholic background, and these were present also in the leadership.

If the war years were years of great expansion for the Y.W.C.A. of Great Britain, of transformation for the young Association of China, and of the organization of potentially significant work in South America, they were also years of no less importance in the changes they wrought in the Association in the United States and in some of the countries of Europe.

When the United States entered the war in April 1917, the Y.W.C.A. was thrust at once into a series of war activities similar to those undertaken by the British Association but on an even larger scale. Under a specially created War Work Council, whose chairman was Mrs. James S. Cushman and whose Executive Secretary was the Associate General Secretary of the National Board, Miss Helen A. Davis, budgets many times the size of those for regular work were raised.[10] Regular activities were enormously expanded to meet mounting needs, and in addition, much entirely new work was organized. Club and recreation centers were opened in communities close to military training camps, and "Hostess Houses" were erected to serve as a meeting place for women and girls with their soldier relatives and friends. Projects in housing for women war workers were undertaken. The special problems of colored young women, and of foreign-born women whose bewilderment and fear were increased by their language difficulties and their incomplete adjustment to American life, were dealt with through the work of special committees. Industrial Service Centers were opened near munition plants and in communities directly affected by the war. The various types of work with younger girls within the Association were drawn together into a national movement called the "Girl Reserves".

Like the British Association, the American Y.W.C.A. was called upon to establish Hostess Houses and recreation centers for the thousands of young women who were serving with the army in France as nurses, signal corps girls, telephone operators, etc. In 1917 and 1918 the Association opened and staffed more than eighty such centers.

It was not, however, this expansion of work at home or the work for American women in war service abroad, important as these were, that was of major significance for the World's Y.W.C.A. It was the work done from 1917 to 1920 by American secretaries directly for and with the women and girls of nine continental European countries, which completely altered the Association map of Europe. To meet the requests for work of many kinds and coming in many ways to the Association in the United States, the Overseas Committee of the War Work Council of the National Board was organized, with Mrs. John R. Mott as its Chairman and Miss Sarah S. Lyon as its Executive Secretary.

The first request came from Russia. Here a group of women already acquainted with the Y.W.C.A. appealed for help in meeting the new conditions of freedom and opportunity for women brought about by the revolution of 1917. From France at almost the same moment, in April 1917, came an appeal from Mademoiselle Fuchs, the head of one of the Y.W.C.A. centers in Paris, who was also a member of the National Council of French Women. Mademoiselle Fuchs asked for aid not for the French Y.W.C.A. as such, but for the thousands of French women and girls forced into industry, chiefly munitions, by the war. In Italy, a year later, it was the National Y.W.C.A. itself that formally requested American help to strengthen and extend its own work, which had been dangerously restricted during the war.

Some of the requests were not for war work as such but for assistance in meeting the tragic conditions, and also the great opportunities, of the days immediately following the war's close. Thus in Czechoslovakia, in 1919, the government, through Dr. Alice Masaryk, daughter of the President of the Republic and herself the head of the Czechoslovak Red Cross, asked for help in making a survey of social conditions among women, on the basis of which future social work might be developed. Work in Poland was undertaken at the instigation of Madame de Turczynowicz of the Polish Reconstruction Association. In Belgium the Y.W.C.A. of the United States responded to a request from Countess Hélène Goblet d'Alviella, who during the war had shared in the work done in France and saw that a similar kind of work was urgently needed for Belgian girls in the difficult post-war period. Roumania, Latvia and Estonia were all entered in response to appeals for help from groups of women in those countries, who felt the crying need imposed by the new post-war social conditions but were aware that their own resources were inadequate to meet it.

Some of these appeals to the Y.W.C.A. of the United States, especially those that came after the end of the war, were made through the World's

Y.W.C.A. But this was not always the case. The Scheme of Relationships adopted at Stockholm set forth procedures which were, in the main, followed even in war years, with regard to work in India, Japan, China and South America. This Scheme, however, had not envisaged any such situation as the war created in Europe. Decisions that must be reached with all speed in order to meet an emergency, often grew out of direct and sometimes telegraphic correspondence between the representatives of a country and the Overseas Committee of the War Work Council of the Y.W.C.A. of the United States.

This work, with one or two exceptions, was not undertaken for the purpose of promoting the Y.W.C.A. The American secretaries came to Europe simply to offer whatever skill and experience the Y.W.C.A. could supply to meet the emergency needs of women and girls.[11] Yet in almost every instance the work done commended itself as something for which there was a permanent need. Hence the years of service in Europe given by the Y.W.C.A. of the United States left a permanent residuum of expanded and more diversified Association program in some countries and of an altogether new Y.W.C.A. in others. The story of the work done in each different country illustrates this fact and at the same time reveals the new European scene of the Association world of 1920.

When the first group of American secretaries arrived in France in April 1917, Madame Avril de St. Croix, the President of the National Council of French Women, and her colleagues urged the desperate need of wholesome pleasure and gaiety for the women workers, "to offset the drab monotony of their work and the enforced sordidness of their living conditions."[12] This need supplied the directive for the work undertaken. Between the arrival of that first "unit" and the withdrawal of the last American workers in 1921, more than thirty club and recreation centers, known as *Foyers des Alliées,* had been established in more than twenty cities and towns. This work, mainly for French women in munition factories, was done in cooperation with the French War Department. In addition, five summer camps, a summer conference, an emergency training school for leaders, and a number of other pieces of work had been carried through.

With the end of the war some Foyers were closed, but for others this was the beginning of a period of enlarged usefulness, in which their leadership and equipment were turned to purposes of reconstruction and permanent work. It had been the policy of the Americans to cooperate with all groups concerned with the needs of women, and not with the Y.W.C.A. alone. After the war, five separate French organizations, of which the Y.W.C.A. was one, unitedly formed a Provisional Committee to arrange for the taking over of the work of the Foyers as the Americans withdrew. While much of the work was left in the hands of other organizations, some of the Foyers became a part of the French Y.W.C.A., which thereby received a permanent contribution in extent and method of work as well as a valuable experience in a cooperative undertaking with other organizations for the women and girls of France.

The hope of those women who asked help for Russia[13] was that the Y.W.C.A. might now be organized for Russian girls, and it was with this in view that the work was begun. It was a piece of good fortune for this endeavor that Miss Spencer, who already knew and understood conditions in Russia and represented to them the World's Y.W.C.A. as well as the Association of the United States, was one of the first two secretaries to go to Russia in 1917. Politically and economically the situation was very difficult, but Y.W.C.A. centers which had considerable success were opened in Petrograd and Moscow and a little later in Samara.

It was planned to send a sufficient staff to promote the movement in other cities as well. The unsettled conditions, however, prevented this, though valiant efforts were made during 1918 and 1919 to retain a foothold for possible future developments. Those who had hoped to do actual Y.W.C.A. work in Russia turned to whatever opportunities offered to serve Russian women and girls. The workers who were forced to leave Petrograd and Moscow joined a summer "farm and home" demonstration on the Volga, an educational project led by the Y.M.C.A. in cooperation with Russian agricultural specialists, the boat being furnished by the Russian government. Later, in the hope of eventually returning to Petrograd and Moscow, some workers went to Archangel, where they set up a Hostess House for American troops stationed there and ran for a brief six weeks a club for Russian girls.

Other units on the way to Russia via Finland and Constantinople, but unable to enter, organized services for Russian refugees. Still another unit, bound for Siberia, was held up in Vladivostock. There, for several months, they carried on a varied program for American soldiers, Red Cross nurses, Russian women and children, and the Russian brides of American army men. In 1920, however, conditions compelled the withdrawal of all American workers and the work so hopefully begun was completely closed.[14]

Though the request for work in Italy had come early in 1918, it was not until after the Armistice in November of that year that the American workers arrived. But peace did not diminish the needs. Indeed, "if war needs were more intensive, the post-war needs as they presented themselves to the Y.W.C.A. were extensive to a degree outreaching precedent or calculation."[15] It was of vital importance to demonstrate what the Y.W.C.A. could do in Italy if given backing, funds and leadership. In a variety of ways the Americans helped the Italian Associations to enlarge and improve their work. For a time they took over the operation of the *Casa Internationale* in Rome, and expanded its usefulness to the full. In Florence the American assistance made possible an enlarged hostel and recreation center, a tea-room and a summer camp in the Tuscan hills. Genoa, Milan, Turin, Naples were all helped to expand their activities. Foyers, restaurants, club rooms for girls working in factories, hostels for students, port work, educational classes, all were used to make clear in a land not used to such activities for girls the possibilities of the Y.W.C.A. Temporary centers were opened to meet emergency needs in Spezia and Trieste. The difficulties of obtaining funds and trained leadership for such an organization as the Y.W.C.A. was bound to be a continuing one, yet the demonstration bore permanent fruit.

Although Poland was the one country in which no permanent work of an organizational character resulted from the response to its appeal for help, the piece of emergency work done was of particular interest. Out of the suggestion of Madame de Turczynowicz there grew a training course for Polish-American social workers which was a cooperative project of the Polish Reconstruction Committee in the United States and the Committee on Work for Foreign-Born Women of the Y.W.C.A. War Work Council. Seventy-five young women took this course in the summer of 1919. Through a commission sent to make official arrangements for entrance into Poland with Premier and Mrs. Paderewski, the Overseas Committee ascertained that the services of these "Polish Grey Samaritans", as they were called, would be warmly welcomed. In the course of the following year, two units went to Poland, accompanied by Y.W.C.A. representatives who were also trained social workers. They devoted themselves at first to the most immediately needed work, that of child welfare under the American Relief Administration. Later their services were extended to other fields under the same agency. Meantime the Y.W.C.A. secretaries opened clubs for girls in Warsaw and Cracow, started emergency work for Polish nurses during the Bolshevist invasion in the summer of 1920, worked with refugees, and in cooperation with the Y.M.C.A. rendered service to the 4,000 women soldiers who made up the Women's Battalion of the Polish army.

In commenting upon the help asked from the Overseas Committee for making a social survey in Czechoslovakia, Dr. Alice Masaryk had said: "It is necessary to think of a working plan for social work in the Czechoslovak Republic, and the survey . . . will make clear thinking more possible."[16] The survey was made with the help of both American and Czech organizations in Prague, and a training course was conducted to provide leadership for social welfare projects. No attempt was made to organize Y.W.C.A. work, but as the survey and the training course proceeded, those who had shared in them saw that the Y.W.C.A. was peculiarly fitted to meet needs in the lives of girls of which they were acutely conscious. Under the leadership of Miss Olga Masaryk, a daughter of President Masaryk, who had herself been a leader before the war in the Student Movement in Bohemia, a formal request was made of the World's Y.W.C.A. for help in the organization of a Y.W.C.A. in Czechoslovakia.

From this time on, the efforts of the American secretaries, in cooperation with their Czech colleagues, were directed toward the forming of a Czechoslovak Young Women's Christian Association—a national organization that should have the development of work throughout the Republic for its concern. Under a Provisional Committee the work continued to grow until in May 1921, a conference of committee and staff at the summer camp at Prerov worked together to produce a national constitution to be submitted to the World's Executive Committee with an application for affiliation with the World's Y.W.C.A.

The first American unit to go to Belgium in response to Mademoiselle Goblet d'Alviella's appeal arrived in Brussels in the autumn of 1919. A small staff continued there until 1923, when the work that had been developed in cooperation with committees of women in Brussels and Antwerp was left entirely in the hands of Belgian leaders. The work followed closely the pattern set in France. Foyers and hostels were opened in Brussels, Antwerp, and several other centers. These were after a time federated in a national organization, "The Federation of Belgian Foyers, Founded by the Y.W.C.A." A summer camp was established. Educational classes and training courses for leaders were important elements in the program carried on in the Foyers.

There were very special problems in Belgium. The sharp racial antagonism between Flemish and French-speaking groups presented a challenge to fellowship. There was also the delicate question of the relation of the new work, so quickly and successfully developed, to the already existing Y.W.C.A. The new work was built upon an inclusiveness of membership, a freedom of method, and a variety of program quite new to Belgian women. The Y.W.C.A., though it had a long history of valiant effort, was strictly Protestant; its *Unions* were closely related to the church, with a program largely limited to religious meetings. The Foyers aimed to reach as many girls as possible, and to that end had a very simple statement of purpose. Their interpretation of Christianity was largely through a spirit which motivated and permeated all activities. Thus, although united by the common purpose of bringing fuller Christian life to girls, the two organizations were sufficiently different in outlook and in method to make union no light and easy matter. The situation as it existed at the close of the period of American service is summed up in the report for 1922-1923:

Both the Unions and the Federation have a work to do which seems best able to be done under their different membership bases. Both groups have the common aim of bringing a fuller life to the girls of Belgium. Both have much to gain from and much to contribute to the great fellowship which centers in the World's Committee of the Young Women's Christian Association. It is the hope of both organizations that when they come to know each other better they may so unite their forces as to ask for affiliation as the Y.W.C.A. of Belgium. Each summer a certain number of places at the summer camp have been reserved for members of the provincial Unions. Young Union leaders who attended a training course in Brussels during Easter week 1923, were at different times the guests of both centers in Brussels. In Antwerp, Mons and Verviers the Union leaders are recruited as volunteer workers for the Foyers. By these various contacts a mutual comprehension is growing among the younger members.[17]

The organization of Y.W.C.A. work in Roumania in the latter part of the year 1919 and the early days of 1920 was the outcome of a combination of factors different from those in any other European country. Early in 1919 Miss Spencer returned to London, and much of the work of the Executive Committee that year was given to making contact with the new situations in Europe. One of the important undertakings was an investigation of conditions in the Balkans, which led the Committee to feel the urgent necessity of work there. At almost the same time a member of the Roumanian government appealed to the Y.W.C.A. of the United States for help for Roumanian women. As a result of consultation between the World's Y.W.C.A. and the Y.W.C.A. of the United States, a commission was appointed to confer with Queen Marie of Roumania in London, and after further consultation, it was decided to send Association workers to Roumania. Thus, in this instance it was not the United States alone but that Association working with and through the World's Committee that initiated this new venture. It was, moreover, a definite plan both to meet a desperate emergency and, as in Russia, to establish the Y.W.C.A. in this Greek Orthodox country. As such it represented not only American aid to Europe but also the fruit of the World's Y.W.C.A. concern for the Balkans, earlier expressed in Miss Spencer's visit to Bulgaria in 1911 and by the years of work carried on there against great odds by Miss Grace Saunders.

Another difference between the work in Roumania and that of the war years elsewhere in Europe was that it was carried by a staff of British and American secretaries. For a time Miss Grace Saunders had a kind

167

of area-secretary relation to it. Miss Elsie Boyd and Miss Theodora Maclagan were members of the unit sent to Bucharest, and Miss Dorothy Brown,
soon to become Executive of the Foreign Department of the British
National Council, and also Miss Elined Prys of the British Y.W.C.A. served
with Miss Anita Hodgkin and other secretaries from the United States.

The Roumanian work, although not large in numbers, made rapid
progress. It had the continued support and sympathy of the Queen and
Princess Ileana. A flourishing center was opened in Bucharest and later
a second one in Jassy. Work was started with girls in industry and in shops,
business girls and girls of leisure, and there was an encouraging willingness of women to undertake responsible committee service. As early as
March 1920, Miss Hodgkin, the Executive Secretary, reports: "Miss Boyd
has been leading a class on the subject of a possible basis for the Roumanian Y.W.C.A."[18] The following year it was reported: "We have now
forty members understanding and working devotedly for the purpose . . .
we have an Association, small in numbers but mighty in spirit. They are
adding slowly to their membership in order that they may be sure that
every member may have a true conception of its Christian basis."[19] A constitution had already been drawn up by a group of Roumanian women,
who held their first meeting as a Y.W.C.A. Council, or Board of Directors,
in April 1921.

American secretaries were not sent to the Baltic States of Estonia and
Latvia until late in 1920 and 1921 respectively, and in both cases it was in
response to an appeal from women leaders of the two countries, encouraged
by the Y.M.C.A. which was already at work there. Here also it was
definitely a request for the organization of a Young Women's Christian
Association.

The repercussions of the war in Europe were felt far outside that continent. In the Near East particularly, upheaval and change followed in its
wake, with tragic consequences to thousands of people. In 1919 the
Y.W.C.A. of the United States, through its Overseas Committee, sent a
secretary to Constantinople. She was followed later by others, and two
types of work were organized. Service Centers in Constantinople, Beirut,
Adana and Smyrna, and relief work, in cooperation with the Near East
Relief, in some centers in the interior. The relief work was ended in
1921; Adana and Smyrna were discontinued in 1922, the latter because
of the catastrophic fire which laid waste the city in the course of the war
with Turkey. In Constantinople and Beirut, however, the work went
forward, carrying on anew that begun by Frances Gage in 1913, which
had been without secretarial leadership after her death in 1917.

The results of this overseas work were important not alone in Europe.

The Y.W.C.A. of the United States issued from the experience of the war years profoundly influenced by having shared its workers and funds with European countries. The Foreign Division in a report said:

> The close association with the women of Europe has given us a true basis for international thinking and for international friendship. . . . The secretaries who have come back after months of living and working in Europe have brought a new appreciation of the historical background and culture of the Old World that is an invaluable contribution to the work with foreign-born women in the United States. And finally, this touch with the women of European countries has meant a new appreciation of their difficulties, their abilities, their devotion and their courage that will make possible our working together for the women of the world with a new understanding and sympathy.[20]

Another result, not mentioned in this memorandum but of great significance, was the entrance of American leaders in person into the councils of the World's Executive Committee. Secretaries and committee members responsible for work in one or another of the countries of Europe were present at almost every meeting of the Executive Committee and of the Extension Committee during 1919. For the first time in the twenty-five years of history of the world organization, the responsible leaders of the National Association of the United States were to be found working continuously and closely with those who administered world policies.

The World's Y.W.C.A. in 1920 was in many ways a new and different movement from that of 1914. The Anglo-Saxon, Protestant tradition might seem still to be dominant in its thinking, its administration and its methods, but the Orient and the countries of Roman Catholic and of Greek Orthodox culture had become a part of the World's Association, not as "receiving" countries only but as contributors to the world mind in the making. In the Anglo-Saxon countries especially, but also to a great extent in other lands, the boundaries of the Association program had been extended far beyond anything thought of before. Yet the World's Y.W.C.A. was never more sure that in aim, purpose, spirit, it was profoundly at one with its earlier days. The creative impulse of Christian love and fellowship and devotion was not lost—indeed it was strengthened in the cruel days of war, though it was being called upon to express itself in new terms, new ways, new fields of endeavor.

169

REFERENCES

[1] Pamphlet, *The World's Y.W.C.A. Since Champéry*, 1920, p. 5.

[2] *The Women's International Quarterly,* April 1917, Editorial, pp. 130-132.

[3] Ibid., p. 133.

[4] *The World's Y.W.C.A. Since Champéry*, p. 5.

[5] *Our Eighty Years*—Historical Sketches of the Y.W.C.A. of Great Britain, 1935, p. 17.

[6] *Our Eighty Years*. p. 17.

[7] *A Study of the Y.W.C.A. of China*, 1933, p. 13.

[8] Fifth World's Y.W.C.A. Conference, 1914, p. 274.

[9] *A Study of the Y.W.C.A. of China*, p. 14.

[10] In the final year of the war, 1918, the budget of the War Work Council was $15,000,000, some of which, however, was used to finance post-war work in Europe and elsewhere.

[11] Reviewing the overseas work after American help had been withdrawn from Europe, the Foreign Department of the National Board thus described its purpose: "The aim of the American Y.W.C.A. in sending workers to Europe was to give first aid to these countries in the special emergency created by the war, but there was also the desire to help the women worn by war and faced with perilous economic, social and religious conditions, strengthen the women's organizations already at work, so that they might be able to measure up to greatly increased opportunities and needs, or to aid them in establishing an organization fitted to do the work needed by women in the new life in which they found themselves after the war." (Memorandum on the American Y.W.C.A. in Europe, p. 9.)

[12] *The Y.W.C.A. Overseas*, 1919, p. 4.

[13] See p. 162.

[14] In 1921 Miss Marcia Dunham, who had been the Executive Secretary for the Y.W.C.A. work in Russia, returned to that country as a member of the staff of the American Relief Association. Through her work with the European Student Relief organization, Miss Dunham continued to have some touch with Russia until 1924. In 1926, in response to an opening for a physical director, the American Association sent Miss Edith Gates to Moscow, but a new government policy compelled her to return without beginning work.

[15] Report of Overseas Committee, War Work Council of the Y.W.C.A. of the United States, 1921, p. 105.

[16] Report of Overseas Committee, Y.W.C.A. of the United States, p. 135.

[17] Risley, Florence. Report, 1922-1923, p. 11.
Note: Belgium at length achieved a national federation of the two movements which was affiliated with the World's Y.W.C.A. in corresponding membership in 1934.

[18] Hodgkin, Anita. Report. March 1920, p. 2.

[19] Jaeger, Martha. Report, February 1921.

[20] Memorandum on the Work of the American Y.W.C.A. in Europe.

*Those who are one in Christ, and the infinite diversity
of development for which "the whole body of Christ"
stands, can take a stand above the usual divisions of
the world. This is not an easy matter, and it involves
individual adjustment and sacrifice; but the Champéry Conference brought home that inspiration of
the World's Young Women's Christian Association
which lies in the fact that the very differences in the
work carried on for women in different parts of the
world make the strength of the one body in which
the Associations are united.*

*The World's Young Women's Christian Association Since
Champéry.*

CHAPTER 13 REUNION: CHAMPÉRY

THE YEAR 1920, when for the first time since
1914 an official meeting of the World's Young Women's Christian Association was held, was the beginning of a new era. Some of the leaders on
whom the movement had relied since its earliest days were no longer
present. Miss Mary Morley, whose faith and sound judgment were for
many years so greatly valued, had died in 1917, and Mrs. Tritton in the
early months of 1919. Miss Reynolds' death was to follow in February
1922. Miss Spencer, who had offered her resignation at Stockholm but
had consented to remain as General Secretary during the war, was now to
retire. The Association itself had taken on new elements, new outlooks
during the war years.

Moreover, there were wide chasms to be bridged within the movement. Many leaders in the German Association felt it a duty to their
country to keep apart from international circles. Leaders in France found
it difficult to meet even with Christians from enemy countries in a spirit
of fellowship and goodwill. The World's Y.W.C.A. was fortunate in having as its president during this critical period a woman who carried on the
evangelical and international tradition of the early leaders and at the same
time was particularly fitted by temperament and by conviction to promote
the spirit of reconciliation and the restoration of world fellowship so
sadly needed.

The Honorable Mrs. Montague Waldegrave, who had been elected to
succeed Mrs. Tritton at Stockholm, was a woman of great insight and judgment, whose love for and understanding of people enabled her to be in

171

an extraordinary way a reconciling force in this time of deep division. Her visit to the German Association in 1920 did much to bridge the chasm between them and the World Movement. Above all, she was a woman of prayer, and it was the depth of her prayer life, her complete reliance upon the guidance of God in response to prayer, that made her in these difficult years a constant source of strength, serenity and power.

The World's Y.W.C.A. was also fortunate in that Miss Bretherton, who carried the heaviest staff responsibility in the absence of Miss Spencer, was especially fitted by her administrative gifts and her experience in the National Association of Great Britain and in the Student Christian movement, to undertake this. When in 1917 Miss Knight left the World's Y.W.C.A. staff to go to France with the women of the British forces, Miss Bretherton took over her responsibility as Secretary for the Extension Committee and in this capacity dealt with the many problems relating to the new situations created by the work of the American War Work Council in Europe.

The task that faced the World's Y.W.C.A. leaders was first of all the re-establishment of fellowship, but it was not only that. It was also to face together the new world in which the Y.W.C.A. must now live and work; to recognize and adjust to new points of view, new aspirations and convictions which the war years had brought to the Associations themselves. There was also a multitude of concrete matters, administrative and otherwise, to be dealt with before the World's Association could function fully and freely in the new day.

The question of how best to take up these tasks was a serious one. In the normal routine there would have been a biennial meeting of the World's Committee in 1916, a World's Conference in 1918, and another biennial meeting of the World's Committee in 1920. Psychologically, financially and practically, from the standpoint of the things to be accomplished, a World's Conference in 1920 was considered inadvisable. Yet something more than a World's Committee meeting was needed, something that should furnish direction and a wider base of understanding for action.

In the light of these facts, a plan was made to call together an International Commission of six carefully chosen delegates from each National Association, who should consider some of the most pressing problems before the World's Association and whose recommendations should give guidance to the World's Committee for its future course. Since a fundamental purpose of such a meeting was also a fresh realization of Christian world fellowship, it was felt that the setting for it should be a quiet spot, free from the distractions and publicity attending a meeting in a city.

The place chosen was the village of Champéry in the Swiss mountains,

172

Fräulein Hulda Zarnack

The Hon. Mrs. Montague Waldegrave

Pach Bros.

Mademoiselle Jeanne Bertsch

Miss Charlotte T. Niven

Miss Gladys E. Bretherton

Miss Mary A. Dingman

high above Lake Geneva. It was decided that there should be no speakers from outside the Association. The meeting would be a family gathering in which there might be united thought, study and prayer, and out of which it was hoped would come a common mind regarding the next steps in the work of the World's Y.W.C.A.

If, however, the Champéry meeting was simple and unostentatious in character, the preparation for it was extensive and arduous. To this was given the largest part of Executive Committee thought and planning throughout 1919. It was with a view to this meeting that Miss Spencer, and also Baroness Olga Meyendorff and Miss Charlotte T. Niven, both of whom joined the staff that year as traveling secretaries, visited not only the older Associations of Europe but the new centers, interpreting the World's Y.W.C.A. and becoming personally acquainted with the new leaders and the new work.

Three fields of thought and action were judged to call for consideration from the International Commission. The first of these was the industrial field, which was increasingly recognized as having an important bearing on the conditions that had brought about the war. The second was the vast shift in populations, which was creating on a huge scale problems of immigration and emigration with all their attendant dangers and tragedies for young women. The third was the integration, in orderly fashion, with the World's organization, of the work done by the Foreign Departments of various countries, particularly that of the United States, in Europe, China and South America.

There were set up, therefore, three sections of the International Commission, one on Industry, one on Emigration and Immigration, and one on Foreign Departments. Questionnaires were prepared on each subject and sent to the National Associations for study. The replies to these were analyzed in the World's office and their information made available to the delegates in advance of the meeting. For carrying out the somewhat intricate detail that these questionnaires involved, the National Board of the United States lent a member of its staff, Miss Katherine Halsey, formerly a secretary in China, to act as a World's Y.W.C.A. secretary especially assigned to preparation for the meeting.

The International Commission met at Champéry from June 2 to 10, 1920, with 126 delegates representing twenty-seven countries. It was cause for deep thanksgiving that no Association had withdrawn from the World's Association during the war, and that every active member Association except Denmark was able to send representatives to this meeting. Out of the discussions, the prayer and the fellowship of this week there came a series of findings that were handed on to the World's Committee which met June 11 to 14. Here these findings were considered and adopted, with some slight modifications, as the directive for the work of the next two years.

The findings of the Industrial Section of the Commission emphasized again the recommendations of the Berlin Conference of 1910, and stressed, as did those, the responsibility of the Y.W.C.A. for the application of Christian principles to the social order. The Champéry resolutions went beyond those of Berlin, however. They definitely recommended cooperation with other bodies striving to improve conditions, and urged that the Association "make every effort to get into touch with industrial workers in far larger numbers through such means as foyers, clubs, camps, canteens and hostels." They proposed that self-government be developed to the fullest possible extent in industrial centers, and social and economic education and training for citizenship be a definite part of the industrial program.

They went even further, and recommended that the Y.W.C.A. "encourage organization among women workers and give opportunity to its members . . . to become acquainted with the principles underlying such organization." They recommended that the World's Y.W.C.A. urge National Associations publicly to approve the standards adopted by the International Labor Conference established in connection with the League of Nations and to support bills concerning these proposals when introduced into their own legislatures. Lastly, to make action along these lines effective, they recommended the appointment of an Industrial Committee and an Industrial Secretary by the World's Y.W.C.A. and by each National Association. At Berlin the emphasis had been upon the responsibility to study and understand social and industrial conditions; at Champéry the demand was for a vigorous and concerted program of social action. A long step had been taken, revolutionary in its import for Y.W.C.A. program and function.

The Section on Emigration and Immigration, noting the immediate human problems arising from the movement of large numbers of people from one country to another and the particular needs of young women, expressed the conviction that this situation offered to the World's Y.W.C.A. a definite and immediate opportunity for service. It therefore recommended the appointment of a standing committee and a secretary to develop a plan for an international service among emigrants, and the cooperation of this committee, when appointed, with existing international organizations working in the same field.

The Section on Foreign Departments dealt with an array of practical problems that had come to light since the adoption of the Scheme of Relationships at Stockholm. It reaffirmed the principle enunciated there that National Associations should give the fullest help of which they were capable to the development of Y.W.C.A. work outside their own countries. On the basis of the experience of the war years, it urged that staffs of foreign secretaries in non-self-supporting countries be international in character rather than all from one country. It recognized the complications that must result from this policy, and took up such detailed matters as selecting and training secretaries for foreign service, and the harmonizing of procedures and standards in different countries in such matters as salaries and furloughs. It made recommendations regarding the relation of foreign staffs to church, community, missionary societies and other organizations. Assuming the correctness of the general scheme outlined in 1914, the Champéry recommendations endeavored to set up standard procedures at specific points where experience had shown further definition to be needed.

The World's Committee meeting that followed the meeting of the International Commission had many matters to deal with. The questions considered and the decisions reached indicated certain trends in the movement. There was an evident desire to make the actual operation of the organization more truly international in character. For example, to the four vice presidents resident at headquarters were added four corresponding vice presidents, each representing an area or a group of countries, Madame Alfred Bertrand of Switzerland for Latin countries, Fröken Netzel of Sweden for the countries of northern and central Europe, Mrs. James Webb of the United States for America, and Miss Kawai, National General Secretary of Japan for Asia.

Other resolutions were directed to the same end. One, while naming London as the continuing headquarters for the present, called for consultation with the national committees and consideration at the next World's Committee meeting "as regards the wisdom of removing the headquarters to another country." Another recommended the appointment of a sub-committee "to work out some plan whereby the Executive Committee may be made more international in character."

There was a new sense of the obligation resting upon the World's Y.W.C.A. to use its strength and influence to espouse openly those movements striving for peace and cooperation among nations. Some National Associations had come to Champéry with the understanding that there would be no discussion of political issues. This prevented the Committee from considering a resolution specifically approving the League of Nations. A resolution was, however, passed, that:

> The World's Y.W.C.A., including as it does women of all nations, shall give itself to the development of public opinion on international questions and relationships such as shall strengthen all those forces which are working for the avoidance

175

of war and the promotion of peace and better understanding among the nations.[1]

Further, the Executive Committee was asked "in view of the urgency of the question . . . to give serious attention to the matter with a view to preparing a statement to be sent to all the National Committees."[2]

The increased responsibility laid upon the World's Committee by the expansion of the war years was recognized in the increase of the budget from the £7,500 recommended by the Executive Committee to £10,000;[3] by the provision for area or group conferences in the years between biennial meetings of the World's Committee; and in the decision to approve the International Commission's recommendations for the appointment of new committees and for increase in staff. That the new era called for considerable reconsideration of organization appears in such resolutions as those providing for the reorganizing of the Extension Committee "to enable it to deal adequately with the greatly increased volume and variety of work now within its sphere of direction"; amending the by-laws to make more definite the requirements of Associations applying for affiliation with the World's Committee; and by the appointment of a sub-committee on the revision of the constitution and by-laws.

In view of the probability that several applications for affiliation would be received from National Associations within the next few years, the sub-committee on amendments to the by-laws was also asked "to give special consideration to the question of the basis, with relation to new national organizations." To this request it replied: "This committee interprets Article V of the Constitution[4] in the sense that no young woman, to whatever branch of the Christian Church she belongs, should be excluded from membership in any branch of the National Association if she is prepared to accept the basis which the World's Committee accepts as the application of its principles to the needs of that particular country."[5] Thus the ecumenical principle adopted at Stockholm was at Champéry interpreted definitely in terms of the practice that should obtain in all newly organized national work. It is doubtful if the full significance of this action was appreciated at the time. It is certain that as its results matured in the life of the Association during the following years there was much questioning with regard to it in a number of countries.

On recommendation of a sub-committee appointed to consider the matter of a new General Secretary, the Committee called Miss Charlotte T. Niven to that post. Miss Niven, like her predecessors in this position, was an American, and like them also she was "a child of the manse", her father having been a Presbyterian minister in the southern state of Virginia who had served as a chaplain in the Confederate Army during the Civil

War of 1860-1865. He later came to Dobbs Ferry, New York, the first Southerner after the war to become the minister of a northern church. At Dobbs Ferry he was largely instrumental in founding the well-known "Miss Master's School for Girls", and it was here that Miss Niven received her education.

After leaving school she served as a voluntary worker in Christodora House, a settlement in New York City which carried an extensive program of work among the Italians living in the neighborhood. In Christodora House, especially through her contact with Miss McCall, the remarkable woman who was its head, her interest and experience in Christian social work were developed. This interest led her, in 1910, to go with a friend to Italy "to see for ourselves the background and conditions from which our immigrants had come." In Italy she became absorbed first in the work of a center for students in Naples, and later in the work of the Y.W.C.A. in Florence, where she went in 1911, at Madame Schalck's request, to open an International Student Hostel. From that time on she was closely identified with the work of the Y.W.C.A. in Italy, going with the Italian delegation to Stockholm in 1914, and serving at various points during the war years. In 1918 she was called to the staff of American workers in Paris, and in 1919 joined the staff of the World's Y.W.C.A. as Area Secretary for Latin countries. Her knowledge of European languages and her wide contacts with and understanding of Latin peoples brought to the World's Y.W.C.A. a valuable and needed contribution in this special field.

Two other actions of the 1920 committee meeting should be recorded. The publication of *The Women's International Quarterly* was discontinued "owing to the financial situation throughout the world, which prevents an adequate circulation"; the funds thus released, it was suggested, should be used to publish more leaflets, "particularly those suitable for use in pioneer countries, and leaflets in French and German and possibly in other languages."[6] It was decided that a simpler and more easily recognized badge than that which was then official might be more useful. This badge, adopted in early days, was a design showing a map of the world surrounded by the World's motto in Hebrew. In place of this, the present design of a blue triangle enclosed in a gold circle was chosen.

These problems that were discussed, these decisions that were made, were all a part of the essential process of beginning again the active functioning of the World's Y.W.C.A. Yet they were, and were felt to be at the time, the less important achievements of the Champéry meeting. The heart of it, that which made all its actions significant, was found in the realm of the spirit.

The National Committees of both France and Germany had at first felt that it would not be possible to meet together in fellowship so soon. That there were both French and German delegates present throughout the conference and that they came through the experience there into deep spiritual communion with one another was a gift of the Holy Spirit, made possible by faith and love, shown especially by Mrs. Waldegrave and Miss Spencer, and above all by Fräulein Zarnack, National Secretary of the German Association, and Mademoiselle Bertsch, National Secretary of the French Association, whose conviction of this oneness in Christ rose above all national barriers. At the beginning of the conference there was for many of the delegates a strong consciousness of inner strain, but as the days passed this strain was overcome, so that "going home we took along the conviction that we had lived through something very rare and great."

This experience of deepening fellowship was realized and expressed in many ways—in the daily periods of prayer and meditation, in the Communion Service in the village church, in conversations between individuals, and in the corporate consideration of the common needs of women and girls and the Association's obligation and capacity to minister to them in new ways. Acutely conscious of their differences and of the seriousness of the problems confronting their nations, the delegates were even more profoundly aware of the faith in which they were all one and of which their very differences were each an individual and partial expression.

"Many associations," it was written later, "cling around the word 'Champéry'. . . . But, as in all mental pictures the ever-changing glory of the mountains overtops all other memories, so the final impression left of the days of fellowship at Champéry is the infinitely varied revelation of the unchanging purpose of the Young Women's Christian Association throughout the world."[7]

REFERENCES

[1] World's Committee Meeting, Champéry, 1920, Minutes, p. 12.

[2] World's Committee Meeting, Champéry, 1920, Minutes, p. 13.

[3] The receipts of the World's Y.W.C.A. for 1922 were £9,035. Following this year, the depressions of the 1920s and 1930s made necessary much smaller budgets. Not until 1942 did the World's Y.W.C.A. achieve the goal of £10,000 which it set for itself in 1920.

[4] See Appendix II, p. 275.

[5] World's Committee Meeting, Champéry, 1920, pp. 10, 11.

[6] World's Committee Meeting, Champéry, 1920, p. 9.

Note: The difficulty of language has been a constant one throughout the history of the World's Y.W.C.A.

[7] The World's Y.W.C.A. Since Champéry, p. 6.

*We meet today from the Old World and the New,
from the East and West, North and South. We gather
together to strengthen each other for the service in
the world which has been given us to do; to give, not
take; to serve, not rule; to nourish, not devour; to
help, not crush; if need be to die, not live. We are
here to serve the girls of the world through the
Y.W.C.A.*

THE HONORABLE MRS. MONTAGUE WALDEGRAVE. Address
World's Committee Meeting, Washington, 1924.

CHAPTER 14 REBUILDING: 1920-1930

THE WAR had brought both gains and losses.
The work of the Young Women's Christian Association had grown and
expanded in many quarters. The World Movement was wider in extent,
more inclusive in its constituency than in 1914. Moreover, the World's
Committee itself had gained a new conviction regarding its own significance
and the field of its operations. Its spiritual life had been quickened and
deepened.

At the same time, it was recognized that the changes which the war
had brought were not uniform throughout the Association. The differences
in point of view within it were more evident. Much of the advance of the
war years had been made without the active participation of the World's
Association, which was therefore to some extent out of touch with developments and must readjust its thought and action. Leadership was depleted
in many countries and the new leaders who were taking up the work were
inexperienced and needed training and help at many points. For all these
reasons the period from the meeting at Champéry in 1920 to the removal
of the headquarters from London to Geneva in 1930 was one of rebuilding
and readjustment.

The World's Y.W.C.A. was faced with new conditions; new work
had to be undertaken; new problems arose. For reasons of both policy and
finance it had been deemed unwise to hold a World's Conference in the
early post-war years. Instead, the business of the organization was transacted at biennial meetings of the World's Committee, in connection with
which a larger group of selected representatives met for consideration of
issues and recommendations of policy. These meetings were held suc-

179

cessively at St. Wolfgang, Austria (1922), Washington, United States (1924), and Oxford, England (1926). The first World's Conference after the war was at Budapest, Hungary, in 1928. At the Washington meeting Mrs. Waldegrave retired as President and was succeeded by Lady Parmoor, whose interest in and contact with other international organizations, particularly those working for peace, was of special significance in these years of widening cooperative efforts among world movements.

One of the most immediate undertakings following Champéry was the setting up of the new lines of work that had been provided for there. Miss Mary A. Dingman was called to the staff as Industrial Secretary, and an Advisory Committee was formed, with Miss Constance Smith, His Majesty's Deputy Chief Inspector of Factories under the British Government, as its Chairman. Miss Smith's deep loyalty to the Christian purpose of the Association, combined with her wide knowledge of international industrial legislation, made her an invaluable leader in this new venture. Miss Dingman brought to the task long experience first as a teacher of economics in a girls' school in the United States, and then as an industrial secretary on the national staff of the Association in the United States. She brought also a knowledge of Europe gained from her work as the Executive Secretary of the program for munition workers in France during the war, and from her contact with industrial and economic conditions in many continental countries.

The first need was to arouse intelligent interest and conviction regarding the Association's responsibility in this field. To do this, Miss Dingman traveled widely on the Continent, held short study courses in Italy, Austria, Hungary, Sweden and Denmark, and in the summer of 1922, a six weeks' summer school in London. "Altogether," says a report of these beginnings, "in the first year of its existence the Industrial Advisory Committee of the World's Y.W.C.A. has made a very definite mark."[1]

The story of the carrying out of the resolution of the section on Emigration and Immigration of the Champéry International Commission reads almost like a chapter from *Alice in Wonderland,* so astonishing and rapid was its development. Following an investigation by the World's Committee at several European port cities, which revealed the need of expert knowledge to deal with this problem, the Y.W.C.A. of the United States lent Miss Mary Hurlbutt, who had already helped to organize the Y.W.C.A. in Czechoslovakia, to act as Secretary to a Migration Committee of which Miss Grace Tottenham, of the World's Executive Committee, was appointed Chairman.

To discover the actual needs to be met, Miss Hurlbutt made an intensive study of emigration from Poland and Czechoslovakia, the two countries from which especially large numbers of persons were migrating.

This investigation, reported in a pamphlet entitled *The Welfare of Migrants,* was the first study to be made by any organization of the specifically human side of emigration as distinguished from its economic and political aspects. The study not only became the basis for the education of the Association leadership in many countries, but was widely used by other organizations also, and by the International Labor Office of the League of Nations.

In the next two years, the Migration Secretary traveled to and fro over Europe, investigating situations, talking with Association leaders and other interested groups, and with their cooperation establishing centers for service to migrants in key cities in France, Belgium, Denmark, Poland, Hungary, Czechoslovakia, and in Constantinople. These centers worked in close cooperation with similar centers in the port cities of the receiving countries, especially Canada and the United States. Workers were selected and trained in the specialized techniques necessary. Each of these workers was brought for a brief period to London, to study in the migration office the methods of record-keeping which had been devised, in order that the system in all countries might be uniform. In most countries the work was supported during this experimental period by the Association of the United States, which drew upon its war funds for the purpose. Denmark, however, from the beginning, supported entirely its own center in Copenhagen, supplying its own worker.

The astonishing rapidity with which the work grew and the way in which it reached out to the far corners of the earth was testimony to the vast human need among migrant peoples. It was recognized from the outset that this service involved families and family life and was not confined to girls and women; also that if its value was proved it should become a permanent program calling for trained case workers. Certain principles therefore were laid down with regard to it: that it should be done in cooperation with all agencies interested in the welfare of migrants; that the service should be entirely non-sectarian and without any form of religious or political propaganda; that while the World's Y.W.C.A. would take responsibility in initiating the work, it would be with the definite aim of relinquishing control as soon as practicable to an independent, representative and cooperative body.[2]

The time for this relinquishment came in the summer of 1923, when the need and the method of meeting it had been amply demonstrated and when decreased income made it impossible for the World's Committee and the Y.W.C.A. of the United States to continue it without encroaching on their permanent work. Accordingly, in that year an independent committee was formed, charged with the setting up of a separate organization, the International Migration Service.

In making the final report on this work to the World's Committee at its meeting in Washington in 1924, the Migration Secretary said:

> Making the International Migration Service independent does not mean relieving the Y.W.C.A. of the work they are doing for foreign-born or foreign-speaking people within the country. . . . Rather will such work on the part of the Y.W.C.A. be increasingly needed. The "follow-up" will always be needed as well as the cooperation of all national and local organizations if the International Migration Service is to solve these problems, made infinitely more complicated and delicate because of the wide distances and differences between nations. And so, though this wonderful bit of work has grown beyond the resources of the Association in finance and organization, it has not grown beyond the resources of its spirit. . . . This child organization you are sending out cannot but bear the fruits of its heritage—a Christian international mind.[3]

In addition to its concern with work in the fields of industry and migration, the World's Committee turned its attention in these years to the fostering of work with younger girls. This was an important step. While in some countries the Association from its earliest days had directed its program largely to girls under eighteen years of age, in other countries it had been concerned chiefly with "young adults", for the most part employed young women from eighteen to thirty. The sense of responsibility for the younger groups had grown, however, through the years, and the numbers reached by the Associations had increased enormously during the war.

The programs in use were many and varied, the most widely used being that of the Girl Guides, which was adopted by the Associations in Great Britain, India, South Africa and a number of European countries. In the United States, during the war years, various programs were drawn together into the Girl Reserve movement. In Canada, the Association and some of the churches cooperated in a program known as Canadian Girls in Training. In other countries Blue Triangle Clubs were organized for teen-age girls.

The need for a better understanding of the psychology of adolescence, for trained leaders, and for sound program methods had been recognized at the World's Conference at Stockholm in 1914, in a recommendation "that some specialists on matters relating to girl life be added to the staff." In the light of the experience of the war years, further consideration of work in this field was felt to be an urgent necessity.

In preparation for the meeting of an International Commission on this subject at St. Wolfgang, Austria, in 1922, a questionnaire regarding work

Delar

Miss M. Marianne Mills

with younger girls was sent to National Associations. The replies to this, together with a series of lectures on adolescent psychology given by Professor Bovet of the Jean-Jacques Rousseau Institute in Geneva, and a series on "The Girl of Today" by Miss Una Saunders, provided the basis for the discussion at the meeting. The findings of the International Commission stressed the special fitness of the Y.W.C.A. for the fuller development of girls' work, and urged the establishment in every National Association of a Girls' Work Department under trained leadership. As a result of the discussions at St. Wolfgang and at later meetings, the World's Committee itself, in 1926, called to its staff Miss M. Marianne Mills, whose previous professional experience had been that of teacher training and settlement work under the Church of England, as a specialist in religious education with primary concern for work for younger girls.

Another pressing post-war task confronting the World's Y.W.C.A. was the integration and further development of the European Associations started or greatly expanded during the war. The extraordinary budget of its War Work Council made it possible for the United States to carry on emergency work to meet conditions created by the war in Europe and the Near East for several years after 1918. The new Associations in Czechoslovakia, Roumania, Estonia and Latvia and the Foyer Movement in Belgium were the results of this.

Although it had been recognized from the start that this American aid was temporary, there were many difficulties in the way of its relinquishment and many questions arose. What should be the basis of the permanent organization, if any, in each country? How would the work be financed? How find and train the necessary leadership? Both the Foreign Division in the United States and the World's Executive Committee were concerned to solve these problems. In 1921, the Foreign Division sent Miss Anna Rice and Miss Marion Vincent to visit the centers in Europe in which American secretaries were at work, to confer with them and with committee women on the questions of basis and of financial plans in preparation for the withdrawal of American aid.

The World's Y.W.C.A. was greatly handicapped in meeting the enlarged opportunities of the post-war decade by the financial situation. The policy of referring all advance work in non-self-supporting countries to the Foreign Departments of National Associations for promotion and support meant, in practice, that new developments were limited to those that could be undertaken by the two largest sending countries, Great Britain and the United States. The Associations in both these countries passed through a difficult financial period after the war. This resulted in a decrease both in the World's budget and the assistance given to Associations in other lands. To meet in some measure the dilemma created by enlarged demands and shrinking funds, the World's Committee, at its Washington meeting in 1924, authorized the further development, through contributions from Associations and individuals, of a special fund that had been created in 1914 by a gift from Miss Grace Dodge, President of the National Board of the United States, and known as the Extension Fund. The Washington resolution further stated: "In cases of special emergency or opportunity, and where it is not possible for the work to be undertaken by any Foreign Department, we recommend that the Executive Committee take action at its discretion, within the limitations of the money available."[4]

The amount secured for the Extension Fund, however, was not large, and Miss Niven, commenting upon the acute limitation put upon the usefulness of the World's Y.W.C.A. by the financial situation, said:

> We have had requests from countries where we have never had work; we have had requests, more urgent, if possible, from countries where there is now a little work being done and where secretaries are bending and breaking under the loads they are carrying. We are in the unhappy position of being almost despairing, certain as we are that nowadays when we transmit these requests . . . to you and to other "sending countries" as we call them, they will be refused. . . . At our own headquarters our Executive Committee has not had the power or funds to respond to these appeals.[5]

For Europe, this curtailment meant, from 1923 on, that little aid came from America save for small grants for special purposes and for the support of the work in the Near East. The European countries themselves, reduced to poverty by the war and still without popular understanding and support of a program such as had been begun by American secretaries, necessarily fell back into a much smaller work. Nevertheless, the seed that had been planted grew, slowly, and with varying fortunes, throughout this decade and bore fruit not only in Czechoslovakia and Belgium but in Roumania and the Baltic States. The work that American secretaries had done was taken over as far as possible by national workers, and the guidance formerly given by American secretaries was replaced by visitation and advisory correspondence on the part of the World's staff and committee members. In the Near East, on the other hand, the United States Association continued to maintain workers in Turkey and Syria, and appointed Miss Ruth Woodsmall as Executive Secretary for this region, to work with a Near East committee.

The World's Extension Committee had been reorganized after Champéry, and its three sub-committees, dealing respectively with Survey Pioneer Work, and Corresponding Associations, carried a heavy load of consultation with these new Associations as well as with the workers in Bulgaria, Greece, Egypt and Palestine, and West Africa.

To meet the crucial problems of leadership in the European Associations in this period, the World's Executive Committee developed a program of leadership training far beyond anything attempted in earlier years. The first step in this was a three months' training course for leaders sponsored jointly by the World's Young Women's Christian Association and the World's Student Christian Federation in Paris in 1919. This course, financed by a grant from the war fund of the Y.W.C.A. of the United States, was attended by some forty students from fourteen countries. In 1922, a special Training Committee was appointed, with Mrs. C. de J. Luxmoore as Chairman and Miss Evelyn Moore of the World's staff as its Secretary. When first appointed, this Committee was charged with "the responsibilities involved in endorsing the applications of students to enter training schools and the providing of reports on their subsequent work."[6] This continued to be an important function of the Committee, since in the succeeding years an extraordinary number of young women from Europe were accepted for longer or shorter periods of study, in the National Training School of the United States Association in New York and in the British training centers, at Duff House and Tudor House, London, and later at Selly Oak, Birmingham.

Almost from the first, however, the Training Committee found itself carrying on an actual program of training as well as recommending students to the two established schools. The Industrial Advisory Committee, later renamed the Social and Industrial Committee, cooperated in this. Two types of training were developed—study courses of several weeks' length, and short training conferences for leaders from special areas or in special lines of work. In addition, the World's Committee members and staff cooperated in many study courses and leaders' conferences carried on by the various National Committees. Some of these projects were general in character, but many dealt with special subjects such as Religious Education, Industry, Work with Younger Girls. Always they included discussions of the World's Y.W.C.A. and of Association methods of work. A listing of some of them reveals their type and variety.

In 1921 a week's leadership training course was held at Sonntagsberg, Austria, in cooperation with the World's Student Christian Federation, for workers from eastern Europe. Forty delegates were present from Austria, Hungary, Turkey, Bulgaria, Czechoslovakia. In the same year, national training courses in which American secretaries in Europe and representatives of the World's Committee shared the leadership were held in Italy, Czechoslovakia and Hungary.

In 1922 the six weeks' International Summer School in London, on Religious, Social and Economic Questions, conducted by the Social and Industrial Committee, was attended by twenty-four students from Austria, Sweden, Denmark, Holland, Belgium, Switzerland, France, Germany, Italy, Poland, Czechoslovakia, Roumania, Spain, Greece and the United States. The chief object of this course was stated by Miss Dingman:

> To develop a more sympathetic understanding of the relation of Christian ideals to social problems and also to give the students some concrete help in the ways in which efforts may be made to realize these Christian ideals.[7]

In 1923 a special conference for leaders of girls' work was held at Sonntagsberg.

In 1924 the World's staff assisted in an international camp in France for workers in Latin countries; in a two weeks' training course in the Baltic States, and in a similar course for the leaders of the *Foyers Belges* in Belgium.

In 1925 the Training Committee planned and administered a course at Visegrad, Hungary, which registered twenty-two students from Bulgaria, Czechoslovakia, Greece, Roumania, Austria, Hungary, Germany and Yugoslavia, and also a month's course at Mons, near Grenoble, France, attended by thirty-seven students from seven countries. This course included lectures in Bible Study, Psychology, Association Technical Work and Program Building. A similar course, held at Storrington, England, before the meeting of the World's Committee at Oxford the following year, was attended by thirty-nine students representing twenty-two countries.

In 1927 a new approach was made to the training of leaders for work with the younger membership, when a conference sponsored jointly by the World's Y.M.C.A., the World's Student Christian Federation and the World's Y.W.C.A. was held at Dassel, Germany, for workers among high school boys and girls. Careful preparation was made for this conference through preliminary papers which outlined the work already being done by various organizations in different countries. The conference, while composed largely of W.S.C.F., Y.M.C.A. and Y.W.C.A. workers, was attended also by leaders of other Christian organizations from Germany, Switzerland and Great Britain. There were 113 delegates, fifty-eight of whom were women, representing twenty-six countries, including Egypt, Palestine, Australia, India, as well as most of the European countries, Great Britain and the United States. The joint approach to the problem of youth was reported to have been of great value:

> This conference, although composed of delegates holding widely differing points of view, yet achieved before its close a wonder-

ful unity, the differences having been very frankly faced at the outset. The sharing of a variety of methods of approach and the comparing of personal experiences has been most enriching, and the experience of bringing together men and women leaders has been unanimously approved.[8]

That same year the Training Committee also conducted a study course in Latvia for the northern countries—Norway, Sweden, Denmark, Fin land, Estonia and Latvia.

The year 1928, the year in which the International Missionary Council met in Jerusalem, naturally found the Training Committee concentrating its efforts on the Near East. In April a conference was held in Beirut, Mrs. Luxmoore and Miss Dingman representing the World's Executive Committee. One hundred seventy-five delegates attended this conference, coming from Egypt, Palestine, Syria and Turkey. Following the confer- ence a three weeks' training course attended by a small number of leaders was held by the World's Y.W.C.A. at Ain Karim, near Jerusalem.

In 1929 an Industrial Study School was held at Schloss Bredeneck, Holstein, Germany. Here thirty-seven students were registered, coming from fourteen European countries and from Australia and the United States.

This type of training for leadership did not come to an end with the close of the decade; two similar courses were organized later—one for leaders from Orthodox countries at Balcic, Roumania, in 1930, and one for leaders from Latin countries at St. Georges, France, in 1931.

The mere recounting of the location and the international character of these courses suggests the difficulties involved in their preparation and administration. In spite of handicaps, however, the World's Committee carried through in these years a program of training remarkable in view of its small budget and staff, by which leadership was developed and new work undergirded in Europe. The importance of this in establishing the new Associations, setting common standards in ideals and programs, creating a common mind and a living international fellowship, can scarcely be overestimated.

A similar emphasis on leadership training was characteristic of other parts of the Association world in these years. The World's Committee minutes frequently record word received of study courses in India, China, Japan, South America, Australia, New Zealand. Though the World's Committee could not function in these countries to the same extent as in Europe, its staff members frequently contributed to them. They were also often "lecturers" at the British training centers and at the National Training School in New York. The latter was helpfully related to the entire training system of the World's Committee during this period by two visits from Mrs. Luxmoore, as Chairman of the World's Training Committee. In 1924, while visiting the United States, she spent five weeks at the school, "taking the whole schedule" as she told the Executive Committee. In 1927 she came again by special invitation, to act as hostess for the summer session. In these ways there was kept in the leadership training of the Association world a unity without suggestion of uniformity.

At the close of the decade, the financial crash of 1929 and the depression which followed served to hasten a reorganization, already long under consideration, of the system of training in use by the Association in the United States. Under the new scheme the National Training School was discontinued in favor of shorter training courses in different parts of the country and more reliance upon recommended courses in the universities. With this change, and with the loss in funds available for scholarships, the flow of workers from other lands to the United States for training was greatly lessened, although other methods by which shorter periods of training were made possible in a number of countries were later developed.

New Associations were by no means the only concern of the World's Committee in Europe in these years. The shifting of national boundaries that occurred with the close of the war involved drastic consequences for some National Associations, especially Austria and Hungary, the former losing one-third of its Associations. The financial situation in these countries was desperate and there was lacking the fresh enthusiasm of newly created national existence which was so large an element in the progress of the Associations in Czechoslovakia, Roumania, Latvia and Estonia. The question of the relationship of branches composed entirely of one nationality to the National Association of a country predominantly of a different nationality arose again with new insistence. This was especially true of the German branches in the Baltic States and in Czechoslovakia.

On the other hand, one of the encouraging developments of these years was the growth of the German movement. Although the early postwar years were for the German Y.W.C.A. years of great hardship and suffering, and in them the national staff was reduced by half, yet the recovery made was remarkable. The representative of the World's Committee who attended the German National Convention in 1921 was much impressed with the progressive spirit of the younger members. Two years later, 3,000 delegates were present at the National Convention in Halle, while a girls' conference at Bremen in 1925 had an attendance of 3,600, including 500 leaders. In 1927 an Industrial Secretary was called to the national staff, in line with the recommendation made to all National Associations at Champéry.

188

Fräulein Zarnack, the General Secretary of the German National Committee, worked closely with the World's Executive Committee in many ways. With Miss Bretherton she visited the Baltic States to confer on the question of the relation of the German branches there to the newly formed Associations of Latvia and Estonia. She spent three weeks in Finland as a leader in their training course for workers. She visited Czechoslovakia, was consulted on problems in Austria, and arranged to have a member of the German national staff give help to the Association in Hungary. Germany also undertook, in response to China's appeal for a truly international staff, to try to send one and perhaps two German secretaries to work in China.[9] In 1926 an international club in Berlin, in existence before the war, was reopened by Fräulein Mensing of the German national staff and reorganized as a part of the Assiciation.

A quite different problem of rebuilding was faced in Portugal. This little Association, affiliated as an active member of the World's Association in 1905, had not grown as had been hoped, owing to the immense difficulties of finding competent leadership. In 1921, realizing the need of help from outside, Portugal asked that it might be given the status of a Corresponding Association and receive special help from the World's Committee. In response to this appeal, Baroness Olga Meyendorff of the World's staff, spent the two years 1923-1925 in Portugal, striving to develop there the part of the Association program which seemed most needed, that with younger girls.

Out of the needs of this period there came a certain amount of regional development among Associations in the same geographical area or having similar conditions or problems. Training courses and leaders' conferences were planned by several countries together. In two instances, in northern Europe and in the Near East, this trend developed into an informal regional organization which has continued to be a fruitful cooperative project. As early as 1919, the northern countries of Norway, Sweden, Finland, Denmark and Iceland created an Intercountry Advisory Committee, and in 1921 called Fröken Ingeborg Olafssen to be its traveling secretary. She spent several months in each country in turn, giving advisory service, holding religious meetings, and speaking on the work of the Association in other lands. The Committee also arranged inspirational conferences for these countries, the first of which was held in Denmark in 1921. This was followed by similar conferences in other countries in later years.

Even before the war it had been suggested that there might be a federation of the Associations in countries bordering on the eastern Mediterranean. In 1923 a conference was held at Ramallah, Palestine, with delegates present from Egypt, Palestine, Syria and Turkey. This conference expressed a desire "to be joined loosely for the sake of conference and mutual exchange of ideas and experience." At its meeting in Washington in 1924, the World's Committee approved this plan. An Eastern Mediterranean Federation was therefore formed, with Miss Woodsmall as its Executive Secretary. This Federation, which replaced the earlier Council for Egypt and Palestine, defined its purpose in its constitution as being: "To strengthen and co-ordinate the work of the Y.W.C.A. in this area; to promote friendly relations with other organizations in the same area; and to strengthen the spirit of fellowship between the various Associations." Its work, like that of the Intercountry Advisory Committee of the northern countries, was accomplished through an advisory relation of Miss Woodsmall to all the countries and through joint training courses and conferences.

Outside Europe, the World's Y.W.C.A. was faced with situations arising out of developments during the war, in the Far East, India and South America. The situation in the Far East was directly related to the work of the Social and Industrial Committee established at Champéry.

Immediately following the close of the Summer School of Industry in 1922, Miss Dingman left London for a year of visitation in Japan, China, Australia and New Zealand. Of the need for work among women in industry in Japan, she wrote: "The modern industrial development of Japan is essentially a woman's problem, as more than half the workers in power factories are women. The time is ripe for a careful, constructive but aggressive program."[10] Australia and New Zealand, with their advanced labor legislation, presented a vivid contrast to Japan and China, but Miss Dingman reported:

> . . . acquaintance reveals that there is a big struggle going on between organized labor and organized capital . . . that the group who have really tried to understand in order to find a Christian solution to these acute controversies is very small . . . the labor group has been able to gain so much by their own efforts that the church and other Christian bodies like the Association have felt very little responsibility for action. . . . Given this background, one can see that the task of Miss Jean Stevenson, our National Industrial Secretary there, isn't easy.[11]

The National Committee of the China Association, realizing its need of guidance with relation to work in the rapidly developing industrial situation, had in 1920 requested the help of an industrial specialist "for at least two years to study the question here and help form and direct our policy." This request led to the appointment early in 1921 of an Englishwoman trained in economics, Miss Agatha Harrison, as the first National Industrial Secretary for China. Both Miss Harrison and the China National

Committee sought to pour all their strength into the most fundamental approach they could discover to the appalling industrial situation. The report from China to the Washington meeting in 1924 said that within a few weeks of Miss Harrison's arrival the National Committee

> instead of deciding on a policy of palliative work of clubs and classes, passed a strong recommendation . . . that the National Committee begin at once to make a direct and accurate study of industrial conditions in typical centers, to equip it with the knowledge which will enable it to serve both employers and employees in the most constructive way and to help to create the public opinion that must precede legislation.[12]

With a view to equipping the Association with the needed knowledge, the National Committee sent a member of the national staff, Miss Zung Wei-tsung, to the International Working Women's Congress meeting in Geneva that autumn. The minutes of the World's Executive Committee record Miss Zung as a visitor at its meeting en route to this Congress. In November of the following year, the China Committee sent another Chinese worker, Miss Shin Tak-hing, to the London School of Economics, where a three-year scholarship was promised, to take up training for industrial work. The National Committee of China also sought from the beginning to cooperate with other agencies in its industrial program. At Miss Coppock's suggestion, the discussion of industrial questions was placed on the agenda of the National Christian Conference of China of 1922. From this and further discussions at a meeting in 1923, a standing Committee on Industrial and Social Problems was formed under the China National Christian Council. The first Y.W.C.A. National Convention, held in October 1923, voted to unite with other Christian forces under the direction of this Committee in a unified policy and program. The end of that year therefore "saw the work of the Y.W.C.A. National Industrial Department merged almost entirely in the work of other bodies."[13]

The next step for the Association was the securing of a permanent National Industrial Secretary to work in this cooperative scheme. Miss Lily Haass, American General Secretary of the Peking Association, was asked to take this position after furlough and special study in the United States. Meantime, the World's Committee acceded to the request that it should lend Miss Dingman to the National Committee of China from the time Miss Harrison left until Miss Haass should be ready to take over, that is, from January 1924 to June 1925.

Another area of concern in these years was India. There had been no official visit from the World's Committee to India since that made by Miss Spencer in 1907. In 1922 the National Committee of India urged a study of the post-war situation there by a special commission composed of representatives of the four countries—Great Britain, the United States, Canada and Australia—which contributed workers and funds to India. Neither Australia nor Great Britain felt able to respond to this request, but a commission of three members, Miss Niven, Miss Greta Finley, a member of the National Committee of Canada, and Miss Sarah Lyon, Executive Secretary of the Foreign Division of the National Board of the United States, made a four months' visit to India early in 1923. Six years later, by an arrangement similar to that by which the World's Committee lent Baroness Meyendorff for two years to Portugal and Miss Dingman for a year and a half to China, Miss Mills spent the entire year of 1929 in India. The reports of these two extended visits, supplemented by reports from Mrs. S. K. Datta, a former General Secretary of the India National Committee, who returned to her post for the years 1925-1928, and from Mrs. F. V. Slack, of the American Foreign Division Committee, who visited India with her Y.M.C.A. husband in 1925-1926, make it possible to see what had been happening to the Y.W.C.A. of India.

Even after fifty years of work—for the Association in India celebrated its jubilee in 1925—the difficulties of developing a truly indigenous movement had proved so nearly insurmountable that Miss Niven could say, "The Association has just begun to touch the Indian community apart from the students" and "all the work accomplished so far is only preliminary to what might be done in the future."[14] These difficulties were, as had been recognized from the early days of the Extra-European and Colonial Division of the British United Central Council, largely inherent in India itself. They were also due to the fact that the Association's early program, though theoretically it included Indian young women, always had been directed in large measure to the needs of the Anglo-Indian young women and tended not to reach out beyond that group.

The greatest handicap to the growth of the work among Indians was, nevertheless, "the serious lack of staff and insufficient funds."[15] Mrs. Datta comments on "the almost constant shortage of staff" and adds that it has hitherto been particularly difficult to secure and maintain an Indian staff.[16] Miss Mills believed that the efforts to strengthen the distinctively Indian leadership in the past had "suffered, among other things, from the lack of cooperation between the student work and the rest of the Association." She notes, however, with satisfaction, the recent opening of new centers of Indian work and the fact that one branch has elected its first Indian President.[17]

There were also new currents running strong in India in the post-war years, which were bound to be significant for the future of the Y.W.C.A. Miss Lyon, reporting on the visit of the Commission to India, said:

> The religious influence of the Association is like a golden thread running through the whole strand. . . . But today's religious trends require a new interpretation and a new presentation of religious truth and religious education.[18]

Among these new trends she called special attention to the mass movement toward Christianity; the impatience of the Indian Christian over Western denominationalism and Western traditions; and the active reform organizations among Hindus and Moslems which were introducing Christian principles into their religions. Miss Mills mentioned four factors that she believed would have a decisive effect on the work in India: (1) the strong and growing feeling of nationalism, with its dislike of foreign influence; (2) the increasing importance of social movements outside the Association; (3) the desire of the non-Christians who were cooperating with the Association, for equality in leadership and control in a specifically Christian organization; (4) the sacrifice demanded of the membership in following a Christian way of life, actuated as they were by a desire also to prove themselves loyal to their country.

At its Quadrennial Conference in 1929, the India Association voted to give primary emphasis during the next quadrennium to religious education. This resolution, Miss Mills reported, "was the outcome of the conviction that there is no place for the Association in India unless it works as a religious movement, bringing together all types of Christians."[19] This was the view also of some who appraised the Association from the outside. Professor Arthur Holt, who headed the India group of Christian leaders who in the years 1929 to 1932 made a survey of the foreign work of the American Y.M.C.A. and Y.W.C.A., stressed "the need of the Association as a fellowship grouped around religious ideals rather than as a promoter of activities."

As for the part foreign secretaries might still play in the development of the Association in India, Miss Mills summed up the opinion of those who were best informed and most understanding of the needs of India:

> Undoubtedly there is a place for the work of foreign women who understand India and can help to train Indian leaders. They must, however, go to India with a clear conviction of why they do so, they must be receptive to new ways of thinking and planning, they must have the gift of imagination. Unless they are able to enter into the hopes and aspirations of India, to see the possibilities of her womanhood as well as to understand her problems, they will not be able to help her through this difficult time.[20]

The India National Committee, in view of the action of the 1929 Quadrennial Conference, asked that the World's Committee lend Miss Mills to India for another two years to work with them on the development of a program of religious education. For health reasons it was impossible for Miss Mills to accept this invitation. The work already done, however, proved a turning point in the relation of the World's Y.W.C.A. to developments in India.

While the experience of the Y.W.C.A. in India was setting before the World's Committee new problems regarding the relation of the Association to the growing spirit of nationalism and to organizations which, under the auspices of other religious faiths, were seeking some of the same goals sought by the Y.W.C.A., the development of the movement in the countries of South America[21] was bringing forward the problem of work within a predominantly Roman Catholic culture with a sharpness not experienced before.

Soon after the arrival of Miss Elizabeth MacFarland from the United States as Continental Secretary in 1918, a Y.M.C.A. Continental Conference was held at Piriapolis, Uruguay, at which that organization, already well established in several South American countries, was considering, among other questions, that of a personal basis of membership for Y.M.C.A.s in these countries. Following this conference a small gathering of women from Argentina, Chile, Brazil and Uruguay was held at Bella Vista, Argentina, to discuss the needs of women and girls and the kind of membership basis best adapted to the development of the Y.W.C.A. The Y.W.C.A. now organized a Continental Committee for the purpose of furthering interchange of thought and experience among the already existing Associations and also for promoting work in other Latin-American countries. Through the acceptance of this Committee as a corresponding member in December 1922, the World's Y.W.C.A. established a constitutional relationship with the South American work as a whole before it was possible to form National Committees in the separate countries.

The goal sought by the Continental Committee was a truly indigenous national movement in each country, one which should serve all young women and draw together in its leadership women from all branches of the Christian Church. With this purpose in view, the constitution of the Continental Committee embodied the following statement on organization and basis:

> In order that the leadership of the local Associations shall be in the hands of those declaredly Christian in faith and practice, this Committee will maintain official relationships with those Associations which accept as voting members those who declare their faith in God as revealed in Jesus Christ, their divine

and only Saviour, the sufficient source of moral strength for the individual and for society; who purpose to be his disciples in doctrine (teaching) and in life and who desire to unite with other Christians, irrespective of their church affiliations, for extending Christ's influence among young women and for enlisting them in his service by the promotion of the study of his life, teachings and work, as revealed in history and Holy Scriptures; or which have a basis similar to this and in accord with the World's Y.W.C.A.[22]

In this same year, 1923, a conference of foreign secretaries and some nationals from the South American Associations expressed the conviction that:

The Association in South America should be an interconfessional movement not organically attached to any church body, Catholic or Protestant. . . . They also agreed to attempt to work out a positive, constructive program, emphasizing the common points of unity in all Christian belief and the necessity of the application of the social teachings of Jesus, omitting all controversial differences and cultivating a spirit of tolerance.[23]

By these policies adopted in South America, the Y.W.C.A. was definitely striving to build a movement that would not only permit but would encourage Roman Catholics as well as Protestants to assume leadership within it. The new statement of basis adopted at Stockholm had prepared the way for such a step. The American secretaries who, with the Latin-American women, worked out the details of this policy and program were doing so in line with the position taken at Stockholm and with the policy adopted by the Y.M.C.A. in South America. They were also following a marked trend in the Association in the United States, which had in 1920 adopted a personal statement of basis for use in student Associations that desired it, and was now considering a similar alternate personal basis for Associations other than student.

In 1927 Miss Niven and Madame Bertrand, one of the Vice Presidents of the World's Y.W.C.A., made an official visit to South America, a visit that Miss Niven described as "one of enquiry as well as encouragement of existing work." She wrote:

These pieces of work that we have been seeing are not just experiment stations, or even Foyers, but Y.W.C.A.s aiming at carrying spiritual quality and significance into every part of their varied program. . . . Women of a fine type are willing to serve on the Committee or to give voluntary service in other ways, and this in the face of serious opposition from the church to which most of them belong, but they serve and will continue to serve because they have come to believe in the Association and desire to serve Christianity in South America, with a co-operative attitude toward all, but owing no allegiance to any one part of the Christian Church.[24]

A situation similar to that in South America existed in the Philippines. Here, in a predominantly Roman Catholic culture, the Association was proving itself able "to extend Christ's influence among young women and to enlist them in his service" within an ecumenical fellowship.

These developments in Europe, the Orient, India and South America, along with the beginning of work in Mexico, the Philippines and Korea, where in each case the environment presented peculiar problems, raised for the World's Committee certain issues, the consideration of which was an important part of its work in this decade.

REFERENCES

[1] Industrial Findings, Champéry, Report on, for 1921.

[2] International Migration Service, Report, June 1922, pp. 5, 6.

[3] Larned, Ruth. World's Committee Meeting, 1924, Report, pp. 69, 70.

Note: In September 1946, at a meeting of its International Committee in Paris, the name "International Migration Service" was changed to "International Social Service". The scope of this service goes far beyond technical advice on emigration and immigration. By collaboration with many organizations it seeks to solve a wide variety of problems which arise in families separated by frontiers.

[4] World's Committee Meeting, 1924, Minutes, pp. 11, 12.

[5] Ninth National Convention, Y.W.C.A.s of the U.S.A., 1926, Report, pp. 138-139.

[6] Executive Committee, February 16, 1922, Minutes.

[7] Dingman, Mary A. "An International Industrial Summer School", *The Association Monthly*, November 1922, p. 530.

[8] Executive Committee, July 21, 1927, Minutes.

[9] Executive Committee, April 2, 1926, Minutes, p. 8.

[10] World's Committee Meeting, 1924, Report, p. 50.

[11] *Ibid.,* p. 51.

[12] World's Committee Meeting, 1924, Report, pp. 56, 57.

[13] World's Committee Meeting, 1924, Report, p. 60.

[14] Executive Committee, June 7, 1923, Minutes, p. 3.

[15] Mrs. Slack, Executive Committee, April 22, 1926, Minutes, p. 3.

[16] Executive Committee, July 7, 1927, Minutes, p. 2.

[17] Executive Committee, January 9, 1930, Minutes, p. 6.

[18] Lyon, Sarah S. "Lookin' Eastward", *The Woman's Press,* September, 1923, p. 562.

[19] Executive Committee, January 9, 1930, Minutes, pp. 5, 6.

[20] Executive Committee, January 9, 1930, Minutes, p. 6.

[21] See Chapter 12, p. 160.

[22] Quoted by Wilson, Elizabeth in *World Cooperation,* 1930, p. 126.

[23] *Ibid.,* p. 126.

[24] Niven, C. T. "At Last—South America", *The Woman's Press,* Sept. 1927, p. 621.

*I have seen the most wonderful things happen . . .
things that absolutely confound all the suspicion and
envy and fear that there is in the world. I have seen,
around tables in our Association households, the beginnings of internationalism come into the minds of
people just because we were table to bring people
together.*

AGATHA HARRISON, Address, Eighth National Convention,
Y.W.C.A. of the United States, 1924.

*We have something inexpressibly precious to share
with each other, and we must give it without fear or
reservation. How wonderful are the gifts comprised
in our World's Association! We cross the barriers
of race, nation and confession and find our unity in
our common purpose and work in the name of our
Lord. To lose nothing that is precious in the Christian heritage in which we were born and bred and
to build our inheritance and experience into the
structure of the World's Young Women's Christian
Association will be a rich contribution to ecumenical
fellowship.*

CHARLOTTE H. ADAMS, Report, Commission on Ecumenical
Questions, 1931.

CHAPTER 15 CREATING UNITY WITHIN DIVERSITY

THE NEED for appraisal of new trends and for
reorientation of the work of the World's Y.W.C.A. in relation to the new
conditions, even more than the practical difficulties of the post-war years,
led to the continuance until 1928 of the pattern established at Champéry—
a World's Committee meeting held in connection with a meeting of carefully selected representatives from active and corresponding Associations.
In these meetings, certain areas of concern appear again and again: the
advisability of changing the location of the headquarters of the World's
Association; the religious message and program of the Association,
especially as it related to social, industrial and international issues; the
interconfessional position of the Association in the light of its recent expansion in Eastern Orthodox and Roman Catholic countries, and with relation to the ecumenical movement in the churches.

The question of the removal of the headquarters from London, discussed at Champéry, was brought up again at St. Wolfgang in 1922. Here it was reported that the National Associations were unanimous in the opinion that it should remain in London. The idea of Geneva as a location for the future grew rapidly, however, in the following years. The establishment there of the League of Nations made Geneva a natural center for many international undertakings. The World's Y.M.C.A., the W.S.C.F., and other Christian bodies were already there, and cooperation with them and with other international organizations was a constantly enlarging function of the World's Y.W.C.A.

At Oxford, in 1926, the World's Committee received a proposal from the 1925 Plenary Meeting of the World's Y.M.C.A. that the two organizations consider securing a joint building or headquarters of their own in Geneva, "in the interest of more effective cooperation in planning and in effort in matters of common concern."[1] In the following year, at the invitation of the President, Lady Parmoor, and Lord Parmoor, a conference of representatives of the World's Y.M.C.A. and Y.W.C.A., and the World's Student Christian Federation was held at their home, *Parmoor*, to discuss the evangelical purpose of the three organizations with relation to the needs of youth and their common concerns as ecumenical movements. At this conference, further plans for cooperation among the three organizations were developed.

This subject of cooperation was therefore a large factor in the discussion of the future location of headquarters at the Budapest Conference in 1928.[2] But it was not the only one. The pros and cons in regard to Geneva were given in the World's Committee report to the conference:

> The question of location of headquarters is bound up with questions of cooperation, but it is also to be studied from the point of view of being a world organization, with all that this involves in willingness to be a part of the great movements in the life of this time. . . . The experience of these two years has shown that much can be accomplished in international cooperation from London as the base of operations. It has also shown certain limitations inherent in the fact of distance from the chief center of modern international cooperation, Geneva. In the opinion of many, these are more than compensated by the positive value of so experienced an Executive Committee. A move to Geneva would almost certainly entail a new type of Committee.[3]

After much discussion and in full consciousness of the losses as well as the gains to be incurred, it was voted unanimously to adopt the recommendation for removal, and the conference authorized the appointment of an International Commission charged with the task of making the neces-

Lady Parmoor

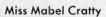Miss Mabel Cratty

sary preparations for the change, including the framing of a new constitution.[4]

As a result of the discussions at biennial meetings of the World's Committee in 1922 and 1924, several important steps were taken with regard to the aim of the World's Y.W.C.A. as it related to social, economic and international issues. The subject of the International Commission which met at St. Wolfgang in 1922, was "The Interpretation of Christ to Young Women Today". The discussions were based on replies to a questionnaire about the attitude of young women to personal and organized religion, to family and community, and to economic and international issues. The findings of the Commission embodied recommendations regarding the practical program of the Association, its work with younger girls, the interpretation of membership, and the responsibility of the Association for interpreting Christ to young women. They called attention to "the serious problems confronting womanhood in all the countries of the world, arising out of the world's negation of the principles which Christ proclaimed," and laid stress upon the distinctive opportunity for dealing with these problems afforded by the wide scope, the varied program, and the flexibility of the Y.W.C.A. They called upon all Associations "to interpret Christ to the individual as one who meets her insufficiency and gives power to be free and strong." They urged the necessity of using the language of today and of approaching young women on the plane of their personal experience; of presenting the Bible vividly and simply; of being fearless and open-minded in facing new ideas, and humble, sympathetic and imaginative in dealing with all groups, nations and creeds; of relating the work of the Association to other movements for social reconstruction and of recognizing fearlessly corporate sin and proclaiming the necessity for corporate righteousness.[5]

At the meeting of the World's Committee which followed the International Commission's meetings, these findings were approved, and the commitment to a social as well as a personal interpretation of Christ was further emphasized by the adoption of a resolution adding to the statement of Aim of the World's Association in the constitution, the following paragraph:

> It also calls all National Associations to promote Christian principles of social and international conduct by encouraging the development of a right public conscience such as shall strengthen all those forces which are working for the promotion of peace and better understanding between classes, nations and races; believing that the world social order can only be made Christian through individuals devoted to the single purpose of doing God's will, and that through obedience to the law of Christ

199

there shall follow the extension of his Kingdom, in which the principles of justice, love and the equal value of every human life shall apply to national and international as well as to personal relations.[6]

In 1924 the first official meeting of the World's Y.W.C.A. outside Europe in the thirty years of its existence took place at Washington. Miss Dingman's report from the Orient, and the increasing pressure for cooperation with other organizations on social and international matters led to further consideration of the responsibility of the World's Y.W.C.A. in these areas. Two resolutions relating to the addition to the aim adopted at St. Wolfgang were passed. One of these suggested a program for carrying out this aim as it related to industrial problems. The second, suggested by Miss Cratty, General Secretary of the National Board of the United States, pledged the members of the World's Committee "to work steadily for the removal of barriers between nations, races and creeds by studying . . . the conditions of social, economic, racial and national life; and to use all the resources we have, alike as citizens and as members of the Association, for influencing public opinion."[7] A third resolution dealt with the authority of the World's Executive Committee to express an opinion or to cooperate with other societies with regard to international matters. It was voted that:

> Whereas the World's Y.W.C.A. has been invited and many, in the future be invited, to give its opinion on international questions or to cooperate with other societies in regard to such matters, we recommend that the Executive Committee be authorized to give such an expression of opinion, or to take such action on behalf of the World's Y.W.C.A. if they believe themselves to be in accord with the mind of the World's Association, it being understood that in no case is any National Association committed by such action, and that where it seems possible that action contemplated by the Executive Committee might embarrass a National Association, such Association should first be consulted.[8]

The biennial meeting at Oxford in 1926 was for those who attended it a deeply moving revelation of the significance of the Association as a part of the ecumenical Christian movement. An address by the Dean of Canterbury Cathedral and the Bible study outline prepared for the meeting by Mademoiselle Suzanne de Dietrich of the World's Student Christian Federation, both dealt with the subject "The Church Universal", while one of the questions sent out in preparation for the meeting was, "How is the function of the Association different from that of the Church?" The experience which was the outcome of the study and discussion of these subjects was summarized in the report of the meeting:

> At Oxford we faced squarely the obstacles that divide us along one important line, our church membership, and in so doing discovered, not only that these differences are many and various, but that the richness of the future perfect unity toward which we are moving is dependent on these very differences. . . . In the inspired moments of the discussion groups, we saw the Association taking its rightful place in the development of the Church Universal, the household of God, in the whole Christian enterprise.[9]

This awakened sense of responsibility for "the whole Christian enterprise" found expression at Oxford in two resolutions, one for closer and more systematic cooperation with the "kindred societies"—the World's Y.M.C.A. and the W.S.C.F.[10]—and the other for sending a memorandum to the International Missionary Council, calling attention to the obstacle to international unity found in economic rivalry, and expressing the hope that on the agenda for the projected World Missionary Conference to be held in Jerusalem in 1928, a large place might be given to the consideration of economic and industrial problems in their relation to mission work.[11]

The year following the biennial meeting at Oxford, the Executive Committee held a conference at High Leigh, near London, in connection with a meeting of the International Commission charged with preparation for the 1928 World's Conference. At this meeting Miss Niven gave a report of the visit of the Madame Bertrand and herself to South America.[12] As she described the work of the Association in these Latin-American countries, the part being taken in it by women belonging to the Roman Catholic Church, and the larger share in its leadership which they might take in the future, there came to some, for the first time, a full realization of the significance of the interconfessional principle which had been adopted at Stockholm in 1914.[13]

By many the fact that this might lead to the establishment of Associations in which Roman Catholic leaders held a large place had not been foreseen. The question was raised whether "the implications of the Stockholm resolutions had ever been fully understood by some countries or, indeed, whether there had been any official or public discussion on that point before they were adopted." It was clear that some Associations were unprepared, without much further consideration, to accept the practical conclusions to which these resolutions now seemed to lead. Distrust of the Roman Catholic Church, fear of its control, and a belief that an evangelistic and Bible study program in the Association would be impossible if members of the Roman Catholic Church were admitted to leadership, made the question one of vital concern. It was also increasingly evident that the ever-enlarging place given to social, economic and international affairs in the program did not carry the approval of all Associations.

For those Associations that from early times had centered their work in the religious appeal to the individual, both these trends seemed to endanger the very heart of the movement. On the one hand, the changing circumstances of life were demanding of Christian organizations teaching and action in the field of social issues and were forcing them to think and act in ecumenical terms. On the other hand, it was easy to make these demands a substitute for the appeal to the individual rather than an extension of it.

As the time for the World's Conference at Budapest in 1928 approached, it was recognized that on both these issues there were profound differences of conviction within the movement, and that a deeper basis of unity than had yet been discovered must be sought for. It was in the light of this that the conference theme was chosen—"The Word of Reconciliation". How far this deeper unity was attained is suggested in the report of the conference and in the actions taken there. An introductory statement to the report says:

> Wherever there is a gathering of people from the ends of the earth (and a glance at the list of the delegates will show from how many points of the compass we came), there will inevitably be immediate, practical need of reconciliation. In our Bible study, in our discussion on Aim and Methods, conflicting opinions in matters of the most profound conviction as well as in more superficial matters were expressed. . . . The two great subjects which were most keenly discussed . . . were (1) our inter-confessional position, nationally and internationally, and (2) our responsibility in regard to social, industrial and economic matters.[14]

In considering the second of these issues, much help was given by two speakers from the International Labor Office, Mr. Johnson and M. Thélin, and by Miss Dingman, "who stirred many of us to see in a quite new light the responsibility of Christians to consecrate the whole of their personalities to the task of bringing the whole of life under the banner of Christ."[15]

There was divergence of opinion also between those who did and those who did not feel an inescapable responsibility laid on the Association in these matters. These opinions were firmly stated in the discussion groups, but "in the end unanimity was developed."

The findings in which this unanimity was embodied made use of another word—"interdependence"—which, with the word "reconciliation", expressed the central thought of the whole conference:

> The fact of world interdependence, daily brought home to us in the common course of national and international existence, bears witness to the solidarity of the whole human race. But this solidarity, with the fellowship which should be the natural consequence, is continually violated by the unjust and unequal conditions which we allow to prevail in our social, economic and industrial relationships. We feel ourselves called to carry our Christian message into the area of these relationships, boldly asserting the claim of our Master to rule every part of the field of human life. This call is the more urgent and compelling because we have been forcibly brought to recognize the grave peril to peace which underlies economic conflict and industrial unrest.

In the light of these considerations, the conference voted unanimously to urge upon local Associations (1) the study of social, economic and industrial questions in their national and international aspects, (2) their responsibility for educating public opinion on these issues, (3) the securing of trained leaders for the development of industrial work, and (4) cooperation in research on social questions with other international organizations.[16]

The interconfessional position of the World's Y.W.C.A. was the issue around which the greatest difficulty centered at Budapest. "It was here that the sharpest divergencies were found; it was here that we all, at the end of the conference, and still more during the closing day of the World's Committee meeting, felt the Spirit of God working among us to bring us to a deeper desire to find a living unity with him."[17] Several resolutions regarding further study were proposed in the conference discussions. In view of the importance of the question, and the impossibility of thorough discussion in so large a body, the matter was at length referred to the World's Committee. After long consideration the Committee voted to urge on National Associations careful study of the World's Y.W.C.A. interconfessional position and to itself collect and distribute the necessary information for such study. Following the conference, the Executive Committee, in order to carry forward this recommended study, appointed an Interconfessional Sub-Committee. In May 1929, this sub-committee sent to affiliated National Associations an historical memorandum tracing the development of interconfessionalism in the World's Association from the original statement of basis, through the experience in eastern and southeastern Europe from 1909 to 1912 which led to the adoption of the new statement of Basis, Aim and Principles at Stockholm, and the further interpretation of these made at Champéry.[18] In an introductory note accompanying this memorandum, the Committee wrote:

> It is quite clear that in 1894, when the World's Y.W.C.A. was organized, the interconfessional question, as we know it today, was not very definitely foreseen, and certainly the word "interconfessional" was not used. . . . It is clear from our own earlier documents that the word "interdenominational" was used to cover much the same idea, that is, relationships outside the Protestant churches as well as within them.

In support of this last statement they quoted the first annual report of the Executive Committee (for 1895) in which Mrs. Tritton said: "Another point we also emphasize is the interdenominational as well as the international character of the World's Y.W.C.A. Every member of every outward and visible church is welcome to join our ranks, provided she can subscribe to our basis."[19] The memorandum summarizes the position as it was at this time in the words of a pamphlet written by Miss Spencer for use in the consideration of the basis in the Associations in the United States:

> The World's Y.W.C.A. is evangelical in character in that it gives a central place in its work and teaching to Jesus Christ, and in its basis and aim presents him as Saviour and Lord. But while affirming its loyalty to the Christian Church, it does not use any church membership test, but is willing to accept any National Association into full fellowship, provided that Association will accept the World's basis or one in conformity with it, and is in harmony with its aims and principles.[20]

Perhaps the most impressive part of this historical memorandum is the list appended to it of the countries having work which touched members of churches other than Protestant.[21]

Later in the year 1929 the Interconfessional Sub-Committee sent to all affiliated Associations, active and corresponding, an analysis of the replies received to questionnaires regarding the position of the National Associations with relation to the religious situation within each country.

These replies, while not complete, revealed the wide range of circumstances within which the Association worked in different parts of the world, and the fact that back of the variety of practices lay historical situations, social, political and religious, of long standing. The confessional type of Association was strong in those countries, chiefly in Europe, where the population was homogeneous and belonged almost wholly to one church, or where the Association was closely related to the State Church or Churches.

The interconfessional type of Association was found in every country where girls whom the Association desired to serve belonged to various branches of the Christian Church. It flourished particularly in those countries of the New World where immigration, coming from many European countries, made for a very mixed population religiously and at the same time offered a peculiar challenge to the Association to meet the need of young women for friendship and service. It was also found in the new post-war countries of Europe, where one of the important functions of the Association was felt to be the building of fellowship between racial groups whose members belonged to different religious confessions, and in countries of a non-Protestant culture. The replies indicated, however, that even in those Associations of most strongly interconfessional character, the genius of the movement and in large part its responsible leadership were Protestant.

It was clear to the Executive Committee that the distribution of this material was but one step in what must be a long consideration of this question. Somewhat similar processes had been going on in the Young Men's Christian Association and the World's Student Christian Federation, both of which had experienced many of the same developments and were meeting like problems. It was therefore decided to appoint an International Commission on Ecumenical Questions which should continue the study within the Y.W.C.A., and should cooperate with similar commissions in the other two movements. At the request of the Executive Committee, Miss Charlotte H. Adams of the national staff of the United States, was lent to the World's Committee to act as Chairman of this Commission. The Commission was composed, in addition to the Chairman, of Miss Una Saunders and Miss Theodora Maclagan representing the Executive Committee, Madame Pannier, President of the National Committee of France, Miss Baimakoff of Latvia, Miss Iliescu of Roumania, Fräulein Doktor Voigt of Germany, Miss te Lintum of the Netherlands and Miss Bretherton and Baroness Meyendorff of the World's Y.W.C.A. staff. The work of this Commission was continued until 1931, and thus spanned the period which saw the closing of the headquarters in London and the opening of the Geneva office.

Two meetings of the Commission were held in 1930, one in Paris in January and a second, enlarged meeting in Geneva following the 1930 World's Committee meeting at St. Cergue, Switzerland. At this meeting, thirty-nine persons, representing twenty countries, were present. There were also two meetings of the Joint Commission of the Y.M.C.A., the W.S.C.F. and the Y.W.C.A. During the fourteen months' life of the Commission, its Chairman visited fourteen countries in Europe, meeting with Association and church leaders, learning from them of their points of view and their problems, interpreting the interconfessional position of the World's Association, and in her reports to the Executive Committee analyzing the significance of the particular conditions and problems in each country for the work of the Association as a whole.

For an understanding of the problems of work in orthodox countries, one of the most important events of the year was Miss Adams' attendance at a "consultation" of representatives of the World's Y.M.C.A. with leaders of the Orthodox Church at Kephissia, Greece. Dr. John R. Mott acted as chairman of this consultation. Of the forty persons present, twenty-four were leaders of the Orthodox Church, both clerical and lay, and represented Bulgaria, Egypt, Greece, Yugoslavia, Roumania and the orthodox work with Russian émigrés in western Europe. Of this gathering Miss Adams reported:

> The Orthodox Church is deeply concerned with the problem of its youth and welcomes the two Asssociations as helpers in the great task of keeping youth in contact with spiritual ideals of life. . . . The consultation opened up the pressing need of youth work which the Church feels and some of the ways in which both of the organizations can help, not only the youth but the Orthodox Church itself, provided we have enough vision and patience to meet this ancient church in a truly ecumenical spirit.[22]

A series of visits to Associations in the countries of northern Europe presented a vivid contrast to the situation in southeastern Europe, as well as to that in non-European lands. Summing up impressions of the Associations in the northern countries, with their almost wholly Lutheran population and their comparative isolation from other countries, Miss Adams said: "The background of one church and the absence of acquaintance and intercourse with peoples of other confessions make interconfessional relationships unreal in experience. . . . It is therefore not at all strange that our northern Associations have found it difficult to understand the procedure of countries whose conditions are so utterly different."

The final report of the Commission on Ecumenical Questions summarizes the situation thus:

> It is evident that two kinds of Associations are affiliated with the World's Y.W.C.A.: the confessional and the interconfessional. Each type reflects the peculiar church environment of the countries where these types of Association exist. . . . Since the Commission has been at work, it has been growing more and more clear that our particular ecumenical problems are by no means peculiar to ourselves. They are shared by the two other Christian youth movements, the World's Y.M.C.A. and the W.S.C.F.

It is also clear that our three organizations are a part of a wider movement in the churches which has set itself to find a solution for the divided church of Christ. . . . There is emerging also . . . a sense of the naturalness of ecumenical fellowship in a movement as rich in diversity as ours. As we learn to know each other better we shall see more clearly that a real unity can exist within a comprehensive diversity.[28]

Although the work of this Commission was brought to a close in 1931, the question itself remained one to which much consideration was still to be given. Doubts concerning the wisdom of the ecumenical position existed in the minds of many of the leaders in some Associations, and these doubts were strengthened by the decrease in emphasis on evangelization and on Bible study that was apparent especially in those Associations of the interconfessional type. In 1930 the National Association of Finland withdrew from affiliation with the World's Y.W.C.A., and in 1931 the National Committee of South Africa did the same. In the latter case, however, two Associations, those in Durban and in Port Elizabeth, dissociated themselves from the action of the National Committee and remained in the World's Association, affiliated as individual Associations in corresponding membership. In these losses to the world fellowship other factors than the ecumenical position of the World's Association were operative. The increasing emphasis on social and industrial questions, the freer and more extensive program in recreation which the war had introduced, also entered into the picture.

The tension involved in maintaining the fundamental evangelical warmth of evangelistic purpose which originally gave rise to the Association movement in the midst of ever more varied conditions, increased interest in public affairs, and an ever more inclusive fellowship, is inherent in the nature of a world organization such as the Young Women's Christian Association.

REFERENCES

[1] World's Committee Meeting, 1926, Minutes, p. 11.

[2] The report of the World's Committee to the Budapest Conference says: "No clearer mandate was given by the World's Committee at Oxford than that relating to cooperation with other organizations. Chief among these were our 'kindred societies', the World's YMCA and the WSCF. . . . During the past two years there has been increasingly valuable relationship to the other international women's organizations. This has been largely through the Joint Standing Committee, which exists to bring women's influence more effectively into the various activities of the League of Nations and the International Labor Office. It has, therefore, many links with Geneva and inevitably draws all its constituent bodies more into the orbit of League matters. . . . The World's YWCA has also had direct touch with the League, with the I.L.O., and with many international interests centering in Geneva, through attendance at conferences and meetings, through reports and requests for advice" (Sixth World's Y.W.C.A. Conference, 1928, pp. 31, 33, 34).

[3] Sixth World's Y.W.C.A. Conference, 1928, Report,, p. 34.

[4] *Ibid.,* p. 10.

Note: One change in the constitution was made at Budapest—the substitution of the World's Committee for the World's Conference as the legislative body of the organization, thus placing final responsibility for policy on the smaller, continuing group of leaders chosen by the National Associations that are in active or corresponding affiliation with the World's movement (*ibid.,* p. 9).

[5] World's Committee Meeting, 1922, Report, pp. 39, 40.

[6] World's Committee Meeting, 1922, Minutes, pp. 8, 9.

[7] World's Committee Meeting, 1924, Minutes, p. 13.

[8] *Ibid.,* p. 11.

[9] World's Committee Meeting, 1926, Report, pp. 5, 6.

[10] See footnote 2 above.

[11] World's Committee Meeting, 1926, Minutes, pp. 9, 10.

[12] See Chapter 14, p. 195.

[13] See Chapter 10, p. 131.

[14] Sixth World's Y.W.C.A. Conference, 1928, Report, pp. 4, 5.

[15] *Ibid.,* p. 5.

[16] Sixth World's Y.W.C.A. Conference—1928, Report, pp. 11-12.

[17] *Ibid.,* p. 5.

[18] See Chapter 13, p. 176.

[19] See Chapter 6, p. 68.

[20] Spencer, Clarissa H., *A Background for Basis Study.*

[21] Countries whose Associations touched members of churches other than Protestant included: Argentina, Austria, Belgium, Brazil, Bulgaria, Canada, Chile, Cyprus, Czechoslovakia, Egypt, Estonia, France, India, Italy, Latvia, Mexico, Palestine, the Philippines, Roumania, Syria, the United States, Uruguay. Other than Protestant churches listed were Roman Catholic, Eastern Orthodox (Bulgarian, Estonian, Greek, Latvian, Roumanian and Russian), Coptic, Syrian and Armenian.

[22] Adams, Charlotte H., Report, April 12, 1930, pp. 3, 4.

[23] Adams, Charlotte H., Report, February 1931, pp. 3, 4.

We are all convinced that we have a very important period before us in our World's Association. Already the circumstances under which we are working, in new surroundings, in constant touch with other large bodies whose work is akin to ours, demand many adjustments. But infinitely more important are the currents of religious and anti-religious thought sweeping through the world, among which we have to take our stand. Against secularism and atheism we want to proclaim clearly and resolutely the message of Jesus Christ, our Saviour and our King. Knowing the emptiness, misery and despair in so many hearts, even among the young, we want to show the way to Him who alone gives life and strength and rest. Seeing so many forces at work for unity in the Church of Christ and for peace and good-will among men we want to join with them.

JONKVROUWE C. M. VAN ASCH VAN WIJCK. "A Message from the New President", *World's Y.W.C.A. News Service,* August 1930.

CHAPTER 16 — A NEW CHAPTER BEGINS: 1930-1934

THE REMOVAL of the World's office from London to Geneva in the spring of 1930 marked the beginning of a new era in the history of the World's Young Women's Christian Association. When the World's Committee met at St. Cergue, Switzerland, in June of that year, headquarters at 2 rue Daniel Colladon had already been secured and equipped through a special fund provided by gifts from individuals and some of the National Associations. The members of the Executive Committee had themselves furnished the "Quiet Room" which was to become the place so often sought for individual or united meditation and worship.

At St. Cergue, the International Commission through its Chairman, Jonkvrouwe C. M. van Asch van Wijck, submitted for adoption the new constitution, the framing of which had been completed at a meeting of the Commission held at Burckhardthaus, Berlin, the headquarters of the German Association, in February 1929. The official language was now to be French instead of English. The name, Basis, Aim and Principles were unchanged. Such alterations as were proposed were made to meet the conditions inherent in the new location and to carry out the desire for a more completely international administration. The most important changes were the substitution of the title "World's Council" for that of "World's Committee" for the legislative body of the organization; the internationalization of the Executive Committee by the requirement that its membership, which was not to exceed fifteen in addition to the officers, must include at least five nationalities; the stipulation that the Executive Committee should meet not less than three times each year,[1] one of these to be an enlarged meeting to which each actively affiliated National Association should be entitled to send a representative; and the setting up of a four-year term for officers of the Association, with the further provision that the President and Vice Presidents should be eligible for re-election for one such other term, after which a period of four years must elapse before re-election.

After the adoption of the new constitution, officers and Executive Committee members were elected as follows:

President: Jonkvrouwe C. M. van Asch van Wijck
Treasurer: Mademoiselle Catherine Picot

Vice Presidents:

Madame Alfred Bertrand	Miss Ruth Rouse
Mrs. C. C. Chen	Miss Una Saunders
Mrs. James S. Cushman	Mrs. Matsu Tsuji
Mrs. C. de J. Luxmoore	Fräulein Hulda Zarnack

Executive Committee Members:

Fru Elsa Cedergren	Lady Procter
Madame Henri Johannot	Mrs. John H. Finley
Mademoiselle Madeleine Chenevière	Fröken Karen Raeder
Miss Theodora Maclagan	Mrs. George S. Huntington
Mrs. S. K. Datta	Miss Elizabeth Victor
Madame J. Pannier	The Honorable Mrs. Waldegrave
Mademoiselle S. de Dietrich	(Honorary Member)

The St. Cergue meeting had taken as its theme, "Presenting the Christian Message", and its addresses and discussions were centered around various aspects of this subject, such as the presentation of the message through teaching, through service, through research, through changing standards, through church fellowship and worship. Among the delegates and visitors were a number of members of the Orthodox Church from Bulgaria, Greece, Yugoslavia, Egypt, and the Russian communities outside Russia, and for these a special service was conducted on Sunday afternoon by a priest of the Russian Orthodox Church in Geneva.

210

G. Maillard Kesslere

Jonkvrouwe C. M. van Asch van Wijck

Mademoiselle Catherine Picot

Boissonas, Geneve

Mrs. James S. Cushman

Madame Alfred Bertrand

The high point of the St. Cergue meeting was the interruption of the business sessions on June 20 for the trip to Geneva, to inaugurate the work there.

We all met at No. 2 rue Daniel Colladon, with a number of residents of Geneva who came to bid us welcome. The new offices were dedicated in a simple but moving ceremony; the hymn "Grosser Gott, wir loben dich" was sung, and Mrs. Waldegrave, Mademoiselle Chenevière, President of the Association in Switzerland, and Fräulein Zarnack, General Secretary of the German Association, led us in prayer, each in her own language. The new premises had been decorated with a quantity of beautiful flowers. . . . Perhaps it is above all to the Quiet Room that the thoughts of many will turn from the distant countries where they work. . . . The next two hours were spent in Madame Bertrand's delightful garden at Champel, where tea was set out under the chestnut trees, and at 5:15, before returning to St. Cergue, we met in the Cathedral of St. Pierre and joined in an inter-ecclesiastical service in which clergy of the Anglican, Swiss Reformed, Lutheran and Russian Orthodox Churches took part. The beautiful singing of the Russian choir added very much to the devotional atmosphere of the service and M. de Saussure's sermon on I Corinthians 12:4 ("There are varieties of talents, but the same Spirit") put before us the true ideal of that unity in diversity in which nothing is abandoned but all contributes to the richness of the whole.[2]

As the long era that had its center in London closed and the new chapter opened in Geneva, the World's Young Women's Christian Association was profoundly conscious of the changes that had been wrought within it. It was not only in the new location of headquarters and in the new constitution that these changes were registered. It was also in the new outlook resulting from the facing of fundamental issues on which wide diversity of opinion existed, and the acceptance of the continuing task of seeking to create unity within that diversity. None of the leaders of the organization, perhaps, appreciated more keenly or welcomed more understandingly the changes and the new opportunities than the members of the Executive Committee in London, for whom it meant the yielding up of a responsibility held in trust by them since the movement first came into existence. The gratitude felt for the vision and the work of this Committee through the years and for the generous confidence with which they now gave over their task to others, was expressed in *The Woman's Press,* the journal of the Association in the United States, by Miss Adams:

The record which this old Executive Committee has made through the almost forty years of its history belongs to the heritage of every Association in the world. . . . Many there are who are willing to carry responsibility, fewer are they who will carry the burden of it year in and year out over a considerable period of time; fewer still are they who, after having given the best that is in them in untiring service for years, can lay down their work with a gallant spirit.[3]

The international situation within which the World's Y.W.C.A. entered upon this new era was one of peculiar and increasing difficulty. The world-wide depression which followed the great financial crash of 1929 severely affected the organization. National Associations as well as individuals were compelled to reduce their support. In the year 1936-1937 the World's Y.W.C.A. budget was, approximately, only half the £10,000 that had been judged necessary at Champéry in 1920. Severe retrenchments in National Associations drastically reduced the number of secretaries sent to other lands.[4] Moreover, the deterioration in international relationships leading to war, first in the Far East and, at the end of the decade, in Europe, was a source of profound anxiety and of uncertainty and limitation in planning and action. Yet the period was of special significance for the World's Y.W.C.A. because of developments within itself as a world movement in contrast to development in the field in which it worked, and because of changes that took place in the methods by which it accomplished its task.

In contrast to the largely British personnel of the earlier leadership, the list of officers and Executive Committee members elected at St. Cergue included eleven from the continent of Europe, coming from seven countries, six from Great Britain, one of whom was a resident of India temporarily living in Geneva, three from America, one of whom was resident in Turkey, one from China, and one from Japan. Although still not entirely well-balanced, the administrative body of the organization was thus far more internationally representative than ever before.

One result of this new alignment was the new volume and importance of the contribution of the leaders from the Associations of the Continent to the formation of World's Council Policy. This contribution was realized only slowly, for the new Committee was at first necessarily less familiar with the problems and less experienced in working together than the homogeneous group of London days. For some, also, their own national background had given far less contact with world affairs than the British leaders possessed. This fact, however, was in itself important, because it meant that one characteristic feature of these years was the growth in experience in dealing with the world-wide issues of the Association of its continental leaders.

The World's Association was exceedingly fortunate in having as its President for the new era Miss van Asch van Wijck, a woman of rare intellectual and spiritual power, who believed profoundly in facing frankly and fearlessly the differences in thought and conviction within the movement and thereby gaining an added richness for the whole. She was a former President of the Federation of Women's and Young Women's Organizations in the Netherlands, which was affiliated with the World's Y.W.C.A., and had been a member of the World's Committee since 1925. She had attended the meetings of the World's Committee at Washington and Oxford, and at Budapest had been appointed Chairman of the International Commission formed to prepare for the move to Geneva, and also of its subcommittee on revision of the constitution. That she was young and free to travel extensively was also of great value in the task of interpretation between Associations having very different environments and points of view.

The ideal toward which the World's Council now worked was not only a more international Executive Committee but also a more widely representative staff. The resignation of Baroness Meyendorff in 1929, and of Miss Margrethe Parm in 1930, left a staff composed entirely of women from Great Britain and the United States. The first effort, therefore, was to add to the staff a member from continental Europe. A call was extended in 1930 to Miss Julia Matouskova of Czechoslovakia, but unfortunately she was forced by illness to resign after barely a year of service. In 1933 the long-held desire for a German member of staff was realized in the acceptance of a call by Fräulein Schmoeckel of the German national staff, but she was obliged to withdraw her acceptance before her work had begun because of pressure to continue vitally important work at home. A permanent member of staff from the Continent was, however, achieved in 1933 by the appointment of Signorina Mary Rossi, formerly General Secretary in Rome.

The widely scattered membership of the new Executive Committee necessitated new ways of working. Three Executive Committee meetings yearly, each several days in length, took the place of the monthly and often even fortnightly meetings that had been held in London. In accordance with the provision in the by-laws of the new constitution, one of these, usually that one held in May or June, was enlarged by the attendance of representatives from National Associations affiliated in active membership. The long interim between Executive Committee meetings made other changes necessary. To advise with the staff in the matter of interim decisions, a "consultative group" was formed of the officers resident in Geneva. Later, this responsibility was carried by means of a series of sub-committees for different subjects, whose reports and recommendations became the basis of the Executive Committee meeting agenda.

A phase of work that presented special problems in the early years in Geneva was that of cooperation with the international organizations.

Although recognition of the need for this cooperation was one of the compelling arguments for the move from London, the extraordinary multiplication of organizations, conferences, meetings to which it seemed that the World's Y.W.C.A. should contribute, and the extent to which this cooperation would absorb the time and energy of both committee members and staff, probably was not foreseen. Miss Niven wrote in 1935:

> We have become a part of an international community of organizations and have found it impossible to hold back our interest and our cooperation from a great number of subjects which are today before the various societies and groups of societies. . . . Those organizations with which there are definite and continuous relations . . . fall into three groups, (a) international Christian organizations, including youth movements, ecumenical church bodies, and the International Missionary Council, (b) women's international organizations, fifteen or more in number at the present time, (c) the two official organizations, the League of Nations and the International Labor Office, and various of their related bodies. . . . Practically every problem, social, moral or international, is too complicated for one organization to attack alone. On the other hand, cooperation can become extremely complicated and time-consuming.[5]

The period was one which challenged fresh study on many subjects, and in the early years in Geneva there was considerable emphasis on such studies, in cooperation with the other Christian organizations on the one hand, and with the international women's organizations on the other. The Christian organizations together opened an International Christian Study Center, which proved valuable as a meeting place for the discussion of a variety of subjects and for increasing understanding and fellowship. Joint study with other Christian groups was carried on in two fields in the years 1930-1934—Ecumenical Relationships and Family and Sex Relationships. The joint Ecumenical Commission, composed of representatives from the Commission on this subject of the World's Y.M.C.A., the World's Y.W.C.A. and the World's Student Christian Federation, which had been formed in 1930, continued to meet during these years, and among other things gave special consideration to the growth of youth movements within the churches. In this connection it added to its membership representatives from the Youth Commission of the World's Alliance for International Friendship Through the Churches and from the Universal Christian Conference for Life and Work. The study of Family and Sex Relationships was pursued jointly with the Y.M.C.A., which had set up a Commission on this subject following its conference at Helsingfors in 1926 and had proposed that the Y.W.C.A. should cooperate in this study through a Commission of its own.

The small staff available and the increasing financial stringency ultimately necessitated giving up the Study Center, but the relationship between the Christian organizations that it represented continued to function through an informal group known as the "Cercle Söderblom"[6] which arranged meetings from time to time for the purpose of hearing special speakers or a member of the Christian organizations. The same reasons forced the discontinuance of the meetings of the Joint Commission on Family and Sex Relationships, which had, however, already done some valuable work in preparing bibliographies and gathering material from different countries on the training of leaders to deal with questions in this realm.

In cooperation with other international women's organizations, the Social and Industrial Committee made studies of unemployment among young women in preparation for the International Labor Conference of 1935, which was to consider especially unemployment among youth. It also continued its studies, begun several years earlier, on the status, conditions of employment, and training of domestic workers in different countries. Its report on this subject, based on replies to questionnaires received from twenty countries, was the first report ever made from a world point of view on this field of employment among women.

More important even than these joint study projects was the study of the Christian purpose of the Association and its expression in the light of new needs and conditions, which was carried on by the World's Council itself throughout this decade and urged by them upon National Associations. Dr. John A. Mackay, addressing the World's Council at St. Cergue in 1930 had said:

> The present hour is characterized by great hesitancy and confusion regarding the Christian message. It may be said that there is a great love of honesty and a hatred of sham, but ours is not an age of faith. . . . In many Christian circles the substance of faith becomes a diminishing quantity, with a resultant sense of weariness and a loss of spiritual insight and vitality. . . . We find at the same time an increasing anxiety to be able to grasp and formulate the essence of Christianity. . . . If Christian organizations do not become vocal on vital matters of faith, they will cease to be, or they will become beached on the banks of the river of life.[7]

The work and the thinking of the World's Y.W.C.A. during these years were dominated by the consciousness of this hesitancy and confusion, this anxiety and hunger, and by its own sense of responsibility for meeting these spiritual conditions on a new level of conviction and effectiveness. Yet in no aspect of the life of the Association did the

215

differences due to historical factors, national environment, psychological and religious inheritance reveal themselves more clearly than in the attitude toward and the expression of the religious purpose of the movement. Deeply conscious of both the need and the difficulties, the conviction of the Executive Committee was expressed in a pamphlet on *The Aims and Practices of the World's Y.W.C.A.*:

> The years that have passed since the Association first came into existence have brought great developments and so wide a variety of methods in use, as well as of areas of life touched by it, that it is now multiform in character. The World's Executive Committee believes that . . . the time is ripe for making a new study of what is already inherent in the statement of purpose, and for looking more deeply into its philosophy and aims.[8]

This pamphlet was published following the enlarged Executive Committee meeting of 1932, when the subject had been much discussed in the light of two series of addresses, one on "The Purpose and Practices of the Y.W.C.A." by Miss Rice of the United States, and the other by Mademoiselle de Dietrich of France on "The Needs of Girls Today". It urged the necessity of adapting the Association program to meet new demands upon it and of cooperating with other organizations "in helping to build a right social order in harmony with the mind of Christ." It suggested four principles as essential for maintaining the balance and vigor of the movement:

1. Loyalty to its deepest religious purpose as expressed in the Basis and Aim of the World's Association.
2. A fellowship which is inclusive rather than exclusive.
3. Recognition of the place of the Association in social, economic and international life.
4. A prepared leadership.[9]

In this same year a second pamphlet, *The Purpose of the Y.W.C.A.*, was published, containing a number of papers written by leaders from different countries.[10] At one in their recognition of the critical nature of the times and in their belief in the saving power of Jesus Christ for the individual and for society, these papers revealed wide differences in approach to and in emphasis on the expression of the purpose in different Associations.

A specific problem in relationships was brought before the new Executive Committee by changes in the work in Turkey. In 1928 the work in syria had been separated from that in Turkey[11] in order that it might grow into a national movement of its own, and that the work in Turkey might be organized on lines especially adapted to the needs of that country, that is, on a basis uniting in one organization Turkish (Moslem) young women and Greek and Armenian Christians for fellowship and common service. A Service Center was established in Istanbul under the leadership of a Y.W.C.A. secretary sent out by the Foreign Division of the United States. The program of this Center was definitely built upon Christian principles, but it was not itself a Y.W.C.A., and its Committee of Management was composed of both Moslem and Christian women.

There was a strong desire, however, that the Center should have some connection with the World Movement of the Y.W.C.A., and in 1931 a proposal was made that contact should be maintained through a small Liaison Committee of women who accepted the World's Y.W.C.A. Basis. The question presented by this proposal was a difficult one. Could the World's Y.W.C.A. recognize any relationship with an organization not completely Christian? The Executive Committee, after long consideration, decided that no organic relationship between the World's Y.W.C.A. and the Service Center was possible. Recognizing, however, the value of an indigenous movement of young women in Turkey, and the need of continuing help in leadership and funds to make this possible, the Committee approved the continuance of such help by the Foreign Division of the United States but recommended that the proposed Liaison Committee be linked with that Foreign Division rather than with the World's Council.

An important recurring question during these years was the relationship of the World's Council to the Associations of the Far East and the means by which their participation in the World Movement might be increased. These Associations were eager for closer links with the World's Council and with one another, for more visitation from World's Y.W.C.A. representatives, and for more opportunity to share in world thinking and policy making. At the World's Committee meeting in Washington, in 1924, the China National Committee had invited the World's Y.W.C.A. to hold the next World's Conference in China. The acceptance of this invitation had twice to be postponed. In 1926, at Oxford, the proposal to move the headquarters to Geneva and the consideration of other issues deeply affecting the European Associations had led to the decision to meet in Europe in 1928. At Budapest in 1928, constitutional and administrative matters connected with the establishment of the new headquarters necessitated a meeting in 1930 near Geneva. But with the move to Geneva accomplished, the matter of securing the full participation of the Associations of the East assumed a primary importance. In view of this, the question of a Council meeting in the Orient presented itself with new urgency.

At St. Cergue, China renewed its invitation, and the World's Committee voted that "a conference be arranged in China, lasting two weeks, ten days of conference work and four days of business sessions." Plans for the conference were discussed. Official languages were to be Mandarin, Japanese and English. The program was to include addresses on "Faith and Purpose", discussions on the Christian expression of the Association, and commissions which would confer on various phases of the work, rural, industrial, student, etc.[12]

At the Executive Committee in February 1931, however, when Miss Ting, National General Secretary of the Association of China was present, it was voted, "in view of the general financial stringency which would make an adequate representation difficult," to postpone the meeting until October 1933, on the understanding that there would be wide visitation by delegates from the West preceding the conference.[13] But in February 1932, a year later, both the political and the financial situations were so much more acute that the Executive Committee, "while reaffirming the importance of an eventual meeting in the East," proposed as an alternative a meeting in Europe in 1933, followed by visitation in the Far East "and possibly a World's Council meeting in the East in 1935 or 1936."[14] This proposal was laid before the National Committees and brought interesting reactions. At the enlarged meeting of the Executive in June 1932:

> Communications were read from various countries of the Pacific urging that a meeting be held in that area. China renewed its invitation in the most definite terms, Japan expressed desire for a meeting in the Orient as soon as possible, and Australia urged the possibility of the meeting being held in some other place in the Pacific area if it seemed inadvisable to hold it in China as planned. The growth of the desire for a World's meeting in the Orient and the need for it was increasingly realized.
>
> Representatives from the different countries present expressed with deepening conviction their feeling that the World's Council should adhere to its plan to hold the next meeting in China, and that the financial obstacles should be overcome in a spirit of sacrifice. . . . It was proposed by Madame Pannier, seconded by Mrs. Luxmoore, and carried unanimously that we recognize a call of God to go to China and reaffirm the decision taken in February 1931 to accept China's invitation to hold the next World's Council in that country.[15]

But at a later session of this same meeting, further decisions as regards date, etc., were postponed in view of a cable from Japan, arriving after the foregoing discussion, advising postponement.

When the Executive Committee met in October 1932, there were before it letters from both China and Japan. Miss Ting expressed the hope that plans for the meeting might go forward but assured the Committee of

218

China's complete acceptance of any decision made by them. Mrs. Tsuji indicated that the problems connected with the proposal were being fully faced but said that "the National Committee in Japan had unanimously agreed to support the holding of the meeting in view of the sense of urgency expressed by other countries." After much discussion, the Executive Committee voted to go forward with plans for the meeting and to send Miss van Asch van Wijck and Miss Niven at once to confer with leaders in both Japan and China regarding the problems involved.[16]

Miss van Asch van Wijck and Miss Niven sailed for the Orient in December 1932. Their first reports, made in the face of increasing political tension between China and Japan, were that "notwithstanding developments" they believed cancellation of the meeting was not justified. In September 1933, however, they met in Shanghai with a group of representative leaders from China, Japan, Korea and the Philippines. This meeting, at which Miss Mills of the World's Y.W.C.A. staff and Miss Lyon, Executive Secretary of the United States Foreign Division were also present, discussed the whole situation, and at length sent a cable to the Executive Committee advising against the proposal. In view of this, the Committee at its meeting in January 1934, after the return of Miss van Asch van Wijck and Miss Niven, voted with much regret that a meeting in China at the present time was inadvisable and decided "for reasons of economy" to hold the 1934 Council meeting in or near Geneva.

Although the visit of the President and General Secretary thus failed to achieve its primary objective—the preparation for a Council meeting—it was nevertheless of great significance. In fact it was a turning point in the relations of the World's Council with the Associations of the East. In the more than a year of their travel, Miss van Asch van Wijck and Miss Niven not only visited Japan and China in the early months of 1933 and again in the autumn, but made a tour of Malaya and spent nearly three months in Australia and New Zealand. Miss van Asch van Wijck paid a visit of several weeks to the Netherlands Indies, and attended a meeting of the World's Student Christian Federation in Java. Miss Niven was present at the Quadrennial Conference of the Y.W.C.A. of India, and visited Korea and the Philippines. Miss Mills also spent almost a year in the Orient in 1933 and 1934, in response to requests for help in training courses for leaders. By this extended visitation and by such intercountry consultation as that at Shanghai in September 1933, the links between the Associations of the East and the World's Council as well as their links with one another were greatly strengthened.

When the President and the General Secretary after their return shared their experiences with the Executive Committee, two convictions stood out clearly:

> First, that in spite of the deep disappointment at the further postponement of the World's Council meeting in the East, the visits of the President and Miss Niven have been infinitely worth while and most warmly appreciated; and second, that never again must so long an interval be allowed to elapse without a visit from World's headquarters to the countries of the Pacific area—or indeed to any of the countries where the Y.W.C.A. exists.[17]

Notwithstanding its seeming preoccupation with the integration of the Associations of the East in these years, contact with other regions was not neglected. There was much travel in Europe by both Executive Committee members and staff. Miss van Asch van Wijck went to America, attending the national conventions of the Associations of the United States in 1932 and 1934, and also visiting Canada. Miss Niven visited America in 1931 and again in 1933, on her return from the Orient. Miss Mills spent the summer of 1931 in the United States and Canada. Miss Moore spent several months in the United States and Mexico in 1931, and in 1933 Miss Dingman made a five months' tour of the Associations in South American countries.

The 1934 Council meeting was held at La Grande Boissière, Geneva. It was preceded by a ten days' study course attended by 120 Council members and experienced leaders. The purpose of the course was to continue with a larger but still selected and responsible group, the consideration of the fundamental purpose of the Association, begun at the meeting of the Executive Committee in 1932. Each delegate to the study course was registered in one or the other of two courses, "Bible Study and the Affirmations of the Christian Faith" and "The Christian Approach to International, Social and Economic Problems".

The Council itself had an attendance of more than one hundred, including representatives of pioneer work, visitors, and fraternal delegates. The meeting was significant for the wide range of subjects considered and for the decisions made that vitally affected future emphasis and policy. Memoranda were submitted on such matters as the organization of work at headquarters; future lines of emphasis; trends in the work of Foreign Departments; cooperation in the Far East; plans for the next Council meeting; the growth of church youth work; the problems created for Christian youth movements by the rising tide of nationalism. These memoranda were discussed at length, and many of them referred to a special Committee on Future Policy of which Miss Curwen, General Secretary of the National Y.W.C.A. of Great Britain, was the Chairman.

Both in the discussions and in the recommendations of the Future Policy Committee, two subjects received special stress—the future emphasis in the work of the World's Y.W.C.A., and the relations with the Associations of the Far East. The opening paragraphs of the Report on Future Policy summarize the thinking on the first of these subjects as it had crystallized in the study groups and the discussions of the Council:

> In a world distraught by economic problems and dominated by tremendous forces reshaping national life and international relations, the World's Y.W.C.A. must face its task with a deepening conviction of its special responsibility and with a spirit of courage to explore new lines of development.
>
> While realizing the values of the diverse forms of expression inherent in the fourfold program of the Association, we recognize the necessity of concentration on certain specific emphases to meet present world needs. This Council has therefore emphasized as its primary responsibility the affirmation of the Christian faith, and seeks as its central objective to deepen the religious life of the individual through a vital Christian experience and to strengthen the spiritual force of the Y.W.C.A. as a Christian movement concerned with the crucial issues of modern life. . . . We would further emphasize the necessity of understanding more clearly the place of women and the service the Association can give in the building of a new social order.[18]

The emphasis of the Future Policy Committee on the need of an understanding of the place of women and the service of a Christian women's movement in building a new social order led the World's Y.W.C.A. to take up the study also of the place and rôle of Christian women in modern life. In the succeeding years of this decade, these two subjects of study were a major concern in the work of the Executive Committee and staff.

The subject of cooperation among the Associations of the Far East received much attention at La Grande Boissière. Miss Gertrude Owen, General Secretary of the National Committee of Malaya, presented a proposal from the Malayan National Conference for a Far Eastern Federation. The National Committee of Japan urged more frequent visitation from headquarters and the appointment in the near future of an Oriental secretary on the World's staff. China again renewed its invitation to hold the next Council meeting in that country, and an invitation for this meeting was also extended by the National Committee of India, Burma and Ceylon.

There was long discussion of these and other possibilities relating to the Far East. It was agreed that "all possible steps be taken to secure that the next Council meeting be held in the Far East," and that the Executive Committee be asked to consider the suggestions made for intercountry conferences and visitation and "a possible enlarged Executive Committee meeting in India in preparation for the Council meeting." It was further voted that up to one-half of the special fund raised for a meeting in the Orient might be used for other forms of cooperation in the Far East.

The Committee on Future Policy approved these decisions, declaring that "for a balanced development of the World's Y.W.C.A. it is essential that all regions be fully represented in the planning of the Association's policy. In the immediate future, it is particularly important to draw in the contribution of the Far East."[19] It recommended further that "at least once between World's Council meetings the Executive Committee should secure by budget provision the attendance of officers or other representatives of regions not usually present at their meetings, thus securing a more truly international thinking on general policy."[20]

The Committee on Future Policy also approved the grouping of Associations within the same region for purposes of consultation and common action, provided this was carried through with a minimum of administrative machinery and its plans made in close consultation with the World's Y.W.C.A. Hearty approval was expressed of a trend in the work of Foreign Departments, illustrated by a report of a new policy adopted for the work of the Foreign Division of the National Board of the United States, toward the substitution of an interchange of services among the Associations of different countries for the old relationship of "sending" and "receiving" countries. This trend was especially welcomed as being in line with a growing feeling on the part of the Executive Committee that the possibilities of the helpful relationship of one Association to another had not yet been fully developed; that it should not be limited to those countries which sent out or received secretaries or financial help but that "interchange of thought and experience can and should be enlarged so that all countries may take their share in it to their mutual advantage."

REFERENCES

[1] Changed at the 1934 Council meeting to "not less than twice a year."

[2] *Presenting the Christian Message,* Addresses given at World's Committee Meeting, 1930, Introduction, p. 4.

[3] Adams, Charlotte H. *The Woman's Press,* July 1930, p. 473.

[4] Between 1930 and 1935 the budget of the Foreign Division of the United States was reduced by more than two-thirds, and the number of its secretaries abroad fell from 100 to 24.

[5] Niven, Charlotte T., *A Fifteen Years' Survey,* 1935, pp. 20, 21.

[6] Named after Archbishop Söderblom of Sweden, founder of the Universal Christian Conference for Life and Work.

[7] *Presenting the Christian Message,* 1930, p. 7.

[8] *Aims and Practices of the World's YWCA,* 1933, p. 1.

[9] *Ibid.,* pp. 5, 6, 7.

[10] New Zealand, France, Germany, Japan, Norway and the United States contributed to this symposium.

[11] See Chapter 14, p. 189.

[12] World's Committee Meeting, 1930, Minutes, p. 13.

[13] Executive Committee, February 1931, Minutes, p. 6.

[14] Executive Committee, February 1932, Minutes, pp. 11, 12.

[15] Executive Committee, June 1932, Minutes, p. 5.

[16] Executive Committee, October 1932, Minutes, p. 10.

[17] *World's Y.W.C.A. News Service,* March 1934, p. 8.

[18] World's Council Meeting, 1934, Minutes, pp. 14, 15.

[19] World's Council Meeting, 1934, Minutes, p. 15.

[20] *Ibid.,* p. 16.

We felt in our hearts anew that the Christian Associations we try to be, transcending many human distinctions and divisions, might "catch some glimmer of the Will of God which brightens the way of men least when they deliberately knock at the gates of heaven and ask for a sign, and most when, in mutuality of friendship and sincere confidence, they sense the Eternal Spirit which dwells in man."

"M. R.", Report on Ceylon Regional Conference (quotation from C. E. SILCOX), *World's Y.W.C.A. Monthly*, February, 1937.

CHAPTER 17   SIGNIFICANT TRENDS

MATERIAL changes in staff followed the 1934 Council meeting. In addition to Miss Evelyn Moore, who had resigned in 1932 after ten years of service to accept a position as head of the new Central Club of the London Association, Miss Niven, Miss Dingman and Miss Bretherton left the World's Young Women's Christian Association in 1935 and 1936 to take up other work. Miss Niven, after fifteen years as General Secretary left to become interpreter of the World's Y.W.C.A. work for the Associations of the United States and Great Britain; Miss Bretherton, after more than twenty-one years of service, to be the head of the British Y.W.C.A. Training College at Selly Oak; and Miss Dingman, after fifteen years, to give her time entirely to the work of the Women's International Committee on Peace and Disarmament, which she had helped to organize in 1931. The loss of so many experienced leaders at so nearly the same time was a severe one, but continuity was maintained through Miss Mills, who had been on the staff since 1926, and Mrs. Evelyn Fox, who had been Miss Dingman's assistant since 1930 and now succeeded her as Secretary for Social and Industrial Questions.

Once again a new General Secretary was called from America. Miss Ruth Frances Woodsmall came of a family in which, as she said, "missions were a vital reality." Her father and mother had founded and developed a Baptist college for Negro students in Alabama, and their home in Indiana, where Miss Woodsmall's high school years were spent, was a center for visiting missionaries as well as for a number of students who later became missionaries. She received her Bachelor's degree at the

University of Nebraska, where she was a classmate of Miss Grace Coppock, later National General Secretary of the Y.W.C.A. of China, and her Master's degree from Wellesley College. She taught for several years in the western states of Colorado and Nevada, and in 1916 spent a year in India with a sister who lived in Bombay. In 1917 she returned to the United States, to be caught up in the war work of the Y.W.C.A., first in a Hostess House in a military camp, then overseas in France, and at the close of the war, in Germany.

The fifteen years between 1919 and her call to the General Secretaryship of the World's Council brought her a wide international experience both within and outside the Y.W.C.A. As a member of the national staff of the Y.W.C.A. of the United States, she was lent to the World's Council to make field studies in the Balkans and in the Baltic States. Under the auspices of several Christian agencies she also made a social survey in Constantinople. From 1920 to 1928 she was the Executive Secretary of the Y.W.C.A. work in Turkey and Syria, and Secretary of the Eastern Mediterranean Federation of the Y.W.C.A. From 1928 to 1930, on a traveling fellowship under the Laura Spelman Rockefeller Foundation, she made a study of Moslem women in the Near East and India. The next two years were spent in the study of missions in the Far East, first as a member of the Christian Education Commission to Japan under the International Missionary Council, and later as a member of both the "Fact Finding" staff and the "Appraisal Commission" of the Layman's Foreign Missions Inquiry in India. Out of these experiences she wrote two books, *Eastern Women Today and Tomorrow,* and *Moslem Women Enter a New World.* In 1932 she returned to the staff of the National Board of the Y.W.C.A. of the United States and it was from that position that she was called to the World's Council.

She was no stranger to its work, for she had been present in one capacity or another at every meeting of the World's Committee or Council since 1920. To the tasks of a period dominated by conflict in the Orient and by gathering war clouds in Europe, by an extraordinary increase in the cooperative relations between the World's Y.W.C.A. and the ecumenical Christian organizations, and by special concentration upon the relation of the World's Council with the Associations of Eastern lands, Miss Woodsmall brought a wealth of knowledge and experience which was of incalculable value.[1]

The new General Secretary began her work in the autumn of 1935. The first Executive Committee meeting that she attended in this capacity was held in London at the invitation of the Y.W.C.A. of Great Britain, in honor of its eightieth birthday—the first meeting of the Executive Committee to be held outside Geneva since the change in location of head-quarters.

Trends that had been gathering strength since 1930 became more clearly embodied in the policy of the World's Council in the later years of this decade. Cooperative relations with other organizations took on new character and significance. Efforts to deepen the spiritual life of the movement and relate its religious message to the special needs of the time were intensified. Intervisitation and interchange between countries increased in variety and extent. Relations between the World's Association and its member Associations in India, the Orient, Australia and New Zealand were strengthened and extended. The study of the place and contribution of women, and therefore of a Christian women's movement, was increasingly stressed.

Regarding the cooperation of the World's Y.W.C.A. with other organizations, Miss Woodsmall wrote in 1938:

> During the past four years the opportunities and demands for cooperation have steadily increased, as the inevitable cumulative result of our location in Geneva and also because of the general trend toward collective effort among international organizations. The World's Y.W.C.A., because of its dual character as a woman's movement and a movement of youth, has unusually wide and varied relationships.[2]

With the League of Nations and the International Labor Office the World's Y.W.C.A. worked continuously in a consultative and advisory capacity. It suggested women for membership on League and I.L.O. commissions, furnished information, recommended young women for the courses of study on international and social questions for which the League and the I.L.O. provided scholarships.[3] Through its correspondent membership on the League of Nations Advisory Committee on Social Questions, it kept in touch with significant developments in the social field.

Much of the World's Y.W.C.A. study and action in social and industrial matters was carried on in cooperation with other international organizations. It was a member of the Committee of Major International Associations (Comité d'Entente), and also of the Liaison Committee of Women's International Organizations, the purpose of which was to serve as a medium of communication and cooperation among the member organizations and to forward the influence of women in international affairs.[4] Studies on such subjects as the Status of Women, Unemployment, Household Employment, were often pursued jointly, and for these the world-wide membership of the Association offered special facilities for gathering information on an international scale. In 1937, on the occasion of a special conference in Java, under League of Nations auspices, on the Traffic in

Miss Ruth F. Woodsmall

Miss Sosa Matthew

Women and Children in the Far East, the World's Executive Committee urged adequate representation of women, and arranged that Miss Woodsmall herself, as well as Y.W.C.A. representatives from China, the Philippines and the Netherlands Indies, should attend the conference. In its work for peace, a special concern in these years, the World's Y.W.C.A. cooperated closely with the Women's Committee on Peace and Disarmament, while consultation and cooperation with the other international Christian organizations having headquarters in Geneva were constant factors in its day by day work.

New and important lines of cooperation emerged in these years from three great ecumenical gatherings: The Oxford Conference on Church, Community and State, in July 1937; the Edinburgh Conference on Faith and Order, in August of the same year; and the International Missionary Conference at Madras in December 1938. Through attendance at these conferences the World's Y.W.C.A. as an international Christian movement was "immeasurably enriched for its own distinctive task" and also given "a new vision of the distinctive contribution it should make to the whole ecumenical movement."[5] These years saw also the formation of a Provisional Committee for a World Council of Churches. Miss van Asch van Wijck was the only woman member of the preparatory committee that formulated the plan for the World Council for presentation to the Oxford Conference. The widening field of ecumenical activity illustrated by these conferences and the relatively small place assigned to women in them emphasized the need, within the general study of the "Place and Contribution of Women", for special consideration of "Women and the Church".[6]

In the field of youth, the World's Y.W.C.A. cooperated with organizations carrying a similar program, such as the International Girl Guides; with ecumenical movements such as the Youth Commission of the World Alliance for International Friendship Through the Churches; with the "kindred societies", the Y.M.C.A. and the World's Student Christian Federation; and with still other groups such as the World Youth Peace Conference. In these various relationships the World's Council shared in the promotion of the World Youth Peace Conference in Geneva in 1936, at which there were thirty-five Y.W.C.A. representatives from different countries; in securing Y.W.C.A. representatives in the youth delegation of one hundred at the Oxford Conference on Church, Community and State in 1937; and in an International Conference for Leaders of Secondary School Youth at Dassel, Germany. The Dassel conference, at which there were forty Y.W.C.A. delegates from eighteen countries, was a joint project of the World's Y.M.C.A., the World's Y.W.C.A., the World's Student Christian Federation, and certain other movements.

Of all the international meetings of youth during these years, however, the World Conference of Christian Youth which met at Amsterdam, Holland, in 1939, on the very eve of war, was of unique significance because it was the first great cooperative effort to bring together a world-wide gathering of Christian youth. This conference, with an attendance of more than fifteen hundred young men and women from some seventy countries, was jointly sponsored by the Provisional Committee of the World Council of Churches, the Joint Ecumenical Youth Commission of the World Alliance for International Friendship Through the Churches, the Universal Christian Conference for Life and Work, the World's Y.M.C.A., the World's Y.W.C.A., and the World's Student Christian Federation. The theme of the conference was "Christus Victor", and in addition to the daily service of worship, the platform addresses and the daily Bible study, the conference met in separate groups for discussion of such subjects as Christian Youth in a World of Nations, in the Nation and the State, in the Economic Order; Christian Youth and Race; Christian Youth and Education; Christian Marriage and Family Life; the Church, Its Nature and Mission.

To the preparation and execution of this conference many members of the World's Executive Committee and staff gave much time and thought. For a few it was a major responsibility for several months. Thirty countries sent Y.W.C.A. delegates, and for eleven of these, representation was made possible by help from the World's Y.W.C.A.

An increase in the cooperative relationship between Associations in different countries was promoted chiefly in two ways—by the extension of regional conferences, and by the development of an interchange of services. The Eastern Mediterranean Federation and the Advisory Committee for the Northern Countries continued to hold regional conferences as in the past. In addition, a Far Eastern Regional Conference was held in 1936 in Colombo, Ceylon. In connection with this conference the Executive Committee held an enlarged meeting, the first official meeting of the World's Association to be held in the East. In 1936 also the South American Associations held an Intercountry Conference at Piriapolis, Uruguay.

This South American conference, attended by Mademoiselle Goblet d'Alviella and Mademoiselle de Dietrich representing the World's Executive Committee, was of particular significance for two reasons: its searching examination of the spiritual basis of Association work in Latin-American countries, and its decision to request the World's Y.W.C.A. to disaffiliate the Continental Committee, through which the Associations in South America were linked to the World's Association, in order to open the way for each country to work toward separate affiliation as a national movement.[7]

228

The Associations of Mexico, the United States and Canada met in a North American Area Conference at Toronto, Canada, in 1937, and two United States-Canadian conferences were held, one in Muskoka, eastern Canada, and the other in Spokane in western United States, following the World's Council meeting in 1938. The Executive Committee suggested a regional grouping of the French-speaking countries of Europe, but it proved impossible to accomplish this at that time.

In 1936 the former Extension Committee was replaced by an internationally representative Committee on Field Planning (later renamed Mutual Service), whose task was to survey and study the needs throughout the Association world and bring recommendations regarding those that should be given priority and the means by which the needs might be met. Miss Clara Roe, formerly General Secretary in Buenos Aires, Argentina, was called to the staff in 1936 with a special assignment to the work of this committee, which was to meet annually in connection with the enlarged meeting of the Executive Committee. These mutual services, in which many Associations shared, were chiefly help in the training of leaders, by means of scholarships, or by visitation in order to gain practical experience; short-time services of secretaries lent by one country to another; and grants of money for special projects.

Interesting illustrations of the kinds of mutual services which were anticipated but were handicapped by the outbreak of war, are found in the Executive Committee minutes and reports of those years. For example: The request of Siam for help in organizing a Y.W.C.A. led to an offer from the Y.W.C.A. of the Philippines to provide training for Siamese leaders in the Association in Manila. The desire of the Iran Mission of the Presbyterian Church to see the Y.W.C.A. established in Iran resulted in the sending of Miss Helen Crawley, secretary in Beirut, to Iran at the expense of the Foreign Division of the United States, to study the situation. The question of beginning work in Fiji as a joint endeavor of Australia and New Zealand was considered, and Australia set aside a sum of money for this purpose when the time should be opportune and the right leader found. India also expressed the hope that it might cooperate if work were begun in Fiji. A successful earlier instance of such mutual sharing was the appointment of Miss Celestine Smith of the Y.W.C.A. of the United States, to a year and a half of special service in Lagos, Nigeria, the expenses of salary and travel being borne jointly by the United States and Great Britain.

The 1934 Council meeting had declared its primary responsibility to be the affirmation of the Christian faith, the deepening of the religious life of the individual, and the strengthening of the spiritual force of the Y.W.C.A. as a Christian woman's movement concerned with the crucial issues of modern life. This statement of responsibility not only influenced the program of all the regional conferences of this period but led to a number of special projects undertaken by the Executive Committee and staff. Early in 1935 a letter was sent to National Associations asking for information about their methods of embodying the Christian emphasis in their program. Thinking on "the contribution of women" was stimulated at the same time by an article by Miss van Asch van Wijck in *The World's Y.W.C.A. Monthly*[8] on the subject "Our Approach to the Study of the Task and Place of Women". Consideration of how the study of both these subjects might be furthered was a major item on the agenda of the 1935 enlarged meeting of the Executive Committee, and also of the November meeting of that year held in London.

To further common thinking and at the same time create understanding of the varying approaches to religion found in different Associations, an outline for Bible study was prepared by Mademoiselle de Dietrich of the World's Student Christian Federation and a member of the Executive Committee of the World's Y.W.C.A., on the theme "Jesus Christ: Who He Is; What He Gives; What He Asks". Leaders representing different countries or different religious traditions were invited to prepare outlines on the same theme, but especially adapted to the needs of their own country or group.

Six outlines were received, three of which were prepared by Association leaders in Germany, the United States and Japan, one by a theological professor in China, one by an English woman in India, and one by a leader in the Eastern Orthodox Church. These studies were sent to National Committees to be used in such ways or with such adaptations as individual circumstances might dictate. In some countries it was thought that "a group might make a comparative study of all the outlines, endeavoring to understand the meaning of the differences in the approaches shown in them."[9]

In 1937 the Executive Committee called Mademoiselle de Dietrich to the staff on a half-time basis as a special worker in the field of religion, and Miss Mills and Mademoiselle de Dietrich together undertook a study of the "Christian Emphasis" within the World Movement, as expressed in the different National Associations. Another stimulating project in this field was the visits made for purposes of discussion and interpretation, by leaders representing one religious tradition to Associations having a different background of experience and point of view. In 1935 Miss Mills spent several months in the Balkan countries and the Near East, working

230

on the "Christian Emphasis" with Association leaders and discussing with them and with other leaders the special problems faced in Orthodox lands. In 1937 Fräulein Doktor Voigt of Germany visited Great Britain for special Bible study courses, and in the autumn of that year Mademoiselle de Dietrich spent three months in the United States and Canada in the interest of the religious work of the Y.W.C.A.

In the expression of their religious purpose, the Associations of the United States and those of the countries of continental Europe often seemed to stand at opposite poles, so that it was difficult for them to find a common meeting ground. For this reason Mademoiselle de Dietrich's visit to the United States had peculiar significance. Her own account of the series of Round Table discussions in which she shared made clear not only the differences within the Association but also the exceeding value of frank face-to-face discussion of them. She wrote:

> My two months in the U.S.A. have been a very fascinating experience. . . . Five "Round Tables" put me in touch with leaders of about eighty-five Associations. Each meeting lasted for two or three days, the main theme being religious trends of thought in Europe and America. The first two sessions were of a descriptive kind, giving the background and stating the main issues at the present time. The following sessions were more definitely a Round Table discussion, a sharing of experiences in Association life as well as of personal conviction.
>
> The method proved very fruitful, the main difficulty being that so many questions were raised that one could never cover the ground adequately and we moved perhaps too quickly from one problem to another. . . . There is a long history behind our continental differences. Several of the speakers felt that very deeply, and analyzed in different but very challenging ways the underlying factors which have contributed to the making of the America of today.[10]

The intention of the World's Executive Committee to have specialists in the field of religion from different countries give, as Mademoiselle de Dietrich had done, a period of service on the World's Y.W.C.A. staff, would have extended further this method of building understanding, and a call to Miss Rice of the United States for a period beginning in 1940 had already been accepted when the outbreak of war unfortunately made the carrying out of this plan impossible.

"In the immediate future it is particularly important to draw in the contribution of the Far East." Of great value in the carrying out of this mandate was the contribution of Oriental leaders called to headquarters, and the Regional Conference and Executive Committee meeting in Ceylon. Rather than try to secure a permanent member of the staff from the East, it was decided to ask different leaders to give several months each to the World's Council, acting both as interpreters of the Eastern Associations to the West, and of the Western Associations to the East.

The two Vice Presidents from the Orient were invited to be the first of such "collaborators", but neither Mrs. Tsuji of Japan nor Miss Ting of China was able to accept the invitation. It was then hoped that Miss Ting might come at a later time, but her death in the early months of 1936 robbed the World's Y.W.C.A. as well as China of the great contribution she would have made to world understanding. In the following year, however, Miss Taka Kato, General Secretary of the Tokyo Association, and later National Secretary of Japan, spent six months as a member of the World's staff, visiting among the Associations of the Continent and Great Britain. A similar service was given in 1939 by Miss Sosa Matthew, District Secretary for South India and soon to become the first Indian General Secretary of the National Association of India, Burma and Ceylon.

The Regional Conference at Colombo, Ceylon, in November 1936, was of peculiar significance both for the Far Eastern Associations and for the World's Council itself. It was the first conference of its kind in this region, bringing together more than seventy delegates from India, Burma, Ceylon, Malaya, the Netherlands Indies, China, Japan, Korea, Australia, New Zealand, the Philippines, and a visitor from Siam. The fact that the Conference Committee invited the Executive Committee to hold an enlarged meeting in Ceylon in connection with the conference, and that this invitation had been accepted, brought to the conference a group of some twenty Executive Committee and Council members from Europe and North America. This enlarged Executive Committee meeting, the first official meeting of the World's Association to be held in Asia, was also the first in the history of the movement in which there was a large representation from Eastern Associations.

Central to the program of the conference was the Christian purpose of the Association and its expression in the actual circumstances and conditions of the Far East. Discussion of the place and contribution of women, of leadership, and of international relations was also on the agenda. A particularly valuable part of the program was the presentation by each country of the problems that the Y.W.C.A. as a Christian organization faced in a time of rising nationalistic feeling, a growing trend toward war, and increasing fear and insecurity, and the frank and realistic discussion that these presentations called forth. The closing service of the conference, led jointly by Miss Tsai of China, Mrs. Uemura of Japan, and Miss Helen Kim of Korea, was a deeply moving experience.

The meeting of the Executive Committee was held at Kandy, a quiet spot of great beauty high above Colombo. It began with a day of retreat. The Committee then heard reports of the regular and special committees, including the groups working on the "Christian Emphasis" and on the "Place and Contribution of Women", and gave special consideration to the plans for the next World's Council meeting, to be held, it was hoped, in China in 1938.

Following the Executive Committee meeting there was wide visitation to Associations in India by the delegates from the West. Miss van Asch van Wijck and Miss Woodsmall attended the Plenary Meeting of the World's Y.M.C.A. at Mysore, India, where Miss van Asch van Wijck gave an address on the contribution of women. After Mysore she visited the Netherlands Indies, and Miss Woodsmall, after attending the League of Nations Conference on the Traffic in Women and Children, in Java, went on to China and Japan for further consultation regarding the Council meeting. She then made a brief visit to Korea and on her return journey attended the North American Area Conference at Toronto.

Although the outbreak of war between Japan and China in July 1937 made necessary the further indefinite postponement of the Council meeting in the Orient, the result of the Regional Conference, the Executive Committee meeting, and the extensive visitation was an inestimable enlargement of understanding and furtherance of participation of the East in the total World Movement.

The enlarged Executive Committee meeting of June 1937 was once again obliged to consider where the 1938 Council meeting should be held. Invitations were received from Canada, Czechoslovakia, the Netherlands, the Netherlands Indies, and the Philippines. The Near East was also considered. There was great difference of opinion within the Committee, some feeling that for reasons of economy the meeting should be in Europe, others having a strong conviction that in a changing world it was essential at all costs for an organization with headquarters in Europe and a large proportion of European leaders to come into contact with the movement in another part of the world, where conditions and viewpoints were different. As for financing a meeting outside Europe, it was argued that the funds "set free" at the Council meeting in 1934 and used for the Ceylon Conference, which had now been restored, might be used again to provide travel for delegates from the Far East.[11] The issue finally narrowed to a choice between Europe and Canada, and the minutes say:

> An informal vote showed lack of unanimity and the discussion was adjourned. Later the Committee met together in prayer for guidance. The next day the discussion was resumed, suggestions were made regarding ways of reducing costs in Canada, and of getting special gifts.

233

At length a resolution proposed by Mrs. Luxmoore (Great Britain) and seconded by Princess Sulkowska (Hungary) carried the decision for Canada.[12] The feelings of the Committee as well as the decisions reached were embodied in a resolution proposed by Princess Sulkowska and seconded by Fröken Bille (Denmark):

> That the Committee expresses its deep regret that it is not possible to hold the World's Council meeting in the Far East in 1938; reaffirms its decision to hold a Council meeting in the Far East as soon as possible; and agrees that the sum of money set aside for that purpose, apart from that set free by the World's Council meeting . . . in 1934, be kept separate and intact for this purpose.[13]

REFERENCES

[1] In May 1945 Miss Woodsmall's Alma Mater, the University of Nebraska, granted her the honorary degree of Doctor of Laws in recognition of her work in the field of international affairs.

[2] Woodsmall, Ruth F., *Report on the Work of the Executive Committee, 1934-1938.* Part I, p. 49.

[3] Under this plan, three Y.W.C.A. leaders, Miss Edna Bayeuth of Syria, Miss Cora Deng of China, and Miss Ella Kirsipuu of Estonia had periods of study in Geneva which enabled them to interpret the League of Nations and the International Labor Organization to their own countries.

[4] *An Experiment in Cooperation*—The History of the Liaison Committee of Women's International Organizations, 1945, p. 4. The organizations represented on the Liaison Committee in 1945 were: The International Council of Women, International Alliance of Women for Suffrage and Equal Citizenship, World's Y.W.C.A., Women's International League for Peace and Freedom, International Federation of University Women, World Union of Women for International Concord, World Women's Christian Temperance Union, St. John's Social and Political Alliance, International Federation of Women Magistrates and Members of the Legal Profession, International Federation of Business and Professional Women, International Cooperative Women's Guild.

[5] Woodsmall, Ruth F., Report on the Work of the Executive Committee, 1934-1938, Part II, p. 83.

[6] At Oxford there were 23 women among the 389 voting delegates; at Madras, 67 out of 450. At Madras the contribution of women was outstanding at a number of points.

[7] Both Argentina and Chile were received into corresponding membership at the World's Council meeting in 1938.

[8] *The World's Y.W.C.A. Monthly,* after 1934, took the place of the former monthly bulletin called the "News Service".

[9] Executive Committee, November 1936, Minutes, p. 8.

[10] *World's Y.W.C.A. Monthly,* February 1938, pp. 3, 4.

[11] The devaluation of the Swiss franc in 1937, while it had increased expenditure had increased receipts even more. It was this which made it possible to refund to the Far East Council Fund the amount borrowed in October 1936 to cover the cost of the Ceylon meeting (Minutes, Executive Committee, June 1937, p. 3).

[12] Executive Committee, June 1937, Minutes, p. 10.

[13] *Ibid.,* p. 11.

It has become clear to us that the Christian Church has again come to a decisive moment in its existence. . . . The tempest of contemporary history is forcing back the church to fundamentals, to such a radically religious conception of life as is revealed to us in the Bible. . . . The Christian Church is awakening to its responsibility to give a clear and unequivocal answer to the questions that arise out of the thunder of events. . . . .In an unprecedented way the sense of need to stand together, to form a united front on a clearly defined basis, has grown in the last years among Christians, and the ecumenical movement is beginning to take root in many a church. . . . A revival of vital religious life is evident in many places. . . . This, too, demands of us a fundamental reorientation. Where are we in all this? Are we ready to take our stand on this front?

JONKVROUWE C. M. VAN ASCH VAN WIJCK. "The Challenge of Today to the World's Y.W.C.A." Opening Address, World's Meeting, Muskoka, Canada, 1938.

CHAPTER 18 RESTUDYING THE TASK

THE 1938 World's Council meeting at Elgin House, Muskoka, in the lovely lake region of Northern Ontario, was the first meeting of the World's Young Women's Christian Association to be held in Canada. In a total attendance, including visitors, of 143, the official delegates represented twenty-nine countries. The atmosphere within which the Council gathered was one of great and growing international tension. The war between Japan and China and the shadow of coming war in Europe formed the background of all the Council's deliberations, and was reflected not only in addresses and discussions but in the business agenda.

It was reported that the work in Austria was temporarily closed; the National Association of Korea, which was not able to send a delegate, announced its withdrawal from the World's Y.W.C.A. as an independent Association in order that it might become the Korean Council of the National Y.W.C.A. of Japan, since this was the only way in which it would be permitted to continue its work. The Y.W.C.A. of Mukden, cut off from the National Association of China by the occupation of

Manchuria, was accepted in direct affiliation with the World's Y.W.C.A. Germany was not able to be officially represented, though two members of the German Association were present unofficially.

The plight of refugees in Europe was brought to the attention of the Council, which voted that a letter be sent to National Associations regarding the appalling need, especially of non-Aryan refugees, both Christian and Jewish, and stressing the responsibility of the Y.W.C.A. in this connection. A report was given also of the response made to the World's Y.W.C.A. appeal to National Associations for aid to China, and of the necessity for continued effort, in view of the tremendous task of the China Association in emergency relief and reconstruction.

In spite of the dark international outlook, the Council recommended the holding of a meeting in 1942, in the Pacific area, and emphasized the need for keeping the Associations in that part of the world in close touch with the World's Association. A forward look to 1944, the Jubilee year, was taken, and the hope expressed that a meeting to celebrate this event might be held in Great Britain and that a History of the World's Y.W.C.A. might be written for the occasion.

Miss Ruth Rouse was elected to the presidency to succeed Miss van Asch van Wijck, who had already served the two consecutive terms provided for in the constitution. Miss Rouse had long been associated with the World's Y.W.C.A., having been a member of its Executive Committee continuously since 1906. She knew the Association all over the world through her work in the Student Christian Movements of Great Britain, the United States and India, and through her travels as a secretary of the World's Student Christian Federation from 1905 to 1924. She had wide contacts also with missions in many lands and had been a secretary of the Missionary Council of the National Assembly of the Church of England from 1924 to 1938. She was an active leader among youth during the first World War. To the presidency of the World's Y.W.C.A. for a period which was destined to be dominated by world-wide conflict, therefore, she brought a fund of experience both within the movement and in those "kindred societies" with which its work was so closely linked, as well as an unshakable faith in the purposes of God and the calling of the Association for a time of crisis.

The Vice Presidents elected were Mrs. Huang Siu-feng of China, Mrs. Uemura of Japan, and Mrs. H. S. Hensman of India for the Far East; Miss van Asch van Wijck of the Netherlands and Fru Elsa Cedergren of Sweden for Northern Europe; Miss Julia Matouskova of Czechoslovakia for Central and French-speaking Europe; Mrs. Harrie R. Chamberlin of the United States for North America; Dr. Georgina Sweet of Australia for

G. Maillard Kesslere

Miss Ruth Rouse

Dr. Georgina Sweet

Fru Elsa Cedergren

Mrs. Tamaki Uemura

G. Maillard Kesslere

Mrs. Harrie R. Chamberlin

G. Maillard Kesslere

Miss Julia Matouskova

Australia and New Zealand. Mademoiselle Picot was re-elected to the office of Treasurer which she had held since 1930.

The Muskoka meeting was of special significance for its consideration of two questions: the varying expression of the Christian purpose of the World's organization as a whole, and its distinctive place and function among other world organizations in a time of international crisis. The theme of the meeting was "Jesus Christ the Center of Life", and a series of addresses on this theme, together with the discussions based upon a report of the "Christian Emphasis" study, brought to a climax the study of the Christian purpose of the Association which had been a major interest during the entire decade. As preparation for these discussions, two brochures had been prepared, one on "Jesus Christ, the Center of Life" and one on "The Rôle of Christian Women". Both these were symposiums to which leaders from different countries had contributed.[1]

The report on the study of the Christian Emphasis analyzed the replies received from National Associations to questions about their religious program as expressed in Bible study, evangelistic effort, and in relation to economic and political issues. Regarding Bible study, the report said:

> The response to the Bible study scheme and the answer to our enquiry about the place of Bible study in our movements have made certain facts very clear: (1) in most Western countries the growing ignorance of the Bible among youth is a fact which must be frankly recognized; (2) there is a real concern among leaders that such a study should be undertaken; and (3) the Bible is generally considered as a book unable to attract youth.[2]

Japan was one of the Associations that made the most use of the Bible study outlines, both their own and that of Mademoiselle de Dietrich, which they translated into Japanese. Great Britain also used widely the outlines sent out from Geneva, and it headed the list for the number of outlines prepared for the use of the membership. The German Association was unique in its thorough study of the Bible:

> While several other European Associations give an essential place to Bible study, none, to our knowledge, has carried it out in so systematic a way. . . . This systematic Bible study implies well-trained leadership, and the Y.W.C.A. Bible School provides for this with its two years' course and its shorter courses for volunteers. . . . This remarkable basis of work is the only explanation of the fact that the German Y.W.C.A. has been able to maintain its influence and carry on its work under actual conditions when it is forbidden any but its strictly religious activities.[3]

The replies to the question regarding evangelistic efforts in the Associations showed that:

Little seems to have been done in the realm of evangelization. Switzerland mentions this as an unsolved problem. Interesting experiments have been made in Norway, partly under the influence of the Oxford Group Movement. . . . Great Britain's principle is to have a constant stream of new people and new ideas flowing into the religious life of the clubs, but the real question is to find the point of contact. China mentions the fact that one-half of the membership of its clubs is non-Christian. Several countries where the background is Roman Catholic mention the difficulty of any direct witnessing, which would immediately be labeled proselytizing.[4]

As regards the relation of the religious emphasis in the Association to the critical economic and political issues of the day, the report says:

This has been earnestly tackled in many countries. The United States of America has certainly taken the lead in study as well as in public action; the Chinese Association has also devoted a great deal of time and thought to this aspect of our Christian responsibility. . . . The European countries, with some exceptions, seem more slow in taking up these issues.[5]

In a closing paragraph the report comments on the divergent approaches to the Christian Emphasis found in different Associations:

When one studies the programs of our Associations throughout the world, one sees that they might be divided roughly into two groups: (1) those who stress mainly the Christian preaching and teaching element and think of themselves as a part of the church; (2) those who are earnest in their will to serve the community as a whole, to study and improve the conditions of life among women and girls, and who regard this social service as their specific and distinct function in the Christian community, leaving the "preaching" as such, to the church. It seems to us that only a few Assocations have succeeded as yet in merging these two tendencies in one organic whole, and here lies our main weakness.[6]

The same divergencies appeared in the papers on "Jesus Christ, the Center of Life". In an introduction Miss van Asch van Wijck wrote:

Let us study these answers. Let us try to visualize the background from which they come, the reasons why they are as they are; the reasons why the one states what seems to some of us superfluous and antiquated; why the next one omits what seems to others among us absolutely essential. Let all these testimonies make us face the challenging question Christ puts to each one of us personally: But *you*, who say *you* that I am?[7]

The papers on the "Rôle of Christian Women" dealt with four areas: Women in the home, in economic life, in the church and in public life. Here also there were divergent opinions presented in each field, though all the writers recognized that changing conditions made necessary the reconsideration of traditional points of view.

In an address at the opening of the Council, Miss van Asch van Wijck dwelt upon the crisis for all Christian bodies inherent in the catastrophic changes in the world scene and the challenge presented to the World's Y.W.C.A.

> We have to express ourselves again, deliberately, in view of the situation today, as we have expressed ourselves during all the years of our existence, in the words of our basis and aim. Are we ready to say that we see Jesus Christ, the living Son of God, our Master and our Saviour, as the center of our life? . . . It is a word of immense significance that we pronounce. Do we dare to do it? Do we see all its implications?[8]

Dr. T. Z. Koo of China, Secretary of the World's Student Christian Federation, brought home to each delegate the fundamental personal issue when he insisted that "Christ cannot become the center of life if he has not already become the center of your life and my life." In resolutions urging that the emphasis on the Christian purpose be continued with no less effort during the next four years, the Council recorded its conviction:

> That the next few years will be a testing time for Christian movements, and that our strength will depend on the depth and reality of our individual and corporate experience. We know that it is only as we strengthen our Christian foundations that we can hope to achieve the task before us.[9]

As a background for the consideration of the World's Y.W.C.A. as a whole, Miss Woodsmall, in her report for the years 1934-1938, analyzed the major issues before the World's Y.W.C.A. as a Christian youth movement; as a Christian woman's movement; in the realm of its ecumenical policy and practice; in the field of social responsibility; and in the building of Christian international relations. In all these areas the events of the preceding years throughout the world, as well as growth within the Association itself, had forced upon the World's Y.W.C.A. new relationships and new responsibilities, and sharpened the need for a clear definition of its distinctive task as a world movement among other international organizations.

The Committee on Future Policy, appointed by the Council to study this report, made detailed recommendations for future guidance of the

Executive Committee in each of these fields, recognizing in each the particular task that belonged to the World's Y.W.C.A. as a Christian organization of both women and girls, and also the necessity of cooperation with other organizations working in the same field but approaching problems from other angles.

In view of the conflict in the Far East and the menace of war in Europe, the Committee's statement regarding international relations was of particular significance:

> We recognize that our very existence as a world Christian movement is an evidence of the unity in Christ which transcends all barriers of race and nation. This lays upon us an inescapable responsibility to work for the creation of an international order which may more nearly exemplify the fundamental basis of the world Christian community, the fatherhood of God and the brotherhood of man. [10]

With special reference to the crisis of the times, the Committee recommended that the Executive Committee be free to express an opinion in critical situations, whether of peace or war, "wherever in its judgment the integrity of our Christian fellowship demands it," taking care that action should be based on accurate and impartial information and as much consultation as possible with the member Associations involved. It further recommended that:

> In times of international strife the World's Young Women's Christian Association should seek every means of assuring Associations in the area of conflict that they are, and will remain, part of our fellowship, and should give all possible assistance to the Associations in the solution of their particular problems[11].

Significant as were the actions taken at Muskoka, the experience of the Council meeting reached a far deeper spiritual level than could be expressed in resolutions. The presence of delegates from both Japan and China, and the extraordinary frankness and Christian spirit with which these two groups in special conference together faced the situation in the Orient and found a basis for fellowship that held across all the barriers raised by war, made a profound impression. The whole gathering entered into the pain of international strife when it became necessary to accept the withdrawal of the Korean Y.W.C.A. from affiliation with the World's Association. The development of events in Europe making for war which took place during the very days when the Council was in session foreshadowed the suffering and isolation that were to come, and made infinitely precious the days of comradeship. This consciousness became a sacrament of fellowship when, on an evening in which the entire Council listened to the radio report that the Prime Minister of Great Britain was on his way to Munich to meet with representatives of the German government, the delegates with one accord gathered silently and spontaneously in the chapel for united prayer. At Stockholm in 1914, the premonitions of coming disaster were only vaguely felt, and that by but a few. The Muskoka meeting closed with a profound appreciation of the crucial nature of the world crisis. It was felt at the time that the meeting had been a direct preparation for the Association's primary task should war come —the maintaining of fellowship with those on both sides of the conflict.

In spite of the threat of war, the year following the Muskoka Council meeting was extraordinarily rich in international contacts. Officers and members of the Executive Committee traveled widely in Canada and the United States, and many of them also attended one or the other of the two Canadian-United States conferences at Muskoka and Spokane which followed the Council meeting. Miss Woodsmall, on her journey to Madras to attend the International Missionary Conference in December, visited Japan, Korea, Mukden, China, Malaya and India. Following this conference, she went to Australia and New Zealand before returning to Geneva via South Africa, where she made a brief stop at Durban and at Cape Town. Other members of the World's staff traveled extensively in Europe and visited the Associations in the Near East. South America was the only major area that had no direct contact with representatives of the World's Association between September 1938 and the outbreak of war in Europe in September 1939.

In the summer of 1939 three significant meetings were held in Switzerland. An informal group of about twenty Executive Committee and staff members met at Grandchamps, near Neuchâtel, for a Round Table discussion on the implications of the Christian faith in the difficult area of social and international relations. In June there was an unusually representative meeting of the enlarged Executive Committee, which considered in detail emergency plans in case war should make necessary the evacuation of the Geneva headquarters. It was decided that if such a move became necessary, an office should be established in Washington. Arrangements were made for such things as the dispersal of funds, and the safeguarding of records. Following the Executive Committee meeting, a Leaders' Study Course attended by sixty Association representatives from twenty-two countries, together with members of the World's Executive Committee and staff, met at Mont Pèlerin, above Lake Geneva, for consideration of "The Christian Basis of Our Calling as Citizens and of Our Social and International Action". Looking back over the summer at a later time, Miss Woodsmall wrote: "We now realize with deep thankfulness that the months June to September providentially furnished a spiritual preparation for the dark days to follow."

REFERENCES

[1] The papers on "Jesus Christ, the Center of Life" came from leaders of the Association in Korea, Czechoslovakia, the Netherlands Indies, the United States, Great Britain, India and France. The list of contributors to "The Role of Christian Women" included women from Canada, Great Britain, Sweden, the United States, India, China, Estonia, the Philippines, Germany, Argentina, France, the Netherlands Indies, Australia.

[2] The Christian Emphasis Study, Report, July 1938, p. 16.

[3] The Christian Emphasis Study, Report, July 1938, p. 15.

[4] *Ibid.*, p. 7.

[5] *Ibid.*, pp. 7, 8.

[6] Christian Emphasis Study, Report, July 1938, p. 17.

[7] *Jesus Christ, the Center of Life*, p. 3.

[8] *Elgin House Papers*, III, p. 10.

[9] World's Council Meeting, 1938, Minutes, p. 23.

[10] World's Council Meeting, 1938, Minutes, pp. 20, 21.

[11] *Ibid.*, p. 21.

I have seen the future in the spiritual tensions of the present, in the Christian minorities that cannot identify Christianity with nationalism, cannot be satisfied with the bitterness and tensions of war, cannot be cut off from the larger Christian Community. Cruelly separated though we are by war, we have never as a movement been more closely bound together. . . . Today we match the power of physical force with the incomparably greater and universal power of the Spirit.

RUTH F. WOODSMALL. Opening Address, Executive Committee, June 1941.

CHAPTER 19 THE WORLD'S Y.W.C.A. IN WORLD WAR II

WHEN, in September 1939, war was declared in Europe, the World's Young Women's Christian Association found itself in a position very different from that of 1914. In the first war the almost entirely British Executive Committee could continue to meet regularly with full attendance. In 1939 one of first effects of war was to cut off some members of the Executive Committee from all attendance at meetings. The first war took the World's Association by surprise and unprepared. When the second came, plans that the now isolated leaders had helped to make were ready to be put into operation. In 1914 to 1918 the World's Committee had been forced very largely to mark time. In 1939 the outbreak of war was the signal for assuming new tasks. In the first war the World's Y.W.C.A. had little effective relationship with other world Christian bodies by which they could jointly face the crisis. In 1939 ten years of cooperation and growing fellowship between the leaders of the Christian organizations having headquarters in Geneva had borne fruit in a sound personal relationship that was ready when the need for it arose.

The day before war was declared, Mr. Tracy Strong of the World's Young Men's Christian Association, Mr. Robert Mackie of the World's Student Christian Federation, Dr. Visser 't Hooft of the Provisional Committee of the World Council of Churches, and Miss Woodsmall met and formed an informal Emergency Committee of Christian Organizations, known throughout the war as ECCO, for the purpose of consultation and exchange of information and opinion. Later, M. Henriod of the World Alliance for International Friendship Through the Churches, and Professor Adolph Kellar of the Committee for Inter-Church Aid, joined the ECCO group. The Committee assumed no administrative functions but met for joint consultation and planning whenever and wherever it was possible for some of its members to get together.

Throughout the winter of 1939 and 1940 it was possible to maintain surprisingly normal contacts with Associations in Europe, though many adjustments were necessary. In spite of hindrances to travel, Miss Woodsmall visited Germany in October 1939 and again in March 1940. She attended the regional conference of the northern countries in Oslo in October, and visited Denmark, Sweden and the Baltic States, making what proved to be the last contact with Estonia. She also visited France and Great Britain. Mrs. Fox visited Germany, Belgium and France, and after the fall of France both she and Mademoiselle de Dietrich were still able to make frequent trips to Unoccupied France. Miss Roe visited Roumania and Spain. Miss Mills spent six weeks with the Associations of Great Britain and made a month's tour of Hungary, Roumania, Bulgaria and Greece. In the spring of 1940 also, Miss Rouse and Miss Woodsmall went to America to attend the national convention of the Associations of the United States.

The Executive Committee at its meeting in December 1939 faced its wartime task in the light of the discussions held at Muskoka and the decisions made at its enlarged meeting in June. The Committee was keenly aware of the responsibility of the World's Y.W.C.A. as an ecumenical organization in a time of world-wide conflict. Beyond the emergency tasks that the war might impose, it was resolved to place primary emphasis on four things: such an interpretation of the Christian message as should help the Association membership, particularly youth, in their spiritual struggle; the maintenance of all possible contact with Associations throughout the world, and particularly with those on opposite sides of the conflict; preparation for peace and reconstruction in the post-war period; the development and extension of the Association in countries which, because they were less directly involved in the war, might be particularly accessible.

With the advance of war it was necessary to abandon plans for the meeting of the Executive Committee in June 1940, and the summer of that year became the period of transition to a wartime set-up. Since Switzerland remained neutral, it was possible to maintain the Geneva headquarters throughout the war. It was clear, however, that the difficulties of operating in a country virtually surrounded by conflict would be such that another center in addition to Geneva was essential to a full functioning of the organization. A temporary office in Washington was therefore opened in September 1940. To the Geneva headquarters were assigned the special functions of maintaining contact as far as possible by travel and correspondence with the Associations of continental Europe; of carrying advisory service for European Associations on their programs of aid to the fast-mounting numbers of refugees and evacuees; and of keeping in touch with the international and world organizations in Geneva. Mrs. Fox, with the aid of Miss Wilhjelm and an office staff, remained in Geneva.

To the Washington office was transferred responsibility for the work of the Executive Committee, general correspondence, production of material, matters concerning regular program, finance, and world support. Miss Mills was placed in charge of this office and in Miss Woodsmall's absence acted in her stead. With her were associated Miss Pearl Carruthers, the Publications Secretary, and Miss Marcia O. Dunham, who now joined the staff as Secretary for World Support. Miss Dunham's previous experience as a member of the national staff of the Association in the United States, as a worker in Russia, and as Executive Secretary of the work in the Baltic States after the first war, added to her value as a member of the World's staff at this time. In 1942, on Miss Carruther's return to England, another secretary with long experience in the national work in the United States, Miss Lucy T. Bartlett, took over the work of publications. The Washington staff was further increased by the coming of Miss Marion Royce of Canada to take the position of Secretary for the Young Adult Membership. Short periods of service were given also by Miss Rose Terlin, formerly a secretary of the World's Student Christian Federation, and Miss Lilian Rohwedder, formerly with the National Board of the United States.

The new arrangement presented many difficulties because of the added expense involved, the smallness of the staff, and the necessity of constant coordination of the work in the two centers. A Washington office, however, proved to be fully justified, while the significance of Geneva as an international center in a neutral zone increased rather than diminished as the war went on. Miss Woodsmall wrote:

> To a degree beyond anticipation there has been movement in and out of Geneva of individual people from different organizations, and Mrs. Fox uses them to the maximum for keeping in touch with leaders who would otherwise be completely cut off from us.[1]

The Executive Committee held its first Washington meeting in December 1940, and met on an average twice each year from that time until the re-establishment of full headquarters in Geneva in the autumn of 1945.

In June 1941 a special meeting of the World's Council was held in Washington to act upon the report of a sub-committee appointed to propose amendments to certain articles in the by-laws which were in need of clarification.

The absence from Executive Committee meetings of almost all members from Great Britain and the continent of Europe was a great loss. However, Miss Rouse, who spent these years in the United States,[2] and Miss Matouskova, one of the European Vice Presidents, who served during the war on the national staff of the Canadian Association, were regularly present. Also Mrs. Arthur Grenfell, President of the National Council of Great Britain and a member of the Executive Commit ee of the World's Y.W.C.A., was present at one meeting in 1942, and again for consultations in 1944, and Fru Elsa Cedergren of Sweden, another European Vice President, attended one meeting in 1944.

For the North American members of the Executive Committee the war was a period of consecutive attendance at meetings such as had never been possible before, a period somewhat comparable for Canada and the United States to that which the years in Geneva in the 1930s had afforded to the continental members. Since many Association leaders from other lands came to America during these years, it was possible also in several instances to find relatively permanent proxies for officers, who thus made a continuous contribution to the deliberations of the Committee. One such was Mrs. Chu Shi-ming, former President of the Chungking Y.W.C.A. and a member of the National Committee of China but now resident in Washington, who served on the Executive Committee during almost all the Washington period, first as proxy for Mrs. Huang and later as her successor as Vice President for Asia. Another was Mrs. Slotemaker de Bruine, who acted as proxy for Miss van Asch van Wijck for the four years 1942-1945 inclusive. Well acquainted with the Association in the Netherlands and also with that of the Netherlands Indies, of which she had been President, Mrs. Slotemaker brought a valuable experience to the Committee.[3] The appointment of Miss Emma R. Kaufman of Canada as member of the Executive Committee to succeed Miss Greta Finley on the latter's resignation in 1942, brought into the Committee a wide and sympathetic understanding of Japan gained through twenty-five years of service with the Tokyo Association.

In addition to these regular members and proxies, an extraordinary number of World's Council members or Association leaders from different parts of the world were present at certain meetings and for purposes of special consultation. China took a larger share than ever before in the inner counsels of the movement, for a number of Chinese leaders, including Mrs. Huang, Dr. Wu Yi-fang, President of Ginling College, Mrs. King

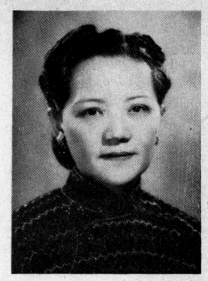

Delar

Mrs. Chu Shi-ming

Mrs. Arthur Grenfell

Pach Bros.

Countess Hélène Goblet d'Alviella

Lung-chang, World's Council member from Kunming, Miss Tsai Kwei, General Secretary of the China National Committee, and Miss Cora Deng, National Industrial Secretary, were present at various times. Mrs. Howard Hannaford of Tokyo, who returned to the United States in 1944, brought a valuable contribution from her recent contact with the Associations of Japan. Latin America, too, shared in the work of the Committee for almost the first time, through the presence at the meeting of the Executive Committee in April 1945 and at the Latin-American "Consultation" which followed it, of Doctora Angela Santa Cruz, President of the Association in Buenos Aires, Argentina, and Señorita Guadalupe Ramirez, President of the National Committee of Mexico. India was represented at this same meeting by Miss Nora Ventura of the staff of the National Committee of India. At one or another meeting during these years, representatives were present also from the Philippines, Siam, Lebanon, Syria, Egypt, Australia, Japan, Belgium and Czechoslovakia.

Meantime, while official Executive Committee action emanated from Washington, the members of the Executive Committee remaining in Geneva, Mademoiselle Picot and Madame Johannot, with the addition of Mademoiselle de Dietrich and Mademoiselle Chenevière, the President of the Y.W.C.A. of Switzerland, acted as an informal consultative group for dealing with the many perplexing problems that arose at headquarters. They also spoke to many groups in Switzerland on the emergency program of the world organization.

The need for an emergency program was apparent soon after the beginning of the war. Early in 1940 it was realized that among those interned as enemy aliens in many lands there were numbers of women and children, and that these stood in peculiar need of such friendly service as the Y.W.C.A. could give. In its service to women internees, developed in response to this need, the World's Y.W.C.A. performed a unique function, parallel, in a way, to Y.M.C.A. aid for prisoners of war, though on a smaller scale and under a different theory of administration. The World's Y.M.C.A. carried directly through its own world organization all the vast aid to prisoners of war given by the Y.M.C.A. The Y.W.C.A., on the other hand, extended this aid through its National Associations, each of which served the internees in its own country, the function of the World's Y.W.C.A. being to promote such service by National Associations and give them aid in the development of their plans. In this it followed a policy that it had pursued in other fields over the years. In 1940 it sent letters to all National Associations, calling their attention to the needs of internees. As they traveled, the World's Y.W.C.A. staff visited internment camps and promoted the work in the National

Associations. Bulletins and pamphlets were issued, giving information and suggestions.[4]

In some countries, however, it was not possible for the National Associations to undertake work for internees. This was the case in both Germany and France, and in these countries the service was carried directly by the World's Y.W.C.A., whose representatives served on the staff of the Y.M.C.A. War Prisoners Aid organization. In Germany, Miss Wilhjelm of the World's Y.W.C.A. staff, served from 1940 to 1942; later Miss Alice Arnold, of Switzerland, was called to the staff as a special worker for this purpose. In France the work was carried by Mrs. Andermo of Sweden, a trained nurse, who had prepared for missionary service in Africa. Miss Arnold's support was carried in part by the Associations of those nations that had women citizens interned in Germany and in part by the Y.M.C.A., Mrs. Andermo's support was carried by her Swedish Mission Board. In Trinidad also, where Germans were interned, Miss Ruth Cowdrey, who had gone to Trinidad as a volunteer representative of the World's Y.W.C.A. to organize a new Association there, was appointed the official representative of the Y.M.C.A. War Prisoners Aid not only for the women's camp but for the men's as well.

As one country after another was cut off, either by actual fighting or by occupation, from any relation with other countries, maintaining contact with the Associations became more complex and difficult. Some were completely hidden behind a curtain of silence. But every possible facility for keeping in touch was utilized, both of committee members and staff. Where a person of one nationality could not enter a country, it was sometimes possible for one of another nation to do so. Travel by air became a commonplace, as some countries could be entered by this means but by no other. Throughout the war, Fru Cedergren was able to make journeys of peculiar significance, visiting Germany, Hungary, Denmark and Switzerland. Mademoiselle Picot and Madame Johannot visited Unoccupied France, and even attended, with Mrs. Fox, a meeting of the French National Committee in 1941. Mademoiselle Goblet d'Alviella, Executive Committee member, herself a refugee from Belgium, assisted in the establishment of Foyers for refugees in Unoccupied France.

A truly Pauline journey of visitation was made in the winter of 1940-41 by Miss Woodsmall. Having visited France in the summer of 1940 and Germany in the autumn, she set forth on a tour, largely by air, which was to bring her for the first time to the Washington office in May 1941. She stopped briefly in Hungary and Bulgaria en route, and then went to the Near East—Turkey, Syria, Palestine and Egypt—and to India, Burma, Siam, Malaya and the Netherlands Indies (Indonesia), conferring with leaders, visiting internment camps, and stimulating the emergency programs of the Associations. She then spent three months in the Orient, visiting Free China (i.e. West China and Hong Kong), Shanghai, and occupied North China, Japan and the Philippines.

In this same period Miss Rouse traveled widely in Canada and the United States and Miss Kaufman, as a representative of the World's Y.W.C.A., toured the Caribbean area, visiting British Guiana, Surinam (Netherlands Guiana), Trinidad and Barbados. Thus, in the first two years of war there was contact with most of the Associations in Europe, . with all those of the Near East and most of those in Asia, as well as with those of North America and the Caribbean area.

The entrance of the United States into the war in December 1941 put further limitations on travel, yet in 1942 Mrs. Grenfell paid an extensive visit to the Canadian Associations, Miss Woodsmall visited Mexico and South America, and Miss Ruth Cowdrey spent several months as a World's Y.W.C.A. representative in the Caribbean area. The military occupation of North Africa and the total occupation of France in November made direct communication between Washington and Geneva impossible except by cable. Sweden then became the main avenue of approach betwen the two centers.

In view of this new isolation, the visit of Miss Woodsmall to Great Britain and Sweden in the winter of 1942 and 1943 was of particular importance. In Sweden, besides invaluable conferences with Fru Cedergren and with Miss Wilhjelm, who worked in Sweden after leaving Germany, she was able to make contact with persons who brought news of the Associations in Estonia and Norway, and to meet Miss Alice Arnold, who came to Stockholm for a conference regarding her work for internees in Germany. It was even possible to talk by telephone with the staff in Geneva. Sweden was, as Miss Woodsmall wrote, "a window into Europe". On her return trip by plane to the United States she stopped at Algeria, North Africa, and made a much appreciated contact with the French Y.W.C.A. center there, then cut off from its headquarters. She also conferred with Miss Jean Begg, who was in charge of the British war services then being opened in North Africa and the Near East.

In the winter of 1943 and 1944 two other important journeys were made. Fru Cedergren came to the United States to attend the World's Executive Committee meeting, where she gave much information about conditions in Europe and important help in the shaping of future plans. She also visited internment camps in the United States and Canada, and on her return journey met with the British members of the Executive Committee in London.

Mrs. Grenfell, having been asked by the National Committees of

Australia and New Zealand to visit them, went en route, as a representative of the World's Y.W.C.A., to the Association centers in West Africa, Egypt, Palestine, Iraq, Iran and India. On her return flight, for this also was a tour by air, she reported to and consulted with the Executive Committee in Washington. Travel in the summer and autumn of 1944 was concentrated on the renewal of contact with liberated countries in Europe—France, Italy, Belgium, Holland and Greece. Miss Woodsmall also made a visit to the Eastern Mediterranean Associations, where she helped them to prepare for a regional conference in that area in July, and was able to return once more to Geneva several months before the actual close of war.

What did this extensive travel reveal about the influence of the war upon the Associations in different parts of the world? Certain effects were common to many Associations. In every country where actual fighting or bombing occurred, there was widespread loss of Association property. The Associations in all these countries emerged from the war greatly impoverished in material things. In some countries the Association suffered not only property loss and damage but destruction of much of its work as well, and persecution because of its loyalty to vital Christian principles which placed it in open opposition to national policy.

The German Association, while it was not dissolved and its property was not confiscated, suffered from a consistent attempt to destroy its influence. It was forced to dissolve its membership of girls under the age of eighteen, and lost many others, since employers were ordered to dismiss older girls who were members of a Christian youth organization. Its publishing department, on which its material for program and much of its income depended, was closed. Only strictly religious meetings might be held. In spite of these measures against it, the German Association survived. "Its staff of traveling secretaries intensified their service. The result was that the contact between the Y.W.C.A. center at Burckhardthaus, the group of leaders, and a great part of the former members remained a very living one." [5]

In Japan the work of the Y.W.C.A. was severely limited. To prove itself a completely Japanese movement, in no way under foreign control, it requested the withdrawal of the three foreign staff members working with it. Any emphasis upon world fellowship in its program was impossible. The government's reorganization, under its own auspices, of all work with students, largely cut off from the Y.W.C.A. an important part of its work, from which it drew most of its leadership. On certain questions of policy, such as that of opening work for Chinese and Japanese girls in the Japanese-controlled areas of China, the Association felt compelled to take an unpopular stand, since it believed such work would be a violation

250

of the rights of the China Y.W.C.A. Yet in Japan as in Germany, the Association, though under great difficulties, continued to carry on, centering its efforts on constructive character education, holding conferences when possible, confining its war emergency program to such things as raising funds for relief. In the report of her visit to Japan in 1941, Miss Woodsmall wrote: "To find a group working steadfastly to conserve essential values and clinging to an inner loyalty at a time of growing outward pressure is an inspiration."

In the occupied countries of Europe and the Orient the experience of the Associations varied from entire dissolution in Latvia and Estonia, to almost normal activity as in Denmark, where except for the limitations of blackout and transportation, the usual program was carried on until the last stages of the war, even to holding a convention with one thousand delegates in attendance in 1943. Denmark, however, was the exception. In most occupied countries, buildings, if not destroyed, were requisitioned, equipment was confiscated, publications drastically curtailed, certain activities—as for example, the Blue Triangle Clubs in the Netherlands—were forbidden. The Belgian Foyers were closed.

In spite of these things, perhaps because of them, the Associations in the occupied countries and areas for the most part not only continued to live but grew in spiritual stature. Meetings were held secretly, leaders and sometimes members braved imprisonment or worse in service to persecuted refugees, and found in the comradeship of dangerous devotion a deepened spiritual fellowship. When Miss Woodsmall met in Sweden two women members of the resistance movement in Norway, they reported regarding the Norwegian Association that though many buildings had been lost, "the work goes on vigorously, the National General Secretary travels much, and the Association has contributed much to the resistance movement."

The close relationship of many European Associations with the church was a source of strength and protection during these years, and one of the outstanding results of the war was to intensify this relationship. There was an illustration of this in France, where early in the war an organization known as CIMADE (Comité Inter-Mouvement auprès des Evacués) was formed by the Y.M.C.A., the Y.W.C.A., the Student Christian Movement, the Scouts, and the National Council of the Protestant Churches. The purpose of this organization in the first instance was service to the population evacuated from the frontier fighting zone in Alsace-Lorraine, but it continued throughout the war in the face of the greatest difficulties and dangers to minister to the ever increasing and ever more tragic evacuees, refugees, and deported peoples in concentration camps.

The situation in China was unique in that all the experiences which it shared with other countries were on a vaster scale. In the occupied cities some Associations were completely closed. On the other hand, the war was the occasion of the opening of much new work in the interior, hitherto almost untouched by the Association.[6] The work for refugees, already very large even before war came to Europe,[7] overshadowed for a time all other work, became in fact almost the whole regular program of the Association. The great contribution of the China Association at this point was the trained leadership it supplied, not merely for the administration of relief but for the development of educational and vocational activities and projects by which refugees could begin to earn a livelihood.

To some extent the Associations of Great Britain, the Dominions and the United States shared the experiences of other countries. In Great Britain the loss of Association property was heavy. The United States and Canada both carried work for refugees, though on a very small scale, except for financial aid given to other countries, if compared with Associations in Europe and Asia. Both the United States and Canada had a special problem in the removal of all Japanese people from their homes on the Pacific coast to "relocation" centers inland.

In Great Britain the war was a period of expansion for the Y.W.C.A., much more so even than in the first World War, through the multiplication of its services for women in the forces in far distant parts of the world, and its work with the multitudes of girls in the home services, in war industries, and on the land. In this increase in its activities, the British Association, like the Associations on the Continent, forged new links in its relation with the church. Significant new forms of cooperation with other organizations also were developed during the war. The government Board of Education initiated a scheme of Service of Youth, in which all young people, both girls and boys, were included. The Y.W.C.A. gave some of its best leaders to become district directors of this inclusive program. In this connection, the Board of Education subsidized the Association's training courses for leaders of youth work. In addition to this cooperative work for youth, the British Y.W.C.A. carried a large coeducational program of its own.

In the United States the emergency service to youth in communities affected by the war as well as that for women employed in the armed services was very largely carried by the U.S.O. (United Service Organizations), of which the Y.W.C.A., the Y.M.C.A., and Roman Catholic, Jewish and other welfare agencies were members. The experience of these organizations in jointly meeting wartime needs will have, no doubt, considerable influence on future cooperative relations.

The Associations of the neutral countries also carried much emergency work. The Swedish Y.W.C.A. contributed with great generosity to many countries, and cared for many women and girls among the refugees from Finland, Norway and Denmark. The Swiss Y.W.C.A. was a member of a committee known as SARCIS (Society for Aid to Refuge Civilians in Switzerland), which developed a constructive program of friendly service to supplement the provision made by the Swiss government for food, shelter and clothing for the thousands of refugees within its borders.

Almost every Association was forced by the war to a fresh examination of the reality of its Christian foundations. In some countries Association leaders were driven by their experiences to a more complete dependence upon the Biblical revelation of God's purpose and to a new search for the bearing of the message of the Bible upon political and international life. Significant also of a number of countries was definite planning for the work of reconstruction. In China, reconstruction went hand in hand with emergency work. The British Associations and also those of several other countries had groups studying particular problems of reconstruction both national and international from the very early days of the war.

Besides fulfilling its primary obligation of keeping contact with all its national movements, the World's Y.W.C.A. was concerned to give every assistance possible to those National Associations most hard pressed by the war. Here a first and principal need was financial aid to those with greatly reduced income or enormously increased burdens or both. Such for example, were the Associations of China, Roumania, Hungary, France, overwhelmed by their flood of refugees; Great Britain, faced suddenly with unparalled expansion at home and a simultaneous demand for a vast extension of services to women in the forces in Europe, North Africa, the Near East, India and the Pacific; the Swiss Association, called upon for an important share, through SARCIS, in the national problem of service to refugees; "orphaned Associations" like the Netherlands Indies, the Danish Hostel in London, the French Association in Algeria, which were cut off from their customary aid from their home Associations.

The World's Council itself usually did not administer the funds by which these needs were met. It recognized that in most instances this was the task of the National Associations. It did, however, undertake to interpret these needs through reports, bulletins and special publications, to the National Associations that were able to render aid in money, or in some cases by lending personnel. Several times the Executive Committee issued direct appeals to National Associations for a special emergency.

Sometimes the funds given by Associations or individuals were sent to the World's Council for transmission to the place of need. More often they were sent directly by one National Association to another. For example, the annual report for 1940-1941 gives the total amount contributed to emergency needs within that year as probably more than $155,000. Of this amount approximately $23,000 was sent through the World's office and $132,000 direct from one Association to another. Since the latter gifts were not necessarily reported to the World's Council, it was impossible to tell at the close of the war what was the total financial responsibility which the Associations had assumed for one another. In the latter period of the war particularly, this responsibility was expressed not only in the contribution of funds and personnel but in large shipments of clothing and bedding sent by national movements as gifts from their local branches.

A major emergency task of the war years was service to refugees. Never before in history had there been such multitudes of homeless, helpless people wandering over the earth. They were to be found in large numbers or in small groups in practically every country of the world, and as very many of them were women and children they were a concern of nearly every National Association.[8] The program of the Y.W.C.A. for refugees was not, except in special cases, one of material relief, since that was undertaken by governments and by the Red Cross. It was one of friendly visitation and the development of programs to meet recreational, educational and spiritual needs.

This vast migration of women and children had a bearing not only on the immediate program of Associations the world around, but on the future of the World Movement as a whole, since it was the occasion of contact and even of fellowship between women of many nationalities, and for many a first experience of the Y.W.C.A. The story of the Polish dispersion is perhaps the most striking but by no means the only illustration of this. The presence of groups of Polish refugees was reported by Y.W.C.A. workers in Roumania, Hungary, France, Switzerland, Great Britain, Algeria, Kenya, Rhodesia, the Union of South Africa, Iraq, Iran, Mexico and the West Indies. India reported a large camp of Polish women and children, "a veritable little Poland". In Palestine there was a camp of 600 Polish girls between the ages of twelve and seventeen. Miss Woodsmall wrote: "The Polish refugees in their Odyssey around the world have found the Y.W.C.A. a haven of service and friendship."

In meeting this problem of refugees the World's Y.W.C.A. was a center for the compilation and dissemination of information regarding both the needs of the refugees and the ways in which various Associations were trying to meet them, thus stimulating concern and aiding in the development of programs. It also issued several appeals for funds for Associations whose burden of work was beyond their power to meet with their own resources.

In the later years of the war, although service to internees was greatly reduced as those interned were released or were returned to their own countries through an exchange of prisoners, there still remained in camps in central Europe a large number of uprooted peoples who for one reason or another were unable or unwilling to return to the countries they had left. In the early months of 1945, the World's Y.M.C.A. and the World's Y.W.C.A. jointly undertook a service to these "displaced persons". In Austria the staff of Y.M.C.A. and Y.W.C.A. workers was under the direction of Miss Alice Arnold of the World's Y.W.C.A. The head of the joint program in Germany was Mr. Royal Thomas of the World's Y.M.C.A. The Liaison Officer with UNRRA[9] for both Germany and Austria was Dr. D. D. Davis of the World's Y.M.C.A. The Y.W.C.A. staffs for this work were recruited from the United States, Sweden, Denmark, France, Belgium, the Netherlands and Switzerland, their salaries being carried by special gifts from some of the National Associations.

This project was of special significance for both the World's Y.M.C.A. and the World's Y.W.C.A. in that it was the first time in the history of the two movements that such an experiment in joint administration had been tried, and it was felt that it might lead to the consideration of other forms of collaboration in the future.

REFERENCES

[1] Annual Report, 1941-1942, p. 22.

[2] In order to write the History of the World's Student Christian Federation, the records for which were in the library of the Yale Divinity School at New Haven, Connecticut.

[3] Others who served for considerable periods as proxies during the war were Mrs. John French, United States, and the Honorable Mrs. Thomas Brand, Great Britain, for Fru Cedergren; Miss Grace Carr and Miss Elizabeth Lamont, United States, for Dr. Sweet; Miss Ruth Cowdrey and Mrs. Orlo Bond, United States, for Mrs. Hensman.

[4] See especially *Women Behind Barbed Wire*, 1944, by Marion Dudley, a Y.W.C.A. secretary in China who was herself interned for several months in Stanley Camp, Hong Kong.

[5] Woodsmall, Ruth F., Report on Germany, January 1946.

[6] It was reported in 1939 that "of the local [city] Associations in China, 9 carry on, some with a very much enlarged program, 9 have been closed, and 7 new places have been opened. Of the rural Associations, 2 remain with great difficulties, 2 have been destroyed, and 3 new centers have been opened" (Executive Committee, Minutes, December 1939, Appendix, p. iv).

[7] In 1941 it was estimated that the number of refugees in China was one hundred million.

[8] A study made by the International Labor Office estimated that in 1944 more than thirty million women and children had been uprooted from their native soil since the beginning of the war. Quoted in *Emergency Service Around the World*, 1944, by M. M. Mills.

[9] United Nations Relief and Rehabilitation Administration.

*As we carry our eyes forward into the future we may
refresh ourselves with the vision of the Association
as it might be, as it should be, as it must be; so we
come back to our immediate tasks and are able to
serve the women of today, that we may go forward
better equipped to meet tomorrow.*

MAY CURWEN, General Secretary, Y.W.C.A. of Great
Britain. Report to Biennial Conference, 1942.

*Lord of all Power and Love, we thy humble servants
in the fellowship of the World's Y.W.C.A. would re-
dedicate to thee for the fulfilment of thy purpose,
every national and local Association, every member
—all for each, each for all. We ask thee, not for a
knowledge of what will come, but for a simpler and
more fearless confidence in thee, the God and Father
of our Lord Jesus Christ; for a higher, wider and
deeper vocation; and for a spirit of instant response
to whatever call is vouchsafed to us.*

RUTH ROUSE. From "A Call to Thanksgiving and Rededication on the Threshold of the Fiftieth Anniversary of
the World's Y.W.C.A.", January 1, 1944.

CHAPTER 20   PREPARING FOR THE
POST-WAR WORLD

As THE war was surging towards its climax
in 1944, the World's Young Women's Christian Association reached its
fiftieth anniversary. It had been hoped that some especially significant
event, perhaps the holding of the long-delayed Council meeting in the
Orient, might mark this occasion. Instead, many Associations were still
hidden behind the barrier of occupation, or were otherwise cut off by the
war from contact with one another. The World's Council, instead of
preparing for a joyous reunion, was absorbed in its emergency tasks and in
the arduous work of maintaining, in spite of war, its fundamental responsibility for the strengthening and deepening of the spiritual fellowship
on which the life of the movement depended. It was also continuing to give
service to such Associations as could be reached, extending the movement
into new areas where this was possible, and at the same time preparing
to meet the post-war need of renewal of contact and of reconstruction.

The war imposed severe limitations on carrying out this program, but it also afforded some peculiar opportunities. The separation of the Associations at the moment in which they were all involved in a common catastrophe was an incentive to reach out to one another through prayer. Miss Rouse, reviewing the period of the war, noted that in these years "the prayer life of the World's Y.W.C.A. and the National Associations has been quickened, and fellowship in prayer has kindled faith, and in no period have richer resources in prayer been given to our members." These resources were shared through certain familiar channels, such as *The World's Y.W.C.A. Monthly,* the "Prayer Circles" in which it had long been the custom to send out thoughts gathered from devotional services at Executive or other committee meetings, together with suggestions for united prayer, and the material prepared each year in cooperation with the Y.M.C.A. for use during the World's Week of Prayer.

New channels were developed in the light of new needs. One of these was a series of three special pamphlets issued in the early years of the war and dealing with problems vitally related to the decisions confronting Christians in every nation. The first of these, "The Christian Basis of Our Social and International Action", contained addresses given at the Mont Pèlerin study course in the summer of 1939. The second and third, entitled "Christian Decisions" and "Paradoxes of Christian Thinking: Freedom vs. Authority; Individualism vs. Community", were symposiums to which Association leaders in different countries contributed. Another new approach was a series of monthly meditations issued every six months during the years 1941-1945. Each series was written by an individual or a group from a different country. Their purpose was expressed in a statement that appeared on the cover page of each series:

> These subjects for monthly meditations have been prepared to
> be used by members of the World's Y.W.C.A. in every land,
> and on both sides of every conflict. They are designed to help
> us to live as children of one Father and to face in his spirit all
> that we are called upon to think, to plan for the future, to
> suffer, to do, and to be.

Articles on spiritual issues which the war raised for individuals, such, for example, as the series by Miss van Asch van Wijck on "What Holds Today", a Bible Study Outline prepared by Miss van Asch van Wijck and by Mademoiselle de Dietrich, and one on "The Christian Community", prepared by a small international group, were circularized and used by groups of leaders in many countries.

The fiftieth anniversary itself became in a perhaps unexpected way a focus for the realization of spiritual fellowship throughout the movement. In the early months of 1944, the World's Council sent out a special service of worship and a "Call to Thanksgiving and Rededication", as well as a radio recording and other interpretative material for use by national and local Associations, together with the suggestion that the celebration of the Jubilee be the occasion for making gifts for post-war reconstruction.

In November, near the date of the first official meeting of the World's Executive Committee anniversary, services were held in the National Cathedral in Washington, and in the Church of St. Gervais in Geneva. A report of the letters received from all parts of the world when the Jubilee year was over, telling of the translation into many languages of the material sent out and of the ways in which the anniversary had been observed, says: "The really wide appreciation of the significance of the World Movement by local Associations was a hopeful surprise." Here at least not alone national leaders and a few world-conscious individuals, but the members of many Association groups as well became aware of their heritage in a world-wide organization of Christian women. China wrote: "In spite of all the uncertainty, all the Associations except Sian (which had been forced to close) held fiftieth anniversary celebrations and made contributions to post-war reconstruction."

Nor did the effort to strengthen the spiritual life of the movement end here. Though international communication was slow and difficult, common thinking on subjects important for the future was promoted by correspondence, and in small groups in both Washington and Geneva. The study of ecumenical questions was continued and a document on "Ecumenical Aspects of the World's Y.W.C.A." was issued. A number of papers discussing the increasingly pertinent questions of the relation of women to the church and the significant development of church youth movements were circulated. These papers summarized the new trends in this field of church relationships which were being noted in many countries. The results of a study carried on largely by correspondence in order to discover the thinking of the Associations on the problem of world order and to stimulate further consideration of this question, were issued as an outline for study called *The Christian Basis of a New Society*.

The effect of war on the life of women was another continuing concern. Through the collection of data from such sources as the International Labor Office, the pulpit, the press, the cinema; by a Round Table discussion in which the United States and Canada shared; by questionnaires sent to National Associations and by material drawn from letters, periodicals and Association reports from many lands, information was gathered for a pamphlet on this subject as a preparation for post-war planning.[1] The contrast between the interchange of thought and experience and the constructive planning for the future which the World's Council was able to promote in 1940-1945, and that which had been possible in 1914-1918, is an indication of the growth in twenty years both of ecumenical Christian consciousness and of the Y.W.C.A.'s recognition of itself as a world movement.

Attention to the development and extension of the Association during the war years centered largely on three areas that offered particular opportunity and called for special study. These were the Caribbean area, Latin America, and East and West Africa.

The Caribbean area included the British West Indies (Jamaica, the Bahamas, Trinidad, Grenada, Barbados and British Guiana); the United States-controlled islands of Cuba and Haiti and the territory of Puerto Rico; Surinam (Netherlands Guiana) and French Guiana.

In the British West Indies some Associations had long been in existence. The tiny center in Georgetown, British Guiana, was first established in 1874, and though later closed, it was revived in 1926. An even smaller center in Grenada dated from 1889. In Jamaica there was a flourishing Association, organized in 1923 by Miss Cecil Heath (who later helped to establish work in West Africa and to develop the work in Palestine), with its main center in the capital city of Kingston and several branches in outlying districts. In the Bahamas an infant Association was opened in 1938. Work in Surinam was started in 1934. In French Guiana and in the United States-controlled islands, no Associations existed, though the organization of work in both Cuba and Puerto Rico had been at various times considered by the Y.W.C.A. of the United States.

In 1940 this whole area, with a population of nine to ten millions composed of many nationalities and races, British, French, American, East Indian, African, Spanish, Portuguese, Chinese, as well as mixed races, was entering upon a new stage of development. In the British West Indies, following a period of acute labor difficulties, the British Government in 1938 had sent a Royal Commission to study the cause of unrest and to propose remedies. The result was a far-reaching scheme of reform, political and social. Included in this was a plan for a central government welfare organization which would carry on an extensive educational and recreational program to supplement and support the work of voluntary agencies. The war was forcing changes also. American naval and air bases established in Jamaica and Trinidad forged new links between these islands and the United States. The development of the Caribbean as a center for air traffic, which the war fostered, seemed destined to be permanent. Trinidad was becoming the crossroads of the western hemisphere. In 1942 an Anglo-American Commission was formed for the purpose of exploring ways by which the British and American governments could cooperate throughout the area.

These developments pointed to new needs and new opportunities for women and girls. The time was ripe for the strengthening and expanding of Y.W.C.A. activities. The comparative proximity of the area to the Washington office made it possible to take advantage of these opportunities. Survey visits were made by Miss Mills to Jamaica and the Bahamas, and by Miss Kaufman of the Executive Committee to British Guiana, Trinidad, Barbados and Surinam. Following Miss Kaufman's visits, Miss Cowdrey spent more than two years in Trinidad as a volunteer worker, organizing in that time an Association in its capital city, Port of Spain. The Canadian Association gave one of its younger leaders, Miss Phyllis Haslam, to become the General Secretary in Trinidad, and made possible a six months' training in Canada for Mrs. Rodriguez, the General Secretary of Georgetown, British Guiana, as well as shorter periods for other leaders. In 1944 a staff member of the United States Foreign Division visited Puerto Rico, Haiti and Cuba, and the followng year an American secretary was sent to assist in the organization of an Association in Puerto Rico.

This expansion in the Caribbean, though the numbers involved were small both in population and in the Associations, was nevertheless significant because of the extraordinary mingling of races, the strategic position of the islands in future world development, and the close interplay required of the Y.W.C.A. with the far-reaching plans for the improvement of the area by the governments of Great Britain and the United States working cooperatively with the governments of the Netherlands and France.

The five years in which the World's Council had an office in Washington afforded also an unusual opportunity for contact with Latin America. While not directly involved in the war, the countries of Latin America were profoundly influenced by it, and the rapidly changing conditions were, as everywhere and always, sharply altering the life of women. It was therefore an appropriate moment for an appraisal of what had been accomplished in these countries and for a study of future needs and possibilities. In 1942 Miss Woodsmall made a five months' survey visit to Mexico and South America for the twofold purpose of strengthening the relationship between the World's Y.W.C.A. and the Y.W.C.A. centers there and studying their present situation. Both Miss Rouse and Miss Royce also made visits of some length to Mexico during the war years.

In the spring of 1945 the World's Executive Committee held a "Latin-American Consultation" in Washington, which brought together a large group of Association leaders with knowledge of these countries, including Dictora Santa Cruz, President of the Y.W.C.A. of Buenos Aires, Señorita Ramirez, President of the National Committee of Mexico, representatives of several other South American countries and members of the National Board and staff of the Y.W.C.A. in the United States, and American secretaries who had worked in Latin America.

Out of this meeting the World's Y.W.C.A. gained a deeper understanding of that "other America" so different from its northern neighbor: Fundamental in the development of the Y.W.C.A. in Latin America was its setting in the midst of Spanish- or Portuguese-speaking countries with a cultural background of continental Europe and a dominantly Roman Catholic religion. Under the impact of modern influences, however, the pattern of life of women was being definitely changed. Though there were wide variations in different countries, in general the number of women in the universities, in the professions, and in business, was steadily growing. Suffrage had been granted to women in some countries, and in a few, notably Brazil, Chile and Uruguay, women were taking an active part in political life. The number of women's organizations, many of them directly controlled by the Roman Catholic Church, was increasing rapidly, particularly in the field of social service. These changes, as well as the rapid emergence in some countries of a middle class and a marked trend toward the reorientation of culture away from Europe and toward North America, all had a bearing upon the future possibilities of the Y.W.C.A. in Latin America.[3]

Looking to the future, it was felt that the primary requisites for the development of the Y.W.C.A. in these countries were an increased number of experienced leaders from the older Associations, the strengthening of the work among students, increased provision for training indigenous leadership, and the building of a vital continental relationship among the Associations, which would strengthen local Associations and increase the significance of the whole movement. The Association of the United States, to whose support in the past the advance already made in Latin America was largely due, would, it was hoped, continue to take a large part in its future development.[4] At the same time, Miss Woodsmall called attention to the need of contact with other countries as well:

> The European tradition and background of Latin America would seem to make it important that leaders from continental Europe should now take some share in the development of the Y.W.C.A. in that area. Great Britain has a special basis for collaboration in areas where English life and thought have had a strong influence, as in Chile and Argentina. Canada is needed alongside the United States to contribute to a larger idea of Pan-Americanism. . . . In fact, the number of nationalities represented in the Latin-American countries would make a more international staff highly desirable, particularly when given in the larger term of reference of a World Movement.[5]

A third field ripe for expansion of its Y.W.C.A. work emerged during this period, Africa, West and East. The British colonial territories of Kenya, the Gold Coast, Sierra Leone and Nigeria, Portuguese East Africa, the Belgian Congo, and Liberia all asked help. The needs of young women in several of these countries had been presented to the World's Executive Committee even in very early days, largely through missionaries. As a result of these early appeals, a few beginnings had been made—at Nairobi, Kenya; in Lagos, Nigeria; and in Freetown, Sierra Leone.[6] Now, however, the stiuation was in many respects a new one. Somewhat the same factors were operative as in the Caribbean. Africa, partly because of the establishment of air bases and the spread of air travel, had suddenly become a new world. Within one generation it was passing from a primitive to a modern industrial society. In the British colonial territories here as in the British West Indies, the government was developing welfare and youth work on extensive lines. In Nigeria, government officials already had appealed to the Y.W.C.A. to establish hostels and other work for girls outside Lagos. Moreover, a century of missionary activity had produced young women capable of leadership.

No steps were taken toward enlarging the work in Africa during the war years, but the World's Executive Committee placed it high in the list of "priorities" for consideration after the war.[7]

Still other opening faced the World's Association as the conflict closed. The war services of the British Y.W.C.A. had awakened a desire to have the Y.W.C.A. in those countries which had seen what it did for the women in the forces. This was particularly true in Iraq, Iran and Eritrea, and by the close of the year 1945 the British Association had plans under way for opening a Y.W.C.A. in Baghdad, Iraq.

Looking ahead to the post-war period the World's Executive Committee recognized that all the wisdom and the resources of the World's Y.W.C.A. and the National Associations would be needed for the task of reconstruction. That task the Committee believed to be:

> To renew and strengthen the bonds that unite the National Associations in a world-wide Christian fellowship that has remained steadfast under the strains and cleavages of war.
> To assist National Associations as they readjust their life and work to a new era in order that they may contribute to the social and spiritual reconstruction of their countries and help to establish national and international life on a Christian basis.[8]

To outline plans for the accomplishment of this task the Executive Committee in 1942 appointed a Commission on Reconstruction composed

262

of representatives of the Executive Committee and staff together with members from National Associations. While, necessarily, some members of this Commission could serve only through correspondence, the American sections of it, composed of those members who were available in the United States and Canada, held several meetings in 1942 and 1943. The proposals of the Commission that were adopted by the Executive Committee included:

The sending of "Emissaries", representatives of the World Movement chosen for their knowledge of and experience in the countries to which they should go, who would seek to re-establish the personal relationships interrupted by war. They would go both from countries that had suffered most and from those that had been comparatively secure, thus through mutual interpretation of their divergent experiences reknitting the fabric of world relationships;

a world survey of needs and resources, to give the World's Y.W.C.A. knowledge of changed conditions;

a further development of mutual service, especially through interchange of leadership among National Associations;

the holding of international gatherings, intercountry conferences and regional meetings, for the renewal of personal contacts and the uniting of the thought of all on the common concerns of the World Movement;

continuing to keep before the National Associations the issues with which a Christian movement must be concerned;

continued cooperation with other Christian world movements and with women's youth organizations in matters of common concern;

contact with intergovernmental agencies for relief and rehabilitation, since moral and social recovery is inevitably linked with relief of physical suffering.

In order to carry out such a program the Commission recommended an early selection of Emissaries, that they might be ready to enter a country as soon as it was open; the addition of temporary members to the World's Y.W.C.A. staff to prepare for conferences and international gatherings; and an increase in the permanent staff in order to supply adequate advisory service in the post-war period. To meet the expense involved in increase in staff and travel and in giving aid where necessary to National Associations, it was voted to raise a special Reconstruction Fund of $80,000.[9]

Under this plan, World's Y.W.C.A. representatives visited the liberated countries of Europe in 1945 and also the Near East, the Philippines, Japan, Korea and Malaya. A conference of the Associations belonging

263

to the Eastern Mediterranean Federation was held in the summer of 1945, and plans were made for an enlarged meeting of the Executive Committee in June 1946. This meeting was to be widely representative, especially of the European Associations. Plans were also made for three conferences in Europe in the summer of 1946, one for national leaders and two for the younger leaders of local Associations in European countries. Six temporary members were added to the World's staff—one Swiss, one Swedish, one Scottish, two American and one Indian—to carry these projects and others that might develop.

An important item in this planning for reconstruction was the decision of the Christian world organizations that had sponsored the World Conference of Christian Youth at Amsterdam in 1939 to arrange for a second such conference at as early a moment as possible after the close of the war.[10] This was felt to be particularly urgent in view of the tragic effects of the war on youth, the phenomenal growth of mass activities for youth, often government-sponsored, and the rapid extension of mixed activities for girls and boys together. In preparation for this conference, and in view of special need everywhere for trained leaders to work with youth, three of the six secretaries temporarily added to the World's Y.W.C.A. staff were assigned to the field of youth work.

To raise the necessary Reconstruction Fund and also meet the larger regular budget required by the extraordinary demands of the time and by the necessity of undergirding the reconstruction program, was no light task. For the special Reconstruction Fund, quotas were assigned to National Associations. The regular budget of the final year of the war, now for the first time in its history well above $50,000, was made possible by increases over previous years in gifts from National Associations, from friends, and from new or special sources such as the Jubilee gifts, contributions from the War Prisoners Aid Committee of the Y.M.C.A. in recognition of Y.W.C.A. work for internees and woman prisoners of war, and emergency contributions in excess of their usual annual contributions made by the National Associations of the United States and Australia. The increases in contributions from National Associations, outside the emergency gifts just mentioned, were of particular interest because, in the case of Canada and the United States, they were made on the basis of a re-study of the relation between their contributions and the number of their members.

Anticipating the need of larger income for the World's Y.W.C.A. program in future years, a special committee, under the chairmanship of Mrs. Harrie R. Chamberlin, gave, during the war years, close attention to the cultivation of financial support. As a result, the annual report for 1944-1945 records that "continued and growing support by the National

264

Associations and individual friends through the war years is a sound basis for confidence that the World's Y.W.C.A. will be financially enabled to carry out its future responsibilities."

Two gifts from members of the Executive Committee were distinguished for vision and wise forethought. One of these was a four-year "working fund" of $20,000 established by Mrs. James S. Cushman, with the emergencies involved in a transfer from war to post-war activities in mind. The other, from Miss Emma R. Kaufman, was a fund of $10,000 "to further the fundamental purpose of the World's Y.W.C.A. especially in the training of leadership," and an additional amount of $75,000, of which $50,000 was to be used at the discretion of the World's Executive Committee for the needs of the Y.W.C.A. in Japan. These, as well as other gifts which though smaller in amount had in view the strengthening of the permanent financial foundation of the World's Y.W.C.A., were encouraging signs of confidence in the organization and belief in its future usefulness.

The work of reconstruction which confronted the World's Young Women's Christian Association was, however, more than the restoration of something that had been destroyed, for these devastated Associations must be rebuilt within a new framework of life, requiring, perhaps, a quite new pattern. Moreover, reconstruction could not be separated from the requirement of extension. The two great continents of South America and Africa, utterly different from one another, each representing a tide of opportunity now at its full but possible of being irretrievably lost, presented to the World's Y.W.C.A. in the opening year of its second half-century a responsibility that would have seemed overwhelming had it not been for the conviction that "the healthiest and most successful periods of · Y.W.C.A. work have been times of crisis, post-war periods, times of reconstruction, trouble and transition, when a 'new woman' was emerging and must be served." [11]

The task called for all the resources of all the Associations everywhere and for the extension of the principle of mutual service beyond any bounds hitherto reached. The National Associations realized this, and a surprising number, in spite of their own desperate needs, found ways to contribute to the needs of others. [12]

In October 1945 the administrative office of the World's Y.W.C.A. in Washington was reintegrated with the Geneva headquarters. A small office, with Miss Dunham in charge, was retained in Washington, to care for certain concerns there, and a "contact office" that had been opened in London some months before the close of the war was retained also, though without allocation of permanent staff. Whether, for the new period on which the movement was entering, Geneva should continue to be the headquarters was a question raised from time to time, but one that could be answered only in the light of trends that were not yet clear, and by official decision taken at a World's Council meeting. In 1945 Geneva was still the chief international center for the Christian organizations to which the World's Y.W.C.A. was most closely related, and for this reason it was a strategic location for the Y.W.C.A. also.

An interim meeting of the Executive Committee was held in November, to make preparations for the first regular post-war meeting of the Committee to be held in June 1946. This enlarged June meeting had an attendance of about sixty people, Council members, representatives of National Associations, visitors and fraternal delegates, in addition to the members of the Executive Committee and of the World's staff. It was a deep sorrow that some of the most beloved and revered members of the Committee were no longer among them. Madame Bertrand of Geneva, Madame Pannier of France, Mademoiselle Goblet d'Alviella of Belgium, Mrs. Cushman of the United States, and Dr. Sweet of Australia, all of whom had died since the Committee last met in Geneva, were profoundly missed and gratefully remembered.

At this meeting, Miss Rouse presented her resignation, and the Committee called Miss van Asch van Wijck to fill the vacancy in the office of President until the next meeting of the World's Council. The Committee also again voted to hold the next Council meeting in China, in October 1947.

It was not easy for those from "both sides of the conflict" to come together with full mutual understanding for the first time after the bitter experience of war. Yet the consciousness of the sin in which to some extent every nation shared, and the even more profound sense of unity in penitence and in desire to be an instrument in God's hand for healing and renewal in a world still under the shadow of fear and suffering and despair, triumphed over all difficulties, making gratitude for the maintenance of unbroken fellowship and rededication to the Association purpose the dominant notes in the experience of those days.

The solemn sense of the crucial nature of the times in which the World's Young Women's Christian Association set its face toward an uncertain but challenging future was expressed for all those present by Miss Woodsmall in her annual report on the work of the year 1945-1946:

This year the life of the World's Y.W.C.A. is set in the framework of heroic events. A year that marked the end of a global war costly beyond all human conception and the beginning of the sacrificial struggle for peace; a year that revealed man's power over the atom and cast a shadow of fear over the world;

a year of continued suffering for millions, hunger and home-lessness and spiritual distress. But a year also of renewed hope. A year that has brought into being the United Nations, which represents another stage in the long endeavor to establish a world order which shall make possible peace with justice.

It is in this crowded setting of momentous events that the World's Y.W.C.A. in 1946 continues to carry on its task. In war or post-war its Christian purpose remains unchanged, to witness in every phase of its work and all its relationships to the relevance of the Christian message for the life of today.

REFERENCES

[1] Royce, Marion, *The Effect of the War on the Life of Women*, 1945.

[2] This Commission was enlarged in 1945 to include representatives of the governments of France and the Netherlands.

[3] See Woodsmall, Ruth F., *The Y.W.C.A. in Latin America*, 1943, pp. 8-17.

Note: The survey made by Miss Woodsmall showed a notable advance in the leadership taken in the Association by Latin-American women themselves, and revealed that both Roman Catholics and Protestants were serving on Boards of Management and staffs. "At the same time, the official attitude of the Roman Catholic Church, which does not recognize the ecumenical character of either the Y.M.C.A. or the Y.W.C.A., creates an atmosphere in which a frank religious emphasis is difficult if not impossible." The danger of religious neutrality inherent in this situation was felt to be a chief problem of the Association. (See *The Y.W.C.A. in Latin America*, pp. 50-52.)

[4] At its national convention in 1946 the American Association presented plans for an advance program in Latin America calling for an expenditure of $250,000, and reported that "progress has been made in realizing this program."

[5] Woodsmall, Ruth F., *The Y.W.C.A. in Latin America*, p. 50.

[6] See Chapter II, p. 138.

[7] In the early months of 1946 Miss Cowdrey, at the request of the Executive Committee, made a survey visit to West Africa, and reported that the time had come to re-think Africa in modern terms; that within the British territories leadership could be found among young women now studying in England; that in Liberia there were young women educated in the United States and now teaching in schools, colleges and hospitals who already knew the Association through connection with it in America.

[8] "Reconstruction Plans of the World's Y.W.C.A." (leaflet) 1944, p. 2.

[9] Later increased to $100,000, as it proved essential to retain temporary additions to staff longer than was at first judged necessary.

[10] In 1946, representatives of the World's Y.M.C.A., the World's Y.W.C.A., the World's Student Christian Federation, and the Youth Commission of the World Council of Churches met in Geneva and made plans for the second World Conference of Christian Youth to be held in Oslo in the summer of 1947.

[11] Rouse, Ruth, *Review of the Wartime Work of the World's Y.W.C.A.*, 1946, p. 2.

[12] The Association of Great Britain took on special responsibility for helping to rebuild the shattered European Associations and the Association in the United States at its national convention in 1946, pledged itself to raise $2,000,000 for a program of reconstruction of Y.W.C.A.s in other countries.

APPENDICES

APPENDIX I

Constitution of the World's Young Women's Christian Association adopted at the first World's Conference, London 1898

ARTICLE I — NAME

This organization shall be called the "World's Young Women's Christian Association".

ARTICLE II — OBJECT

The object of the Association shall be the federation, development, and extension of Young Women's Christian Associations in all lands.

ARTICLE III — BASIS

The World's Young Women's Christian Association seeks to unite those young women who, regarding the Lord Jesus Christ as their God and Saviour, according to the Holy Scriptures, are vitally united to Him through the love of God shed abroad in their hearts by the Holy Spirit, and desire to associate their efforts for the extension of His Kingdom among all young women by such means as are in accordance with the Word of God.

N.B. — The basis of the Evangelical Alliance may be appended where locally desired.

ARTICLE IV — MEMBERSHIP

Section 1. — The World's Association shall include National Associations organized on this basis, together with corresponding membership of those countries having Associations on this basis, but without national organization.

Section 2. — National Associations shall be entitled to Active, i.e., voting, Membership, in the World's Association.

Section 3. — Countries not having a National Association but having Associations on this basis, shall be entitled to Corresponding Membership in the World's Association.

ARTICLE V — THE COMMITTEE

Section 1. — The supervision of the work of the Association shall be entrusted to a Committee, to be called the "World's Committee of the Young Women's Christian Association".

Section 2. — The World's Committee shall consist of an executive body (composed of at least seven members resident at headquarters), together with representatives nominated by the countries holding membership in the World's Association, all to be elected by the World's Conference.

ARTICLE VI — OFFICERS

The Officers of the Committee shall be a President, two Vice Presidents, Corresponding Secretary, at least one Recording Secretary, a General Secretary, and a Treasurer, all residing at headquarters. The officers of the Committee shall also be officers of the Association. The officers, with the exception of the General Secretary, who shall be a woman, may be either men or women, at the discretion of the Committee.

The General Secretary shall be of a nationality other than that of the country in which the headquarters of the Committee are located, unless it is otherwise decided by a four-fifths vote of the Committee.

ARTICLE VII — MEETINGS

Section 1. — The Association shall meet in a World's Conference at the call of the World's Committee, at such a time and place as shall be decided at the preceding Conference.

Section 2. — At the opening of each World's Conference, a Committee shall be appointed to report on the Report of the World's Committee.

ARTICLE VIII — AMENDMENTS

This Constitution may be amended by a two-thirds vote at any World's Conference, provided such amendment has received the approval of three-fourths of the entire Committee; notice of such amendment having been sent to every country represented in the Association, at least one year before the meeting at which the amendment is put to vote.

BY-LAWS

ARTICLE I — ELECTION OF COMMITTEE

Section 1. — The World's Committee shall be (a) of Active Members representing the National Associations; (b) of Corresponding Members representing the countries holding Corresponding Membership in the World's Association; (c) together with at least seven members residing at headquarters who shall form the Executive Committee.

Section 2. — Each National organization shall be entitled to representation in the World's Committee by one active member. National organizations having over 300 Associations in separate centers shall be entitled to two active members, and for every additional 300 Associations, an additional active member.

Section 3. — Each country holding Corresponding Membership in the World's Association shall be entitled to representation by one member on the World's Committee.

Section 4. — The nominations for both active and corresponding members shall be sent to the headquarters, at least two months before each Conference.

Section 5. — The Committee to which is referred the Report of the World's Committee at each Conference shall present these nominations, together with those for resident members, for election by the Conference.

Section 6. — Any vacancy in the Committee, occurring between the Conferences, may be filled by the remaining members of the Committee.

ARTICLE II — DUTIES OF OFFICERS

Section 1. — The President shall preside at the business meetings of the Committee, appoint all Standing Committees, subject to the approval of the Executive Committee, and shall perform the other duties incumbent upon this office, being an ex-officio member of all the Committees.

Section 2. — The Vice Presidents shall assist the President in all duties, and perform the same in the absence of the President.

Section 3. — The Corresponding Secretary shall assist the President in all correspondence relative to the extension of new fields, in securing information concerning the enlargement and development of special departments, and in all points pertaining to growth. She shall be an ex-officio member of the Standing Committees.

Section 4. — The General Secretary shall be employed by the World's Committee as its Executive Officer. She shall visit the various countries as may be required, organize new territory, secure and develop workers, all subject to the direction of the Committee. She shall be an ex-officio member of the Standing Committees.

Section 5. — The Recording Secretary shall keep full minutes of all meetings of the Committee, send notices of the elections, appointments and meetings, collect and classify statistics of the work throughout the world, collect and fill as complete a file of Association literature as possible, and shall be an ex-officio member of the Publication Committee.

Section 6. — The Treasurer and Finance Secretary shall have charge of the funds of the World's Association, and keep all financial accounts. The Finance Secretary shall pay all bills on written orders signed by the Treasurer. The Treasurer shall be Chairman of the Finance Committee.

ARTICLE III — STANDING COMMITTEES

Section 1. — There shall be five Standing Committees appointed from the World's Committee immediately after each Conference, namely: (1) The Committee for the European Continent; (2) The Committee for Corresponding Associations; (3) The Committee on Publications; (4) The Committee on Finance; (5) The Secretarial Committee or the Committee for Selection of Workers.

Section 2. — Duties:

(a) The Committee for the European Continent shall seek to develop the existing Associations in the unorganized countries of Europe, shall study new fields with reference to the extension of the work, and assist in forming National organizations where practicable.

(b) The Committee for Corresponding Associations shall undertake the same duties for other parts of the world.

(c) The Committee on Publications shall arrange for the printing and distribution of such literature as shall be of general value to Associations throughout the world, and shall assist the Recording Secretary in the collecting and filing of statistics and literature.

(d) The Committee on Finance shall devise ways and means of raising funds sufficient to carry on the work of the World's Association, shall keep a careful record of all Associations and individuals subscribing to the work, and arrange for the audits of all financial accounts at the close of the year.

(e) The Secretarial Committee or the Committee for Selection of Workers shall have the selection and training of all workers to be sent abroad under the World's Committee.

Section 3. — Each Standing Committee shall consist of at least two active and one corresponding member of the World's Committee; the Chairmen shall be members of the Executive Committee.

Section 4. — Each Standing Committee may add to its number such additional members as shall be approved by a vote of the Executive Committee.

Section 5. — The Standing Committees shall each hold a meeting preceding the regular meetings of the Executive Committee; shall appoint a Secretary to keep full minutes of the same, which shall be submitted to the Executive Committee at their meetings.

Section 6. — Special Committees shall be appointed as needed.

ARTICLE IV — MEETINGS

Section 1. —The Meetings of the World's Executive Committee shall be held monthly, except in vacation time.

Section 2. — The Committee shall hold an Annual Meeting in the month of January, at which the year's reports shall be presented. A meeting of the World's Committee shall be held during the meetings of the Conference.

Section 3. — The following order of business shall be observed at the regular monthly meetings:

Devotional Exercises
Reading of Minutes.
Reports
   a) Treasurer
   b) General Secretary
   c) Standing Committees
   d) Special Committees
Miscellaneous Business

ARTICLE V — RULES

Section 1. — The Executive Committee, residing at headquarters, shall transact all business of the World's Association during the interval between the World's Conferences. Five members shall constitute a quorum.

Attendance at the committee meetings shall be obligatory. . Absence from two

274

consecutive meetings shall be considered equivalent to resignation, but the Committee shall be at liberty to consider and accept as valid written excuses for enforced absence.

Section 2. — The World's Association shall not have legislative power which may interfere with the local affairs of any Association or National organization.

ARTICLE VI — AMENDMENTS

The above By-laws may be amended at any regular meeting, by a two-thirds vote by the entire Committee, the vote of non-resident members being secured by correspondence, provided a copy of the proposed amendment has been sent to each member at least three months before the meeting at which it is put to vote.

APPENDIX II

Alliance Universelle des Unions Chretiennes de Jeunes Filles
World's Young Women's Christian Association
Christlicher Weltbund Weiblicher Jugend

Constitution [1]
as adopted in 1930 and amended in 1941

ARTICLE I — NAME

This organization shall be called the World's Young Women's Christian Association.

ARTICLE II — BASIS

Faith in God the Father as Creator and in Jesus Christ His only Son as Lord and Saviour, and in the Holy Spirit as Revealer of Truth and Source of Power for life and service, according to the teachings of Holy Scripture.

ARTICLE III — AIM

The World's Young Women's Christian Association seeks to organize, develop and unite National Associations which, accepting its basis or one in conformity with it, endeavor to extend the Kingdom of God according to its principles, and to bring young women to such knowledge of Jesus Christ as Lord and Saviour as shall manifest itself in character and conduct.

It also calls all National Associations to promote Christian principles of social and international conduct by encouraging the development of a right public conscience such as shall strengthen all those forces which are working for the promotion of peace and better understanding between classes, nations and races, believing that the world social order can only be made Christian through individuals devoted to the single purpose of doing God's will, and that through obedience to the law of Christ there shall follow the extension of His Kingdom, in which the principles of justice, love, and the equal value of every human life shall apply to national and international as well as to personal relations.

ARTICLE IV — PRINCIPLES

The World's Young Women's Christian Association desires to be representative of all sections of the Christian Church in so far as they accept the basis. It includes in the field of its activities young women without distinction of creed, and desires to enlist the service of young women for young women in their spiritual, intellectual, social and physical advancement, and to encourage their fellowship and activity in the Christian Church. The World's Young Women's Christian Association also pledges itself to assign a primary position to Bible study and prayer.

[1] The original document is in French.

ARTICLE V — MEMBERSHIP

Section 1. — The World's Association shall include National Associations organized in accordance with Articles II, III and IV above. Such Associations shall have as leaders women who will promote the full Christian purpose of the Association, an organized voting membership, and a number of branches in reasonable proportion to a program for touching every part of the country and every type of young woman. They shall also show promise of continuity and progress in matters of general organization. Such National Associations shall be entitled to active, i.e., voting membership, in the World's Association.

The World's Basis must be quoted in full in the Constitution of all National Associations. This clause shall be understood not to be retroactive in the case of National Associations already affiliated.

Section 2.—A National Association which shows promise of reaching the above standard for active membership in the World's Association, or an isolated local Association or group of Associations organized in harmony with the above Articles and with a view to being eventually incorporated in a fully organized national Association, shall be entitled to corresponding membership in the World's Association.

Section 3.—Should a National Association desire to withdraw from active or corresponding membership in the World's Association, notice must be given not less than one year before it takes effect.

Section 4.—Should a National Association cease to fulfill the above requirements, the World's Council after ample investigation may decide, with a three-fourths majority of the votes cast, which must also represent a two-thirds majority of the countries affiliated in active membership, that this National Association be no longer considered as an active member of the World's Association.

ARTICLE VI — WORLD'S COUNCIL

Section 1. — The legislative body of the World's Association shall be the World's Council.

Section 2. — The World's Council shall consist of:

(a) *with voting power*

1. Representatives of the countries holding active membership in the World's Association, to be elected by their National Associations: (1) two representatives from each Association having 15,000 members or less, and one member for each additional 15,000 members or part thereof to the limit of twelve; (2) the National President, and National General Secretary.

2. The President, Vice Presidents and Treasurer of the Association, to be elected by the World's Council.

3. Representatives of the Executive Committee, to be elected by the said Executive, the number of these representatives to be fixed in the By-laws.

(b) *without voting power*

1. One representative for each country holding corresponding membership in the World's Association.
2. The members of the Executive Committee not included in 3. above.
3. The secretaries of the World's staff.

ARTICLE VII — EXECUTIVE COMMITTEE

In the interval between World's Council meetings, the business of the World's Association shall be transacted by an Executive Committee to be elected by the World's Council. This Executive Committee shall consist of (a) the officers of the World's Association, and (b) at least seven other members. Mode of election, functions and responsibilities thereof to be defined in the By-laws.

ARTICLE VIII — OFFICERS

The Officers of the World's Association shall be:

a) the President.

b) the Vice Presidents to the limit of eight, at least four thereof, as far as possible, drawn from the various racial and national groups in the Association.

c) the Treasurer.

d) The General Secretary.

Mode of election or appointment to be fixed in the By-laws.

ARTICLE IX — MEETINGS

Section 1. — A meeting of the World's Council shall be held as a rule once in two years and at least once in four years, due notice thereof and agenda of the subjects to be discussed having been posted in time to be received at all national headquarters five months previously.

Section 2. — An extra meeting of the World's Council shall be held if called for by one-third of the countries affiliated in active membership.

Section 3. — World Conferences, Regional Conferences or Commissions relating to special subjects shall be called by the World's Council or Executive Committee as needed. Such Conferences shall have power to make recommendations to the World's Council with a view to legislation.

Section 4. — Resolutions of the Council shall be passed by a majority of the votes cast, unless otherwise stated in this Constitution or By-laws. In the event of there being no majority, a resolution shall not be proceeded with. The President shall not have a deciding vote.

Section 5. — At least one representative each from two-thirds of the countries affiliated in active membership shall constitute a quorum for any meeting of the World's Council of which due notice has been given according to Section 1. of this Article. In the event of this quorum not being present, any resolution passed shall be submitted to all absent members of the World's Council and shall not be acted upon until ratified by correspondence by a sufficient number of absent Council members to make up the required quorum.

ARTICLE X — FINANCE

The Funds of the World's Association are furnished by:

a) contributions of the National Associations as provided for in the By-laws.
b) donations, subscriptions and legacies.
   These contributions and donations alone guarantee the liabilities of the World's Association, to the exclusion of all personal responsibility on the part of its members.
c) sale of publications, etc.

ARTICLE XI — POWERS

The World's Council shall not have any legislative power which may interfere with the local affairs of any Association or national organization.

ARTICLE XII — INCORPORATION

The World's Association has its headquarters at Geneva (Switzerland); it is an incorporated body and possesses civil personality in accordance with Article 60 and following of the Swiss Civil Code. The power of official signature on behalf of the World's Association shall be vested in the President or a Vice President, together with one of the other officers as appointed by the Executive Committee.

ARTICLE XII — AMENDMENTS

This Constitution may be amended by a three-fourths majority of the votes cast at any World's Council meeting, notice of such amendment having been posted to every country represented in the Association at least one year before the meeting at which the amendment is put to the vote. Articles I, II, III, and IV shall not be changed unless the proposed amendment is passed by two successive meetings of the World's Council.

BY-LAWS

ARTICLE I — WORLD'S COUNCIL MEETINGS

Section 1. — At each regular World's Council meeting the Council shall:

a) receive a report from the Executive Committee on the work done in the interval, including an account of the work of every Standing Committee. The Council shall appoint a sub-committee consisting of one member from every National Association affiliated in active membership represented at the meeting of the Council to consider this report;
b) receive an account of the management of the World's funds. A report on this account shall be prepared by a sub-committee composed as in Section 1 (a) above;

c) consider and approve the general lines of a budget prepared by the Executive Committee for the coming two years;

d) elect the officers and members of the Executive Committee according to the rules laid down in these By-laws for their election;

e) appoint members of staff according to the rules laid down in these By-laws;

f) decide on requests for affiliation in active or corresponding membership, each member having received a report from the Executive Committee on each request six months previously;

g) decide on the general policies for the coming years with reference to the work of the committees and staff, and the means to be taken in fulfilling the Aim of the World's Association;

h) select date and place for the next meeting of the World's Council.

Section 2. — Representatives from countries affiliated in active and corresponding membership shall be understood to be elected if possible for four years. The question of eligibility for re-election shall be left to each National Association. Proxies may be appointed by their respective National Associations for attendance at World's Council meetings. The members of the Executive Committee mentioned in Article VI, Section 2 (b), 2, of the Constitution may be asked to exercise a vote on behalf of their National Associations.

Section 3. — Representatives from countries not yet affiliated in active or corresponding membership may be invited by the Executive Committee to attend meetings of the World's Council without vote.

Section 4. — The Executive Committee shall be empowered on request from the National Associations to invite visitors to attend meetings of the Council, such visitors not to exceed one-third of the total membership of the Council.

Section 5. — Each person with voting power shall be entitled to use only one vote.

Article II — Executive Committee

Section 1. — During the interval between World's Council meetings the Executive Committee shall carry out the general policy as expressed by the Council at its meetings. It shall keep the members of the Council regularly informed of its work. It shall be responsible to the Council for its work and for the management of the funds of the World's Association.

Section 2. — The members mentioned in the Constitution, Article 7, Section (b), shall not exceed the number of fifteen and shall include at least five nationalities. The retiring President shall become an honorary member of the Executive Committee, without vote, for the four years' period following her term of office.

Section 3. — The members of the Executive Committee referred to in the preceding section shall be elected for a period of four years, or until the Council meeting following the expiration of their term of office. They shall be eligible for re-election for another two periods, after which a period of four years must elapse before their re-election.

280

Section 4. — The World's Council at each meeting shall appoint a small interim Nominating Committee to act until the next Council meeting. This Committee shall be responsible for receiving names for Executive Committee members from the National Associations (not from individual members of these Associations) and from Executive Committee members, and for sending them out to the National Associations in time for them to be received not less than five months before the meeting at which the election takes place. If other candidates are approved by two-thirds of the voting Associations present at the Council meeting, such names may also be presented to the Nominating Committee for consideration. At the time of the Council meeting, a sub-committee formed as provided for in the By-laws Article I, Section 1 (a), shall prepare a final list of nominations to be presented to the Council for election.

Section 5. — The Executive Committee shall as a general rule meet three times and not less than twice a year, due notice thereof, with the agenda, having been sent round at least one month previously. One of these shall be an enlarged meeting, at which the year's reports and accounts shall be presented and to which each National Association affiliated in active membership shall be entitled to send one representative.

Section 6. — Members of the World's Council shall have the right to attend, without voting power, any meeting of the Executive Committee. The Executive shall have the right to invite such other persons at it may deem necessary to attend one or more of its meetings without voting power. Vice Presidents and Treasurer have the right of proxy, such proxies to be chosen by consultation between the Vice Presidents and the Treasurer concerned and the President and General Secretary of the World's Y.W.C.A.

Section 7. — The Executive Committee shall appoint seven among its members to act as voting members at meetings of the World's Council.

Section 8. — The Executive Committee shall have power to fill vacancies in its membership to serve until the next World's Council meeting.

Section 9. — Five members shall constitute a quorum for a meeting of the Executive Committee.

ARTICLE III — OFFICERS

Section 1. —The President shall preside at the business meetings of the Council, and shall perform the other duties incumbent upon this office. She shall be an ex-officio member of all committees and sub-committees.

Section 2. —The Vice Presidents shall assist the President in all duties and perform the same in the absence of the President.

Section 3. — The General Secretary shall be employed by the World's Council as its executive officer. She shall have power to attend the meetings of all committees and sub-committees.

Section 4. — The Treasurer shall have charge of the funds of the World's Association. She shall oversee the keeping of accounts and payment of bills in accordance with the budget. The Executive Committee shall have the power to appoint one or more deputy treasurers if needed.

Section 5. — The interim Committee appointed in accordance with Article II, Section 4, of the By-laws for the election of members of the Executive Committee shall follow the same procedure for the election of officers.

Section 6. — These officers shall be elected for not less than four years.

Section 7. — At the end of four years, or at the next Council meeting following the expiration of their term of office, the officers, except the Treasurer, shall retire; the Treasurer shall be eligible for re-election. The President and Vice Presidents shall be eligible for re-election to the same office for one such other period, after which a period of four years must elapse before re-election to that office. In the election of officers due regard shall be given to the need for continuity.

Section 8. — Vacancies occurring between meetings of the Council may be filled by the Executive Committee until the next meeting of the World's Council.

ARTICLE IV — STAFF

Section 1. — The Executive Committee shall have power to appoint members of the staff. Their appointment shall be ratified at the next World's Council meeting, notice thereof to be given previously to the affiliated National Associations.

Section 2. — For all proposed members of staff, information as to nationality, previous work, etc., shall be sent to the affiliated National Associations.

ARTICLE V — COMMITTEES

The Executive Committee shall appoint such Committees as it may deem necessary for the carrying out of its work.

ARTICLE VI — FINANCE

The contributions of the National Associations shall be voluntary. The Associations affiliated in active membership accept as the standard according to which they ought to contribute to the funds of the World's Association the equivalent of 30 centimes (gold) for every member of their Association. The accounts of the World's Association shall be audited annually by two chartered accountants.

ARTICLE VII — AMENDMENTS

These By-laws may be amended at any regular meeting of the World's Council by a two-thirds majority of the number of votes cast, notice of such amendment having been posted to every affiliated National Association at least six months before the meeting at which it is put to the vote.

APPENDIX III

List of World's Y.W.C.A. Meetings

DATE	MEETING	PLACE
1898	First World's Y.W.C.A. Conference	London
1902	Second World's Y.W.C.A. Conference	Geneva
1906	Third World's Y.W.C.A. Conference	Paris
1910	Fourth World's Y.W.C.A. Conference	Berlin
1914	Fifth World's Y.W.C.A. Conference	Stockholm
1920	World's Y.W.C.A. Committee and International Commission	Champéry, Switzerland
1922	World's Y.W.C.A. Committee and International Commission	St. Wolfgang, Austria
1924	World's Y.W.C.A. Committee	Washington
1926	World's Y.W.C.A. Committee	Oxford
1928	Sixth World's Y.W.C.A. Conference	Budapest
1930	World's Y.W.C.A. Committee	St. Cergue, Switzerland
1934	World's Y.W.C.A. Council	Geneva
1938	World's Y.W.C.A. Council	Muskoka, Canada
1941	World's Y.W.C.A. Council	Washington

APPENDIX IV

Presidents of the World's Y.W.C.A.

1894-1946

Mrs. J. H. Tritton	1894-1902 and 1910-1914
Mrs. George Campbell	1902-1906
Miss Mary Morley	1906-1910
The Hon. Mrs. Montague Waldegrave	1914-1924 and 1928-1930
Lady Parmoor	1924-1928
Jonkvrouwe C. M. van Asch van Wijck	1930-1938 and 1946-
Miss Ruth Rouse	1938-1946

APPENDIX V

General Secretaries of the World's Y.W.C.A.

1894-1946

Miss Annie M. Reynolds	1894-1904
Miss Clarissa H. Spencer	1904-1920
Miss Charlotte T. Niven	1920-1935
Miss Ruth F. Woodsmall	1935-

APPENDIX VI

National Associations in Active Affiliation
with the World's Y.W.C.A. in 1946

(in chronological order of affiliation)

Country	Date of Affiliation
Great Britain	1894
United States of America	1894
Norway	1894
Sweden [1]	1894
Canada	1895
India, Burma, and Ceylon	1897
Germany	1898
France	1900
Italy [2]	1901
Denmark	1902
Hungary	1904
China	1906
Japan	1906
Netherlands	1907
Australia [3]	1925
New Zealand [3]	1925
Switzerland	1926
Iceland	1926
Jamaica	1930
Korea	1930
Malaya	1934
Estonia [4]	1938

[1] See p. 56, Reference 9, Note.
[2] Previously affiliated as Federation of Northern Italy in 1896.
[3] Australia and New Zealand were jointly affiliated from 1907 to 1925.
[4] Not functioning since 1940.

APPENDIX VII

List of National Associations in Active Membership, with Dates of
Formation of the National Organization

(in alphabetical order)

Date	Country
1925	Australia [1]
1895	Canada
1905	China
1902	Denmark
1932	Estonia
1894	France
1893	Germany
1884	Great Britain
1904	Hungary
1926	Iceland
1896	India, Burma, and Ceylon
1901	Italy
1923	Jamaica
1905	Japan
1921	Malaya
	Netherlands
1907	Formation of first national group
1920	Formation of present Federation
1925	New Zealand [1]
1894	Norway
1896	Sweden [2]
1926	Switzerland
	United States of America
1877	Formation of International Women's and Young Women's Christian Association (United States and Canada)
1886	Formation of International Young Women's Christian Association (United States and Canada)
1906	Formation of present national organization

[1] Australia and New Zealand were jointly affiliated from 1907 to 1925.

[2] See page 56, note under Reference 9.

APPENDIX VIII

Countries Having Organized Y.W.C.A. Work

(in alphabetical order)

Country	Approximate Date of Beginning of Work	Date of Affiliation with World's YWCA	Classification
Algeria	....	....	(Through France)
Argentina	1890	1907	Corresponding Member
Australia[1]	1880	1925	Active Member
Austria	....	1912	(Not functioning since 1938)
Bahama Islands (B.W.I.)	1936	....	Pioneer Association
Belgium	1875	1934	Corresponding Member
Bolivia	1930	....	Pioneer Association
Brazil	1920	....	Pioneer Association
British Guiana	1874	1930	Corresponding Member
Bulgaria	1922	....	Pioneer Association (not functioning since 1944)
Canada	1870	1895	Active Member
Chile	1921	1938	Corresponding Member
China	1897	1906	Active Member
Cyprus	1924	....	Pioneer Association
Czechoslovakia	1919	1922	Corresponding Member
Denmark	1883	1902	Active Member
Egypt[2]	1876	1934	Corresponding Member
Estonia	1920	1938	Active Member (not functioning since 1940)
Finland	1896	1903 to 1928	Active Member (withdrew in 1928)
France	1849	1900	Active Member
Germany	1855	1898	Active Member
Great Britain	1855	1894	Active Member
Greece	1900	....	Pioneer Association
Grenada (B.W.I.)	1889	....	Pioneer Association
Hungary	1884	1904	Active Member
Iceland	1889	1926	Active Member
India, Burma and Ceylon	1875	1897	Active Member
Indonesia	1929	1938	Corresponding Member
Italy[3]	1894	1896	Active Member
Jamaica	1921	1930	Active Member
Japan	1905	1906	Active Member

Kenya	1911	1918	Corresponding Isolated Center
Korea	1905	1930	Active member
Latvia	1921	....	Pioneer Association (not functioning since 1936)
Madagascar	....	....	(Through France)
Malaya	1897	1934	Active Member
Malta	1886	1895	Corresponding Isolated Center
Mexico	1922		Pioneer Association
Morocco	....	....	(Through France)
Netherlands	1878	1907	Active Member
Newfoundland	....	....	(Through Canada)
New Zealand [4]	1878	1925	Active Member
Nigeria	1906	....	Pioneer Association
Norway	1887	1894	Active Member
Palestine [5]	1890	1930	Corresponding Member
Philippine Islands	1921	....	Pioneer Association
Portugal	1897	1921	Corresponding Member
Roumania	1919	1938	Corresponding Member
Sierra Leone	1915	....	Pioneer Association
South Africa [6]	1886	1905 to 1931	Active Member (withdrew in 1931)
Surinam	1934	....	Pioneer Association
Sweden	1885	1894	Active Member
Switzerland	1855	1926	Active Member
Syria and Lebanon	1911	1934	Corresponding Member
Tunisia	....	....	(Through France)
Uruguay	1912	....	Pioneer Association
United States of America	1858	1894	Active Member

Note: There are also Association groups, which are not yet recognized as Pioneer Associations, in the Gold Coast, Iraq, Liberia, Peru, Puerto Rico, and Siam.

From 1932 to 1938 the Austrian Association was united with that of Germany.

[1] Affiliated 1907 — 1925 jointly with New Zealand.
[2] Affiliated 1918 — 1934 jointly with Palestine.
[3] Affiliated 1896—1901 as the Federation of Northern Italy.
[4] Affiliated 1907—1925 jointly with Australia.
[5] Affiliated 1918—1934 jointly with Egypt.
[6] The Associations of Durban and Port Elizabeth, after separating from the National Council of South Africa, affiliated with the World's YWCA in 1934 as Corresponding Isolated Centers.

INDEX

INDEX

Burckhardt, Pastor Johannes, 20, 23, 25, 34, 99; Hanna, 140.
Burckhardthaus, 209, 250.
Burma, 7, 73, 74, 98, 248 (see also India).
Burton, Margaret, 123.
Butt, Miss, 14.

Campbell, Mrs. George, 58, 63, 65 rf 6, 92.
Camps, 11, 28, 163, 164, 166, 174.
Canada, 3, 7, 14, 36, 38, 39, 42, 43, 44, 53, 56 rf 10, 69, 91, 98, 99, 100, 111, 112, 118, 146, 181, 182, 220, 228, 235, 241, 246, 248, 249, 251, 264.
Canadian Girls in Training, 182.
Caribbean Area, 248, 259, 260.
Carr, Grace, 255 rf 3.
Carruthers, Pearl, 245.
Cassels, May, 72, 134, 135.
Castro, Julia, 71.
Cedergren, Fru Elsa, 210, 236, 246, 248, 249.
Cercle Söderblom, 214.
Ceylon, 7, 73, 74, 98, 228, 232 (see also India).
Chamberlin, Mrs. Harrie, 236, 264.
Champéry, International Commission (1920), 157, 171, 173-175, 178, 198.
Chen, Mrs. C. C., 210.
Chenevière, Madeleine, 210, 211, 247.
Chile, 161, 234 rf 7, 261.
China, 1, 14, 28, 45, 53, 84, 86, 88, 89, 90, 93 rf 11, 98, 100, 112, 117, 118, 148, 158, 188, 190, 212, 217-219, 221, 227, 230, 231, 232, 233, 234 rf 3, 235, 236, 239, 241, 246, 248, 250, 266; Y.W.C.A. of, 86, 87, 100, 102, 118, 120, 158-160, 190-191, 236, 238, 246, 251, 253, 255 rf 6, 258; National Christian Council of, 191.
Christian Basis of a New Society, The, 258.
Christian Basis of Our Social and International Action, The, 257.
Christian Decisions, 257.
Christian Emphasis, Study of the, 230, 232, 257, 258.
Christian Missions, 3.
Christian Purpose of the Y.W.C.A., The 215, 232, 237, 239, 244, 252, 266.
Christian Social Union of Great Britain, 125.
Christian Women, Place of, 221, 226, 230.
Christian Work in Latin America, Congress of, 160.
Christian Youth Association, 27, 152 rf 24.
Christian Youth Movements, 220, 239.
Christianisme Social, Le, 125.
Chu, Mrs. Shi-ming, 246.
Church, Community and State, Oxford Conference on, 227.

Church Universal, 200, 201.
Church Youth Work, 227, 228, 258.
Churches, Relationship with, 23, 24, 26, 182, 194, 195, 204, 251, 258.
Churches, World Council of, 227, 228, 243.
CIMADE, 251.
Citizenship, 150.
Clubs, Blue Triangle, 182, 251; Girls', 26, 28, 60, 157, 163, 164, 165, 174, 238, 251 (see also Foyers).
Coldstream, Mrs., 13.
Colonial Division (see Extra-European and)
Comité d'Entente, 226.
Conferences, World's Y.W.C.A. (see World's Y.W.C.A. Conferences).
Congo, 28.
Continental Committee (South America), 194, 228; Secretary, 160.
Continental Division (see Foreign and Continental).
Constantinople, 135, 164.
Constitution and By-Laws, World's Y.W.C.A., 51-54, 56, 61, 66, 98, 112, 118, 121 rf 3, 128, 130, 131, 150, 176, 198, 199, 209, 210, 213.
Consultative Group, 213.
Conventions, National (U.S.A.), 43, 44, 63, 99.
Cooperation, 142, 148, 163, 168, 174, 185, 191, 198, 199, 200, 201, 207 rf 2, 213, 214, 215, 220, 247, 251, 252, 253, 254.
Coppock, Grace, 158, 159, 160.
Coptic Church, 129.
Corresponding Associations, 53, 184, 189, 234 rf 7.
Corresponding Membership, 54, 71, 82, 152 rf 24, 170 rf 17 *Note,* 206.
Corresponding Secretary, 82.
Cortez, Elisa, 160.
Couvé, Daniel, 125.
Cowdrey, Ruth, 248, 249, 255 ft. 3, 260, 267 rf 7.
Cox, Miss, 13.
Cratty, Mabel, 96, 200.
Crawley, Helen, 229.
Cuba, 259.
Curwen, May, 220, 256.
Cushman, Mrs. James S., 161, 210, 264, 266.
Czechoslovakia, 162, 165, 180, 181, 183, 184, 186, 188.

Dassel Conference on High School Work, 186, 227.
Datta, Mrs. S. K., 191, 192, 210.
Davis, Dr. D. D., 254.
Davis, Helen A., 161.

291

292

Institutes, 9, 11.
Interconfessional Position, 197, 201, 202, 203, 204; Subcommittee, 203, 204 (see also Ecumenical Questions).
Intercountry Advisory Committee, 189, 228; Conference, 202, 203, 204.
Interdependence, World, 202.
Interdenominationalism, 11, 17, 23, 27, 32, 37, 70, 101, 129, 130, 203, 204.
International Alliance of Women for Suffrage and Equal Citizenship, 234 rf 4.
International Centers, 139, 142, 164, 188; Christian Study Center, 214; Homes and Hostels; 141, 142.
International Commissions, 126, 172, 173; on Ecumenical Questions, 205-206.
International Committee (U.S.A. and Canada), 42, 43, 44, 45, 46; Conference, London (1892), 45, 48, 50-51, 79.
International Cooperative Women's Guild, 234 rf 4.
International Federation of Business and Professional Women's Clubs; of University Women; of Women Magistrates and Members of the Legal Profession, 234 rf 4.
International Labor Conference, 174, 215; Office 181, 202, 207 rf 2, 214, 226.
International Migration Service, 180-181, 195 rf 3 Note.
International Missionary Council, 186, 201, 214, 225, 227, 241.
International Relationships, 16, 240, 241.
International Social and Economic Problems, The Christian Approach to, 220.
International Summer School, (1922) 185.
Internees, 247-248, 254.
Iran, 229, 249, 262.
Iraq, 249, 262.
Ireland, 10, 67, 92, 98, 99.
Italy, 7, 13, 30-32, 53, 67, 69, 70, 91, 92, 99, 162, 164, 177, 180, 185, 249.
Jaeger, Martha, 170 rf 19.
Jamaica, 139, 259, 260.
James, Mrs. Gardner, 22.
Japan, 14, 45, 74, 75, 84, 87, 88, 89, 92, 98, 99, 102, 112, 115, 117, 118, 120, 126, 129, 148, 190, 212, 218, 219, 231, 232, 235, 241, 246, 248, 263; Y.W.C.A. of, 100-101, 221, 237, 250, 265.
Jesus Christ the Center of Life, 237, 238, 239, 242 rf 1.
Johannot, Madame Henri, 210, 247, 248.
Joint Commission on Ecumenical Questions, 205, 214.
Joint Standing Committee, 207 rf 2.
Journal de la Jeune Fille, 20, 23.
Jubilee, Wordl's Y.W.C.A., (1944) 236, 256, 257, 258.

Kaiserwerth, 24.
Kato, Taka, 232.
Kaufman, Emma, 246, 248, 260, 264.

Kawai, Michi, 99, 118, 124, 175.
Kellar, Professor Adolph, 244.
Kenya, 139, 152 rf 12, 261.
Kephissia Consultation, 205.
Kim, Helen, 232.
King, Mrs. Lung-chang, 246.
Kinnaird, Mrs. Arthur (Lady), 8, 9, 12, 59; Honorable Emily, 15, 19 rf 2, 46, 48, 50, 51, 52, 58, 59, 60, 62, 63, 72, 74, 99, 103, 137; Honorable Gertrude, 46, 74; Lord 45.
Kjaer, Mr. 27.
Knight, Ethel, 99, 103, 154.
Knuth, Countess, 34 rf 12.
Koo, Dr. T. Z., 239.
Korea, 195, 219, 232, 235, 240, 241, 263.

Labor Conference (see under International).
Ladies' Christian Association, 36, 37.
La Grande Boissière, Council Meeting, 220-222.
Lamont, Elizabeth, 255 rf 3.
Lapland, 28.
Larned, Ruth, 185 rf 3.
Latin America, 54, 129, 160, 247, 260, 261, 266 rf 3 Note, 267 rf 4.
Latin-American Consultation, 247.
Latin Countries, 175, 177.
Latvia, 162, 168, 183, 188, 250.
Leaders' Study Course, (1939) 241.
Leadership Training, 43, 60, 63, 86, 91, 116, 156, 159, 185-188; Volunteer, 64, 86, 111, 159.
League of Nations, 174, 175, 181, 198, 207 rf 2, 214, 226, 233.
Lebanon, 247.
Legislation Affecting Women, 106, 107.
Leisure, Girls of, 8, 25, 30, 31, 167.
Le Seur, Pastor [Paul], 124.
Lewis, Mrs. Robert, 87.
Liaison Committee, Women's International Organizations, 226, 234 rf 4.
Liberia, 261, 267 rf 7.
Lintum, Miss te, 205.
Location of Headquarters (see Headquarters).
Lorantffy Zsuzanna, 30.
Lutheran Church, Relationships with, 17, 27, 206, 211.
Luxmoore, Mrs. C. de J. 185, 187, 210, 218, 233.
Lyon, Sarah S., 162, 191, 192, 219.
Lyon, Williard D., 86.

Macdonald, Caroline, 100, 101, 112, 125.
MacFarland, Elizabeth, 160, 193.
Mackay, Dr. John A., 215.
Mackie, Robert, 243.
Maclagan, Theodora, 167, 205, 210.
Madagascar, 22.
Maillet, Pastor, 22, 51.
Malaya, 7, 155, 219, 221, 232, 241, 248, 263.